William Shakespeare

CORIOLANUS

Edited with a Commentary by G. R. Hibbard
Introduced by Paul Prescott

PENGUIN BOOKS

PENGUIN BOOKS

Published by the Penguin Group
Penguin Books Ltd, 80 Strand, London WC2R ORL, England
Penguin Group (USA) Inc., 375 Hudson Street, New York, New York 10014, USA
Penguin Group (Canada), 90 Eglinton Avenue East, Suite 700, Toronto, Ontario, Canada M4P 2Y3
(a division of Pearson Penguin Canada Inc.)
Penguin Ireland, 25 St Stephen's Green, Dublin 2, Ireland (a division of Penguin Books Ltd)
Penguin Group (Australia), 250 Camberwell Road, Camberwell, Victoria 3124, Australia
(a division of Pearson Australia Group Pty Ltd)
Penguin Books India Pvt Ltd, 11 Community Centre, Panchsheel Park, New Delhi – 110 017, India
Penguin Group (NZ), cnr Airborne and Rosedale Roads, Albany, Auckland 1310, New Zealand
(a division of Pearson New Zealand Ltd)
Penguin Books (South Africa) (Pty) Ltd, 24 Sturdee Avenue, Rosebank, Johannesburg 2196, South Africa

Penguin Books Ltd, Registered Offices: 80 Strand, London WC2R ORL, England

www.penguin.com

This edition first published in Penguin Books 1967
Reissued in the Penguin Shakespeare series 2005

3

This edition copyright © Penguin Books, 1967
Account of the Text and Commentary copyright © G. R. Hibbard, 1967
Further Reading copyright © Michael Taylor, 1995
General Introduction and Chronology copyright © Stanley Wells, 2005
Introduction, The Play in Performance and additional Further Reading copyright © Paul Prescott, 2005

Set in 11.5/12.5 PostScript Monotype Fournier
Designed by Boag Associates
Typeset by Palimpsest Book Production Limited, Polmont, Stirlingshire
Printed in England by Clays Ltd, St Ives plc

ISBN-13: 978–0–141–01649–8
ISBN-10: 0–141–01649–3

Contents

General Introduction

Every play by Shakespeare is unique. This is part of his greatness. A restless and indefatigable experimenter, he moved with a rare amalgamation of artistic integrity and dedicated professionalism from one kind of drama to another. Never shackled by convention, he offered his actors the alternation between serious and comic modes from play to play, and often also within the plays themselves, that the repertory system within which he worked demanded, and which provided an invaluable stimulus to his imagination. Introductions to individual works in this series attempt to define their individuality. But there are common factors that underpin Shakespeare's career.

Nothing in his heredity offers clues to the origins of his genius. His upbringing in Stratford-upon-Avon, where he was born in 1564, was unexceptional. His mother, born Mary Arden, came from a prosperous farming family. Her father chose her as his executor over her eight sisters and his four stepchildren when she was only in her late teens, which suggests that she was of more than average practical ability. Her husband John, a glover, apparently unable to write, was nevertheless a capable businessman and loyal townsfellow, who seems to have fallen on relatively hard times in later life. He would have been brought up as a Catholic, and may have retained

Catholic sympathies, but his son subscribed publicly to
Anglicanism throughout his life.

The most important formative influence on Shakespeare was his school. As the son of an alderman who
became bailiff (or mayor) in 1568, he had the right to
attend the town's grammar school. Here he would have
received an education grounded in classical rhetoric and
oratory, studying authors such as Ovid, Cicero and
Quintilian, and would have been required to read, speak,
write and even think in Latin from his early years. This
classical education permeates Shakespeare's work from
the beginning to the end of his career. It is apparent in
the self-conscious classicism of plays of the early 1590s
such as the tragedy of *Titus Andronicus*, *The Comedy of
Errors*, and the narrative poems *Venus and Adonis* (1592–3)
and *The Rape of Lucrece* (1593–4), and is still evident in
his latest plays, informing the dream visions of *Pericles*
and *Cymbeline* and the masque in *The Tempest*, written
between 1607 and 1611. It inflects his literary style
throughout his career. In his earliest writings the verse,
based on the ten-syllabled, five-beat iambic pentameter,
is highly patterned. Rhetorical devices deriving from classical literature, such as alliteration and antithesis, extended
similes and elaborate wordplay, abound. Often, as in
Love's Labour's Lost and *A Midsummer Night's Dream*, he
uses rhyming patterns associated with lyric poetry, each
line self-contained in sense, the prose as well as the verse
employing elaborate figures of speech. Writing at a time
of linguistic ferment, Shakespeare frequently imports
Latinisms into English, coining words such as abstemious,
addiction, incarnadine and adjunct. He was also heavily
influenced by the eloquent translations of the Bible in
both the Bishops' and the Geneva versions. As his experience grows, his verse and prose become more supple,

the patterning less apparent, more ready to accommodate the rhythms of ordinary speech, more colloquial in
diction, as in the speeches of the Nurse in *Romeo and
Juliet*, the characterful prose of Falstaff and Hamlet's
soliloquies. The effect is of increasing psychological
realism, reaching its greatest heights in *Hamlet*, *Othello*,
King Lear, *Macbeth* and *Antony and Cleopatra*. Gradually
he discovered ways of adapting the regular beat of the
pentameter to make it an infinitely flexible instrument for
matching thought with feeling. Towards the end of his
career, in plays such as *The Winter's Tale*, *Cymbeline* and
The Tempest, he adopts a more highly mannered style,
in keeping with the more overtly symbolical and emblem-
atical mode in which he is writing.

So far as we know, Shakespeare lived in Stratford till
after his marriage to Anne Hathaway, eight years his
senior, in 1582. They had three children: a daughter,
Susanna, born in 1583 within six months of their marriage,
and twins, Hamnet and Judith, born in 1585. The next
seven years of Shakespeare's life are virtually a blank.
Theories that he may have been, for instance, a schoolmaster, or a lawyer, or a soldier, or a sailor, lack evidence
to support them. The first reference to him in print, in
Robert Greene's pamphlet *Greene's Groatsworth of Wit*
of 1592, parodies a line from *Henry VI, Part III*, implying
that Shakespeare was already an established playwright.
It seems likely that at some unknown point after the birth
of his twins he joined a theatre company and gained
experience as both actor and writer in the provinces and
London. The London theatres closed because of plague
in 1593 and 1594; and during these years, perhaps recognizing the need for an alternative career, he wrote and
published the narrative poems *Venus and Adonis* and *The
Rape of Lucrece*. These are the only works we can be

certain that Shakespeare himself was responsible for putting into print. Each bears the author's dedication to Henry Wriothesley, Earl of Southampton (1573–1624), the second in warmer terms than the first. Southampton, younger than Shakespeare by ten years, is the only person to whom he personally dedicated works. The Earl may have been a close friend, perhaps even the beautiful and adored young man whom Shakespeare celebrates in his *Sonnets*.

The resumption of playing after the plague years saw the founding of the Lord Chamberlain's Men, a company to which Shakespeare was to belong for the rest of his career, as actor, shareholder and playwright. No other dramatist of the period had so stable a relationship with a single company. Shakespeare knew the actors for whom he was writing and the conditions in which they performed. The permanent company was made up of around twelve to fourteen players, but one actor often played more than one role in a play and additional actors were hired as needed. Led by the tragedian Richard Burbage (1568–1619) and, initially, the comic actor Will Kemp (d. 1603), they rapidly achieved a high reputation, and when King James I succeeded Queen Elizabeth I in 1603 they were renamed as the King's Men. All the women's parts were played by boys; there is no evidence that any female role was ever played by a male actor over the age of about eighteen. Shakespeare had enough confidence in his boys to write for them long and demanding roles such as Rosalind (who, like other heroines of the romantic comedies, is disguised as a boy for much of the action) in *As You Like It*, Lady Macbeth and Cleopatra. But there are far more fathers than mothers, sons than daughters, in his plays, few if any of which require more than the company's normal complement of three or four boys.

The company played primarily in London's public playhouses – there were almost none that we know of in the rest of the country – initially in the Theatre, built in Shoreditch in 1576, and from 1599 in the Globe, on Bankside. These were wooden, more or less circular structures, open to the air, with a thrust stage surmounted by a canopy and jutting into the area where spectators who paid one penny stood, and surrounded by galleries where it was possible to be seated on payment of an additional penny. Though properties such as cauldrons, stocks, artificial trees or beds could indicate locality, there was no representational scenery. Sound effects such as flourishes of trumpets, music both martial and amorous, and accompaniments to songs were provided by the company's musicians. Actors entered through doors in the back wall of the stage. Above it was a balconied area that could represent the walls of a town (as in *King John*), or a castle (as in *Richard II*), and indeed a balcony (as in *Romeo and Juliet*). In 1609 the company also acquired the use of the Blackfriars, a smaller, indoor theatre to which admission was more expensive, and which permitted the use of more spectacular stage effects such as the descent of Jupiter on an eagle in *Cymbeline* and of goddesses in *The Tempest*. And they would frequently perform before the court in royal residences and, on their regular tours into the provinces, in non-theatrical spaces such as inns, guildhalls and the great halls of country houses.

Early in his career Shakespeare may have worked in collaboration, perhaps with Thomas Nashe (1567–*c.* 1601) in *Henry VI, Part I* and with George Peele (1556–96) in *Titus Andronicus*. And towards the end he collaborated with George Wilkins (*fl.* 1604–8) in *Pericles*, and with his younger colleagues Thomas Middleton (1580–1627), in *Timon of Athens*, and John Fletcher (1579–1625), in *Henry*

VIII, The Two Noble Kinsmen and the lost play *Cardenio*. Shakespeare's output dwindled in his last years, and he died in 1616 in Stratford, where he owned a fine house, New Place, and much land. His only son had died at the age of eleven, in 1596, and his last descendant died in 1670. New Place was destroyed in the eighteenth century but the other Stratford houses associated with his life are maintained and displayed to the public by the Shakespeare Birthplace Trust.

One of the most remarkable features of Shakespeare's plays is their intellectual and emotional scope. They span a great range from the lightest of comedies, such as *The Two Gentlemen of Verona* and *The Comedy of Errors*, to the profoundest of tragedies, such as *King Lear* and *Macbeth*. He maintained an output of around two plays a year, ringing the changes between comic and serious. All his comedies have serious elements: Shylock, in *The Merchant of Venice*, almost reaches tragic dimensions, and *Measure for Measure* is profoundly serious in its examination of moral problems. Equally, none of his tragedies is without humour: Hamlet is as witty as any of his comic heroes, *Macbeth* has its Porter, and *King Lear* its Fool. His greatest comic character, Falstaff, inhabits the history plays and *Henry V* ends with a marriage, while *Henry VI, Part III*, *Richard II* and *Richard III* culminate in the tragic deaths of their protagonists.

Although in performance Shakespeare's characters can give the impression of a superabundant reality, he is not a naturalistic dramatist. None of his plays is explicitly set in his own time. The action of few of them (except for the English histories) is set even partly in England (exceptions are *The Merry Wives of Windsor* and the Induction to *The Taming of the Shrew*). Italy is his favoured location. Most of his principal story-lines derive from printed writings; but the structuring and translation of these narratives into dramatic terms is Shakespeare's own, and he invents much additional material. Most of the plays contain elements of myth and legend, and many derive from ancient or more recent history or from romantic tales of ancient times and faraway places. All reflect his reading, often in close detail. Holinshed's *Chronicles* (1577, revised 1587), a great compendium of English, Scottish and Irish history, provided material for his English history plays. The *Lives of the Noble Grecians and Romans* by the Greek writer Plutarch, finely translated into English from the French by Sir Thomas North in 1579, provided much of the narrative material, and also a mass of verbal detail, for his plays about Roman history. Some plays are closely based on shorter individual works: *As You Like It*, for instance, on the novel *Rosalynde* (1590) by his near-contemporary Thomas Lodge (1558–1625), *The Winter's Tale* on *Pandosto* (1588) by his old rival Robert Greene (1558–92) and *Othello* on a story by the Italian Giraldi Cinthio (1504–73). And the language of his plays is permeated by the Bible, the Book of Common Prayer and the proverbial sayings of his day.

Shakespeare was popular with his contemporaries, but his commitment to the theatre and to the plays in performance is demonstrated by the fact that only about half of his plays appeared in print in his lifetime, in slim paperback volumes known as quartos, so called because they were made from printers' sheets folded twice to form four leaves (eight pages). None of them shows any sign that he was involved in their publication. For him, performance was the primary means of publication. The most frequently reprinted of his works were the nondramatic poems – the erotic *Venus and Adonis* and the

more moralistic *The Rape of Lucrece*. The *Sonnets*, which
appeared in 1609, under his name but possibly without
his consent, were less successful, perhaps because the
vogue for sonnet sequences, which peaked in the 1590s,
had passed by then. They were not reprinted until 1640,
and then only in garbled form along with poems by other
writers. Happily, in 1623, seven years after he died, his
colleagues John Heminges (1556–1630) and Henry
Condell (d. 1627) published his collected plays, including
eighteen that had not previously appeared in print, in the
first Folio, whose name derives from the fact that the
printers' sheets were folded only once to produce two
leaves (four pages). Some of the quarto editions are badly
printed, and the fact that some plays exist in two, or even
three, early versions creates problems for editors. These
are discussed in the Account of the Text in each volume
of this series.

Shakespeare's plays continued in the repertoire until
the Puritans closed the theatres in 1642. When performances resumed after the Restoration of the monarchy in
1660 many of the plays were not to the taste of the times,
especially because their mingling of genres and failure
to meet the requirements of poetic justice offended
against the dictates of neoclassicism. Some, such as *The
Tempest* (changed by John Dryden and William Davenant
in 1667 to suit contemporary taste), *King Lear* (to which
Nahum Tate gave a happy ending in 1681) and *Richard
III* (heavily adapted by Colley Cibber in 1700 as a vehicle
for his own talents), were extensively rewritten; others
fell into neglect. Slowly they regained their place in the
repertoire, and they continued to be reprinted, but it was
not until the great actor David Garrick (1717–79) organ-
ized a spectacular jubilee in Stratford in 1769 that
Shakespeare began to be regarded as a transcendental

genius. Garrick's idolatry prefigured the enthusiasm of critics such as Samuel Taylor Coleridge (1772–1834) and William Hazlitt (1778–1830). Gradually Shakespeare's reputation spread abroad, to Germany, America, France and to other European countries.

During the nineteenth century, though the plays were generally still performed in heavily adapted or abbreviated versions, a large body of scholarship and criticism began to amass. Partly as a result of a general swing in education away from the teaching of Greek and Roman texts and towards literature written in English, Shakespeare became the object of intensive study in schools and universities. In the theatre, important turning points were the work in England of two theatre directors, William Poel (1852–1934) and his disciple Harley Granville-Barker (1877–1946), who showed that the application of knowledge, some of it newly acquired, of early staging conditions to performance of the plays could render the original texts viable in terms of the modern theatre. During the twentieth century appreciation of Shakespeare's work, encouraged by the availability of audio, film and video versions of the plays, spread around the world to such an extent that he can now be claimed as a global author.

The influence of Shakespeare's works permeates the English language. Phrases from his plays and poems – 'a tower of strength', 'green-eyed jealousy', 'a foregone conclusion' – are on the lips of people who may never have read him. They have inspired composers of songs, orchestral music and operas; painters and sculptors; poets, novelists and film-makers. Allusions to him appear in pop songs, in advertisements and in television shows. Some of his characters – Romeo and Juliet, Falstaff, Shylock and Hamlet – have acquired mythic status. He is valued for his humanity, his psychological insight, his wit and humour, his lyricism, his mastery of language, his ability to excite, surprise, move and, in the widest sense of the word, entertain audiences. He is the greatest of poets, but he is essentially a dramatic poet. Though his plays have much to offer to readers, they exist fully only in performance. In these volumes we offer individual introductions, notes on language and on specific points of the text, suggestions for further reading and information about how each work has been edited. In addition we include accounts of the ways in which successive generations of interpreters and audiences have responded to challenges and rewards offered by the plays. The Penguin Shakespeare series aspires to remove obstacles to understanding and to make pleasurable the reading of the work of the man who has done more than most to make us understand what it is to be human.

                                                    Stanley Wells

The Chronology of
Shakespeare's Works

A few of Shakespeare's writings can be fairly precisely dated. An allusion to the Earl of Essex in the chorus to Act V of *Henry V*, for instance, could only have been written in 1599. But for many of the plays we have only vague information, such as the date of publication, which may have occurred long after composition, the date of a performance, which may not have been the first, or a list in Francis Meres's book *Palladis Tamia*, published in 1598, which tells us only that the plays listed there must have been written by that year. The chronology of the early plays is particularly difficult to establish. Not everyone would agree that the first part of *Henry VI* was written after the third, for instance, or *Romeo and Juliet* before *A Midsummer Night's Dream*. The following table is based on the 'Canon and Chronology' section in *William Shakespeare: A Textual Companion*, by Stanley Wells and Gary Taylor, with John Jowett and William Montgomery (1987), where more detailed information and discussion may be found.

The Two Gentlemen of Verona	1590–91
The Taming of the Shrew	1590–91
Henry VI, Part II	1591
Henry VI, Part III	1591

Macbeth (revised by Middleton)   1606
Antony and Cleopatra   1606
Pericles (with George Wilkins)   1607
Coriolanus   1608
The Winter's Tale   1609
Cymbeline   1610
The Tempest   1611
Henry VIII (by Shakespeare and John Fletcher;
    known in its own time as *All is True*)   1613
Cardenio (by Shakespeare and Fletcher; lost)   1613
The Two Noble Kinsmen (by Shakespeare
    and Fletcher)   1613–14

Introduction

A mother waits for her son, her only child, to return from the battlefield. He has fought so fearlessly that from now on he will be nicknamed after the city he has helped to defeat. She is excited to see the fresh gashes on his shoulder and left arm, the latest incisions on his war-torn body. Trumpets sound. Her son has returned:

> These are the ushers of Martius. Before him he carries noise, and behind him he leaves tears.
> Death, that dark spirit, in's nervy arm doth lie,
> Which, being advanced, declines, and then men die.
> (II.1.151–4)

It is a chilling distillation of maternal pride in the services her son has performed for their city. Few mothers take pleasure in thinking of their sons as killing machines. But this is no ordinary mother, son or city. What Volumnia says of her son, Caius Martius Coriolanus, might also be true of the tragedy that bears his name. Before him he carries noise, and behind him he leaves tears. Shakespeare's play begins explosively with a group of armed, mutinous citizens, poised on the edge of insurrection. It is this noise that sets the volume and tempo for the fractious violence of the events which follow. The play ends with tears. Certainly with the tears of Martius himself; in a telling euphemism he talks of sweating compassion at the impossibility of choosing between his own life and the lives of his mother, wife and son (V.3.197). But Martius also perhaps leaves tears of remorse in the eyes of his rival and effective assassin, Aufidius. And, this being tragedy, might we not also expect to be moved ourselves, as readers and audience members, to some kind of physical response at the sufferings of others? 'Before him he carries noise, and behind him he leaves tears' thus points to beginnings and endings, the before and after of a hurricane-like, cataclysmic disaster. But what is the nature of that disaster? What does the sound and fury of *Coriolanus* signify? What happens between the noise and the tears?

Coriolanus is Shakespeare's most overtly political play. A series of events in the early history of the Roman republic formed the skeleton that the playwright fleshed out into a full-blooded, vivid piece of theatre. The play thrives on conflict and derives much of its considerable energy from the clashing of mighty opposites, whether these clashes are physical, ideological or emotional, or, typically, an intractable combination of all three. Indeed, one of Shakespeare's great achievements in *Coriolanus* is to show the ways in which class, tribal and family backgrounds form individual identity and the faultlines and tensions inherent in such a diversity of influences. As one character puts it, 'violent'st contrariety' (IV.6.74) is the thematic and structuring principle of *Coriolanus*.

The story of Coriolanus dwelt in Shakespeare's mind from an early point in his career. In what is probably his first tragedy, *Titus Andronicus* (1592), it is said of the exiled Lucius that he promises 'in course of this revenge to do | As much as ever Coriolanus did' (IV.4.67–8) – a strange analogy given that Coriolanus never exacts his revenge. Towards the end of his career, probably sometime in 1608, Shakespeare decided to make Martius and Rome the protagonists of his last tragedy. There are a number of reasons why he might have been drawn to the material at this particular personal and historical moment. His main source for the play, Plutarch's *Parallel Lives*, translated into English by Sir Thomas North as *The Lives of the Noble Grecians and Romans* (1579) had lain open by Shakespeare's side when he wrote *Timon of Athens* (1605) and *Antony and Cleopatra* (1606). In *Timon*, Alcibiades is banished from Athens and seeks revenge on his mother city. Plutarch found the comparison sufficiently instructive to structure the biographies of Alcibiades and Caius Martius as 'parallel' lives. But other, more urgent parallels must also have inspired Shakespeare's composition of *Coriolanus*. James I's relatively recent accession to the throne, his scrapes with parliament and his denigrating description of parliamentary critics as 'Tribunes of the people' – all this meant that theories of leadership, government and the distribution of power were keenly felt and debated by his subjects. Equally topically, a combination of bad harvests, hyper-inflationary prices and apparent food-hoarding by the gentry had led in the years 1607–8 to a series of riots and protests by peasants in north and central England. Like their counterparts in Shakespeare's play they were inflamed by hunger and incensed by the greed of a privileged minority. Talk of authority, absolutism, abundance and deprivation was in the air. Furthermore, it is also possible that in recreating the character of Martius, Shakespeare was holding a mirror up to any one of the brave and arrogant noblemen who populated the courts of Elizabeth and James. The careers and personalities of both Robert Devereux, second Earl of Essex, and Sir Walter Raleigh offered immediate examples of the benefits and dangers of the warrior-aristocrat. Finally, Shakespeare may have been influenced in the composition of *Coriolanus* by the theatrical vogue for Roman settings. His friend and rival Ben Jonson had recently produced two Roman political tragedies, *Sejanus* (1603) and *Catiline* (1607). Shakespeare's private reading merged with public events and theatrical fashion to force Plutarch's source to the front of his creative mind. It was a narrative ripe for 'th'interpretation of the time' (IV.7.50).

Unfortunately, we cannot be sure how Shakespeare's audience received *Coriolanus*. There is no hard evidence for the date or venue of the first theatrical production of the play, although it is highly probable that it not only played at the large, popular outdoor Globe Theatre, but that it was also one of Shakespeare's first plays written for the smaller, more elite indoor theatre at Blackfriars. Given the central theme of class antagonism, it is tempting to speculate how these different theatres and their respective clienteles might have affected and received the first performances of *Coriolanus*. But no eyewitness account exists. Furthermore, no text of the play appears to have been published before 1623, when it was collected into the first Folio, the original 'Complete Works' of Shakespeare.

If we cannot know for sure how Shakespeare's first audiences interpreted *Coriolanus*, the play's subsequent stage history bears rich testimony to the extreme and vivid responses the play provokes. The title of Nahum Tate's *The Ingratitude of a Commonwealth; or, The Fall of Coriolanus* (1681) answers the question that Shakespeare's play leaves unresolved. Tate's play is strictly about the ignorant plebeians' out-casting of an irreplaceable hero.

In case we were in any doubt, Tate wrote in his dedication that 'The Moral therefore of these Scenes [is] to
Recommend Submission and Adherence to Establisht
Lawful Power, which in a word, is Loyalty'. Those
seventeenth-century capitalizations give the impression
of a man writing at the top of his voice, shouting down
Shakespeare's careful political ambivalence. Since Tate,
Coriolanus has been frequently adapted, invariably to suit
the political tastes of the adaptor, which are rarely
moderate. For conservatives and those 'o'th'right-hand
file' (II.1.21–2), like Tate, the play is 'about' the inability
of the masses to think wisely and clearly and the need,
therefore, for strong, authoritarian leadership. For left-
wingers, *Coriolanus* exemplifies the dangers of such
leadership and the repressive victimization of the
working-class upon which such power depends. Bertolt
Brecht's adaptation *Coriolan* (1964) emerged from his
somewhat wishful interpretation of the play as 'the
tragedy of a people that has a hero against it' (*Brecht on
Theatre*, p. 258). In its historical context Brecht's play was
an understandable attempt to reappropriate *Coriolanus*:
the play had been so popular with the Nazis that the
American forces who occupied Berlin in the aftermath of
the war banned it.

As simplistic, ingenious, laughable or sinister as some
adaptations have been, they do reveal an underlying desire
of readers and audience alike in responding to *Coriolanus*:
the desire for certainty. *Coriolanus* is a tricky, controversial play because Shakespeare's own politics seem to be
up for grabs in the critical and stage interpretation of the
piece. What Shakespeare *really* thought of the working
classes, the aristocracy, the military, and of mothers and
sons would appear to be tantalizingly present somewhere
in the text. So adaptors, critics, directors and actors

understandably seek for some flash of interpretive or intuitive light to resolve the ambivalence, to reveal whose side Shakespeare took, and, by extension, to let us know where our own sympathies should lie. Simulations of certainty have also been offered by literary critics, old and new historians, doctrinaire Marxists, Freudians, cultural materialists and feminists apparently convinced that their key unlocks the interpretative deadlock. In Aufidius' image of successive interpretations, 'One fire drives out one [critical] fire; one nail one nail' (IV.7.54). While much criticism has been revelatory and truly illuminating, the play seems to have an inbuilt mechanism that resists definitive judgement. It is almost perversely even handed: no character – with the exception of Martius' wife, Virgilia – escapes criticism or is uncontaminated by the corrupt and confused world of the play. As with most art, great or otherwise, opinions on *Coriolanus* will often reveal as much about the observer as the observed. And so it is with Martius himself.

'ALL TONGUES SPEAK OF HIM'

Caius Martius is a celebrity. Born into a powerful elite of politicians and military leaders, fame is his birthright, and from an early age he has been accustomed to public attention. His mother remembers how as a boy his 'youth with comeliness plucked all gaze his way' (I.3.6–7). 'Pluck' is used elsewhere as a verb of violence, as in Martius' heated wish to 'pluck out | The multitudinous tongue' (III.1.155–6), where the action is a sudden sharp pull: even when Martius attracts people, it is through a form of force. At the age of sixteen, when he was still fresh-faced and 'tender-bodied' (I.3.5–6), his celebrity status was sealed as he proved himself a man by killing on the battlefield in defence of Rome. His adult life has taken him from one theatre of war to another, and in every campaign he has fought so fiercely and fearlessly as to outshine all other warriors. He is now, as Ophelia says of Hamlet, the 'observed of all observers' (III.1.155), the charged centre of the city's attention. The slaughterous ability of his 'nervy arm' (II.1.153) has made him the most famous man in Rome.

But not the most popular. The first of the many perspectives on Martius in the play is uttered by the tongue of the First Citizen. His is the first distinct voice we hear and his description of Martius as 'chief enemy to the people' (I.1.7–8) creates an initial impression that all subsequent opinions and appearances will have to confirm, qualify or contradict. Virtually every character in the play has an opinion of Martius – that is the nature of celebrity – and none of those opinions is disinterested. The First Citizen points to his own motivation in calling for Martius' death: 'the gods know I speak this in hunger for bread, not in thirst for revenge' (22–3). The working class of Rome is desperately hungry, and accuses the patrician class, the aristocracy, of hoarding food. In *The Merchant of Venice* Nerissa tells her pampered employer that 'they are as sick that surfeit with too much as they that starve with nothing' (I.2.5–6), but given the choice we would all choose to suffer from the 'sickness' of the first group, the rich. Of all the patricians, Martius is the least able to hide his disgust with the plebeians. He takes a grim pleasure in itemizing their unwashed faces, rotten teeth and stinking breaths (II.3.59–60, III.3.120–21). His assassination would represent a symbolic blow to the heart, or rather the strong arm, of the establishment. The Second Citizen objects: what about Martius' military record? Has that not been for the good of Rome and all who dwell in her? In a play typified by the instant rebuttal, the First Citizen quickly rejoins with an argumentative sleight of hand. Rather than considering the objective value of Martius as a warrior, he counters with an almost tabloid deconstruction of the celebrity's motivation: 'Though soft-conscienced men can be content to say it was for his country, he did it to please his mother and to be partly proud' (I.1.35–7).

When the play opens Rome is at peace with its neighbours. In such a context, albeit perhaps temporary, the status of the warrior and the military in general is precarious. Aufidius, in listing the possible reasons for Martius' eventual fall from grace in Rome, dwells on the soldier's inability to adjust to ceasefires. It is in Martius' nature

> Not to be other than one thing, not moving
> From th'casque [helmet] to th'cushion, but commanding
>   peace
> Even with the same austerity and garb
> As he controlled the war ... (IV.7.42–5)

The question of how a warrior conducts himself when not on the battlefield had occupied Shakespeare many times before, not least in explorations of characters, such as Richard III, Othello and Macbeth, who had been 'bred in broils' (III.2.81), but who spend most of their stage-life in a weaker time of peace. In the first decade of the 1600s, in the context of intermittent military campaigns for the English army, the issue clearly held contemporary relevance. One aristocrat, Lord Burghley, wrote a letter to his son advising him not to train his offspring to be soldiers. Like a career on the stage, professional soldier-ship was not a stable profession: 'it is a science no longer in request than in use: soldiers in peace are like chimneys in summer' (quoted in Jorgensen, *Shakespeare's Military World*, p. 220). Martius accuses the plebeians of being no more reliable, 'no surer, no, | Than is the coal of fire upon the ice | Or hailstone in the sun' (I.i.170–72). But what if the violent contrasts were reversed? What use is the chimney in the summer? What value the firebrand hot-head in the cooler time of peace? What if Martius himself is the unseasonable anachronism?

It is clear that Martius is indeed dislocated when not in battle. His first entrance is fuelled by the pent-up testosterone of the prize fighter between bouts. In a Rome that is experimenting with new forms of government, his dedication to old models of feudal rule, combined with an apparent inability to accommodate the opinions of others, makes him a political liability. Politics is the art of the possible and requires compromise. From this perspective Martius is, like the chimney in summer, a symbol of redundancy. Indeed, Shakespeare's earlier plays contain many examples of inflexible, heroic characters passing into history as they are superseded by a new generation of versatile, opportunistic and pragmatic rivals. In Hotspur and Hal, Richard II and Bolingbroke, or Antony and Octavius Caesar, the idealist gives way to the politician.

Yet, as with so much in this play, Shakespeare is interested in complication rather than explanation. Why else would he follow Plutarch and actually make Martius the only patrician with a grasp of the total political situation? Furthermore, Shakespeare makes it clear that peace between Rome and its neighbours is a provisional condition. The Volsces are a belligerent tribe, seemingly always on the point of attacking Rome. At the opening of the third act it is announced that, while Rome has been preoccupied with internal dissent, Aufidius has regrouped his army. As Martius summarizes: 'So then the Volsces stand but as at first, | Ready, when time shall prompt them, to make road | Upon's again' (III.1.4–6). The intention to attack is later confirmed when the Volscian Adrian informs the Roman deserter Nicanor that the Volsces are 'in a most warlike preparation' (IV.3.15), hoping to conquer the already divided Romans. In this cycle of attritional repetition Martius is far from superfluous.

Whatever else Shakespeare wants us to think of Martius, one thing is certain: more than anywhere else in the canon, Shakespeare wanted to impress us with the spectacle of a warrior in action. Many of the plays contain battlefield clashes, some between armies, others between individuals, such as the hand-to-hand climactic duels through which Macbeth and Richard III meet their bloody ends. But no soldier in Shakespeare fights like Martius: he is peerless. And we *see* Martius' military prowess. It is not merely reported. Shakespeare's dramaturgy here obeys the old theatrical principle: don't tell, show! He makes Martius enter the city of Corioles alone, whereas in Plutarch, Martius is joined by a few daring soldiers. Shakespeare's alteration to his source probably made practical sense; as an actor-manager-director he may not have had enough actors as soldiers for a handful to split off with Martius and still give the impression of being a tiny minority. But more importantly, he was at pains to stress the lonely, suicidal and breathtaking courage of Martius.

The image of a fearless warrior, flanked by fresh corpses and picking his way through a besieged city, had occurred to Shakespeare before. In *Hamlet* the arrival of the players reminds the prince of a gory, melodramatic

speech he once heard at the theatre. It recounts Pyrrhus'
slaughter of King Priam during the fall of Troy. Having
made his way into the enemy city, Pyrrhus is described:
'Head to foot | Now is he total gules [red], horridly
tricked | With blood of fathers, mothers, daughters,
sons . . .' He is, in the pompous and archaic diction of
the remembered play, 'o'er-sizèd with coagulate gore'
(II.2.454–6, 460). Hamlet is amazed that such a speech
can move the First Player to tears. While the description
of a warrior covered in blood is presented in *Hamlet* as
inflated and improbable, in *Coriolanus* we see Shakespeare,
in his final tragedy, literalizing and embodying this image
for his audience, confronting them with its extremity.
'Who's yonder | That does appear as he were flayed?'
(I.6.21–2) asks Cominius, who later describes Martius
during the battle as 'a thing of blood' (II.2.107). Perhaps
our nearest frame of popular reference for Martius'
physical exploits can be found in the unbelievable,
solitary feats of the muscle-bound hero of the Hollywood
blockbuster: Rambo, the Terminator, and other cine-
matic individuals with a genius for self-preservation and
a flair for mass destruction against all rational odds.
(Indeed, posters advertising the Royal Shakespeare
Company's 1994 London transfer of *Coriolanus* depicted
a gory Toby Stephens glowering above the headline
'Natural Born Killer', an attempt to cash in on the noto-
riety of Oliver Stone's hyper-violent film.) Through
playing such parts, embodying such primal glamour, one
can evolve into a senior politician. The improbable ascent
of Arnold Schwarzenegger to the governorship of
California in 2003 testified to the enduring appeal of the
fictional warrior. The difficulty, as Martius discovers, is
when you become mechanically stuck in the role of the
terminator, when you can play no other part.

Within the military ethos of Rome, then, Martius is
the supreme embodiment of *virtus*, the quality of valour
in the service of the state. Cominius begins his long speech
of praise by framing Martius' achievements within the
context of Roman ideology:

> It is held
> That valour is the chiefest virtue and
> Most dignifies the haver. If it be,
> The man I speak of cannot in the world
> Be singly counterpoised. (II.2.81–5)

And he is right: *if* valour is the guiding principle and the
highest virtue, Coriolanus is, to paraphrase Cleopatra's
epitaph, a lad unparalleled. He is also, as the threat of the
ever-encroaching Volsces testifies, probably indispens-
able. The Tribunes' decision to push for his banishment
or execution is remarkably short sighted, failing as it does
to address an overwhelmingly uncomfortable question:
would the populace prefer to live under a home-grown
aristocratic tyranny or under the yoke of occupation by
an outside, foreign military elite? Is the devil you know
really preferable to the one you have yet to meet? This
then is the burden and substance of Martius' celebrity:
he is Rome's saviour but also, as Aufidius' spies inform
him, 'worse hated' in Rome than even the Volscian
general (I.2.13). In Brecht's play *Life of Galileo* (1938)
Galileo's pupil Andrea despairs at his master's recanta-
tion to the Inquisition: 'Unhappy the land that has no
heroes!' Galileo offers the correction: 'No. Unhappy the
land that is in need of heroes.' Rome, an unhappy city,
needs Martius.

'WHAT IS THE CITY BUT
THE PEOPLE?'

What is this unhappy land that cannot quite do without
its hero? And who are its people? The word 'Rome' is
spoken eighty-eight times in *Coriolanus*, more than in
Julius Caesar and *Antony and Cleopatra* combined. In
addition to Plutarch's *Parallel Lives*, Shakespeare probably also consulted the ancient historian Livy's *Ab Urbe
Condita* ('From the founding of the city'), a biography
of Rome, and a work brought back into prominence in
the Renaissance by Machiavelli's *Discourses* (1531), which
offered a commentary on its first ten books. Counter-
balancing Plutarch's emphasis on the individual, Livy
stressed the life and character of the city and its emer-
gence as a model of civilized society. Named more often
than 'Martius' or any of the play's other characters, Rome
is one of the chief protagonists of *Coriolanus*.

At the close of *Henry IV, Part II* the dying King Henry
advises his son that the best way to avoid civil war and
domestic unrest is 'to busy giddy minds | With foreign
quarrels' (IV.5.213–14). Waging war abroad has always
been a useful way for governments to distract attention
from shoddy domestic records; 'foreign quarrels' ask a
populace to forget hardship and inequality by inviting it
to revel in the bonds of patriotism and a common enemy.
According to Aufidius' servingmen, peace 'makes men
hate one another' because 'they then less need one
another' (IV.5.236–9). War manufactures social cohesion
and without it Rome is dangerously dysfunctional. In
Plato's *The Republic* Socrates described how any state
'always contains at least two states, the rich and the poor,
at enmity with each other; each of these in turn has many

subdivisions, and it is a complete mistake to treat them all as a unity' (p. 124). Any attempt to describe a city will always be a tale of many cities. This internal division, in which the rich live cheek by jowl with the hungry and the destitute, is a constant of city life. According to the First Citizen, Rome's affluent class even takes pleasure in this radical inequality: 'The leanness that afflicts us, the object [i.e. the sight] of our misery, is as an inventory to particularize their abundance' (I.1.18–20). This is the first critique we hear of the patricians and it is devastating. Shakespeare has given the speaker a complex and sophisticated mode of self-expression – this is not the bumbling malapropist or monosyllabic grunter so common in negative representations of the working class or mobs. According to this testimony the Roman aristocrat is living in an ethical vacuum. The sight of the poor starving gives him pleasure. It reminds him of his next meal. The First Citizen later details the tactics by which this perverse pleasure is maintained: the hoarding of grain, the encouragement of loan sharks and the introduction of anti-plebeian legislation (78–82). The choice for the plebeian is whether to die in warfare or starve in Rome. It is staggering that, throughout *Coriolanus*, the patricians rarely make any attempt to deny these charges. The longest denial of patrician responsibility comes from Menenius and is based on a very different idea of Rome from that of subdivided cities of rich and poor.

Menenius' first tactic is denial: there is no excess corn. Pray to the gods, he advises, they are responsible for the dearth (I.1.70–72). He then offers one of the most famous extended analogies in Shakespeare. Rome, he argues, is like a body: whole, organic, coherent and functional. Conventional analogies between political systems and the human body figure government or monarchy as the head, the elevated seat of reason, wisdom and vision. But this convention does not suit Menenius' purpose. If the aristocrats' storehouses are indeed 'crammed with grain' (79), as the First Citizen claims, some positive spin must be put on this embarrassment. Rather than the head, then, the patricians are the belly of Rome's body. All resources – food, money, power – must pass through them if they are to be fairly distributed through the arteries of the city. It is merely a matter of time before the goods they enjoy will be shared equally. Although this redistribution may not be perceptible when it happens, yet, says the Belly, 'I can make my audit up, that all | From me do back receive the flour of all, | And leave me but the bran' (142–4). Making one's audit up is both to balance the books and to be prepared for God's judgement. In Menenius' fable, the patricians somehow manage to be selfless, sinless *and* well fed.

The theory that economic intervention in favour of the super-rich creates a stronger economy and thus eventually benefits all sections of society is called 'Trickle Down'. Menenius' fable offers a 'Trickle Around' model. But, shorn of its charm and rhetoric, it is an abnegation of responsibility: If you're satisfied, thank us. If you're hungry, blame the gods. It is not surprising that Karl Marx was fascinated by this section of the play, nor that the left-leaning social and theatre critic William Hazlitt stated flatly in 1817: 'The whole dramatic moral of *Coriolanus* is, that those who have little shall have less, and that those who have much shall take all that others have left. The people are poor; therefore they ought to be starved' (Bate (ed.), *Romantics on Shakespeare*, p. 285). The First Citizen, at least, is not fooled by the fable: 'It was an answer' (I.1.145). If Menenius stalls the potentially riotous citizenry of Rome with long-winded spin, we then immediately see the naked, unspun truth of the patrician attitude to the masses. Martius enters.

The fable of the belly establishes one image of Rome, that of separate limbs and organs with distinct functions and talents but working for a common goal. The arrival of Martius, perhaps the noisiest stage debut in Shakespeare, smashes that image. The body politic is blasted apart. In the contest to define Rome, he offers a new model:

> They say there's grain enough!
> Would the nobility lay aside their ruth [pity]
> And let me use my sword, I'd make a quarry
> With thousands of these quartered slaves as high
> As I could pick my lance. (I.1.194–8)

After Menenius' emollient story-telling this is astonishing. From the outset, Martius makes us aware of his belief in class genocide. This fantasy of a plebicide is confirmed when he receives news that the Volsces are preparing for war: 'I am glad on't. Then we shall ha' means to vent | Our musty superfluity' (223–4). The superfluity (abundance) of grain the citizens speak of as growing musty in the patricians' storehouses is here reimagined: it is the citizens themselves who are surplus to requirements, growing mouldy through lack of gainful employment. The upcoming confrontation with the Volsces solves two problems for Martius: first, his sense of self-worth is far more comfortable in war than in peace, while the prospect of re-meeting Aufidius positively titillates him; second, the war 'solves' the problem of working-class hunger: 'The Volsces have much corn. Take these rats thither | To gnaw their garners' (247–8). In Menenius' fable, the people had been represented as mutual participants in the 'whole body' of Rome (101–3). Martius, conversely, denies both their Roman-ness and their humanity. In the fierce, bestializing imagery so typical of this play, they are rats, curs, hares and geese. Such animals are expendable.

It is notable that when Volumnia first imagines Martius in battle he is not only beating Aufidius and scattering Volsces, he is also railing at his own troops:

> Methinks I see him stamp thus, and call thus:
> 'Come on, you cowards! You were got in fear,
> Though you were born in Rome.' (I.3.33–5)

Of the eighty-eight times 'Rome' is uttered in the play, it is almost invariably invoked by a patrician. No plebeian ever mentions the name of the city in which he dwells. Being Roman is a patrician concept. The plebeians are *unter*-Romans, living *in* the city but not of it. Being born in the city is not qualification enough: 'I would they were barbarians, as they are, | Though in Rome littered; not Romans, as they are not, | Though calved i'th'porch o'th'Capitol' (III.1.237–9). As Volumnia predicted, Martius does indeed turn on his soldiers in the battle of Corioles, offering the self-fulfilling prophecy that, unless they mimic his recklessness, he will 'leave the foe | And make my wars on you' (I.4.39–40). Martius' decision to join Aufidius in exile and offer his service in order to kill Romans thus appears as the logical conclusion of this class antagonism. If the city is the people, the city must suffer.

Into this enormous gulf of misunderstanding between plebeians and patricians step the Tribunes, politicians elected to represent the interests of the working class. Martius announces that five Tribunes have been

appointed, but in a typical Martius moment that is part
anger, part amnesia, he won't or can't tell us the others:
'One's Junius Brutus, one | Sicinius Velutus, and – I
know not' (I.1.214–15). It is hard to admire Brutus and
Sicinius. They are, by any standards, cynical, manipulative and duplicitous. Yet they would not be necessary if
the aristocracy was fulfilling the 'belly' role of Menenius'
parable. It is noticeable that for the patricians the
definition of a plebeian is one who works – Volumnia
refers to the people as the 'occupations' of Rome
(IV.1.14). Then, as now, this is the vast majority of
society. And it is this majority that Martius has been taught
to define himself against; the apparently objective First
Officer who sets the cushions in the Capitol believes
Martius to be 'a worthy man' (II.2.33) but nevertheless
recognizes that 'he seeks [the people's] hate with greater
devotion than they can render it him, and leaves nothing
undone that may fully discover him their opposite'
(17–20). Clearly the people need representation of some
sort, but it is symptomatic of the play's disillusionment
with political processes that those representatives are
Brutus and Sicinius. The greatest argument in the
Tribunes' favour is the all-too-transitory picture of a
peaceful Rome presented in Act IV, scene 6. From their
brief cameo in this scene the working classes do indeed
appear to be happier: 'Our tradesmen singing in their
shops and going | About their functions friendly' (8–9).
If happiness for the greatest number, rather than valour,
is the chiefest virtue of a society, the Tribunes would
appear to have brought it about. But then news of an
imminent invasion arrives to puncture this fragile
prosperity.

'SAY, WHAT'S THY NAME?'

In the interaction between classes, if blows cannot be used, it is words that must take their place. Politics, an urban art form, is impossible without language; to dwell with others in a city requires a system of communication on which all can agree. The connection between language, action and community is announced in the very first line of the play: 'Before we proceed any further, hear me speak.' For all the emphasis on the importance and eloquence of action in *Coriolanus*, this is a world in which words matter. People listen closely to each other, picking up on strange words, querying new ones, interrogating narratives, paying obsessive attention to names. One of Aufidius' servingmen describes Martius as 'he that was wont to thwack our general', to which his colleague instantly rejoins, 'Why do you say "thwack our general"?' Later, he again queries his workmate's choice of words: 'Directitude? What's that?' (IV.5.183–6, 216). These interchanges offer a comic illustration of a serious problem: how do we collectively agree on what things mean? This question is particularly acute when society is in a state of transition, when common values and standards are under stress, and when, as with the First Citizen's opening line, people are speaking in order to change the world.

Politics is partly about knowing when to speak and when to stay silent. In *King Lear*, when Lear asks his daughters which of them loves him most, Cordelia's near-silent response shows immense integrity after the elaborate effusions of her sisters, but is politically disastrous. Martius shares with Cordelia a high-minded distrust of rhetoric and a fear that to use words is to run the risk of betraying oneself. It is often said of Martius that he is proud; it is perhaps the chief accusation the Tribunes make against him (II.1.18–19). But in everyday life pride is not something we can necessarily confer on ourselves; we generally need the recognition or reassurance of others that what we have done is of value before we allow ourselves to feel proud. Not so with Martius. For him it seems that fighting is not the means to fame but a successful end in itself. The passage from deeds to words can only be an embarrassing approximation of what it was actually like to be there. It further implies that the action is not self-sufficient, cannot speak for itself, but requires others to speak for it: 'For if he show us his wounds and tell us his deeds, we are to put our tongues into those wounds and speak for them' (II.3.5–7). This is to cede power from the agent to the witness, from the actor to the historian. Martius' pride curiously resembles an almost pathological modesty. After the Volsces have been successfully 'Fluttered' (V.6.116) in Corioles, Cominius and Lartius offer Martius excited and voluble praise. He interrupts: 'Pray now, no more. My mother, | Who has a charter to extol her blood, | When she does praise me grieves me' (I.9.13–15). When the whole army joins in with shouts, the casting up of caps and with a musical flourish, Martius' response takes us to the heart of his phobia:

> May these same instruments which you profane
> Never sound more! When drums and trumpets shall
> I'th'field prove flatterers, let courts and cities be
> Made all of false-faced soothing. (41–4)

Martius already suspects the integrity of life in courts and cities, based as it is on the give-and-take, the collective struggle towards compromise that is communal living. The battlefield should be different; there, men should act communally but without compromise, as in the great moment when Martius is hoisted up: 'make you a sword of me' (I.6.76).

That Martius is indeed proud of his bravery and daring at the battle of Corioles can be adduced from his later explosions against the Tribunes and his climactic, supreme boast to Aufidius, 'Alone I did it' (V.6.117). But in the series of scenes in the second act of the play, when the patricians are seeking to manoeuvre him into the consulship, Martius continues to display the arrogance/modesty shown in the battle's aftermath. When Cominius is invited to offer the official version of his deeds, Martius rises to leave, admitting that often, 'When blows have made me stay, I fled from words' (II.2.70). A blow would appear to be outside the world of interpretation. You know if you've been hit; it's less easy to know with certainty whether what you've just heard is a compliment, an insult, or a combination of the two. Cominius' speech would indeed have troubled Martius. It is elaborate, full of rhetorical devices. We saw Martius re-enter the city, and while undoubtedly impressive, the image could not live up to Cominius' description of their striking Corioles 'like a planet' (112). This is indeed an 'acclamation hyperbolical' (I.9.50).

The relationship between deed and word, reality and representation, identity and symbol, is acute in one of the most natural and universal of human activities: the giving of names. The arbitrary chanciness of this activity is most famously expressed in Juliet's radically simple: 'What's in a name? That which we call a rose | By any other name would smell as sweet' (*Romeo and Juliet*, II.2.43–4). Shakespeare was fascinated by the question.

In *Julius Caesar* Cassius attempts to demystify the power of Caesar's name: 'Brutus and Caesar. What should be in that "Caesar"? | Why should that name be sounded more than yours? | Write them together, yours is as fair a name' (I.2.141–3). But, however arbitrary, names are important: a frenzied mob, whipped up by Mark Antony's rhetoric, murder a poet named Cinna because he happens to have the same name as one of Caesar's assassins. 'I am not Cinna the conspirator', cries the poet; 'no matter, his name's Cinna', answers an assailant; 'pluck but his name out of his heart' (III.3.32–4).

Coriolanus explores further the complexities and paradoxes of naming. The triple title Caius Martius Coriolanus – first name, surname and the name he gains for the victory at Corioles – represents three distinct identities, those of the individual and the family, and that conferred on the individual by society. These identities are vulnerable to internal and external pressure. As if to underline this vulnerability, Shakespeare has Martius forget the name of the 'poor host' (I.9.86) whose freedom he requests after the battle of Corioles. What's in a name? In this instance, at least one man's life and liberty. The way Martius is addressed throughout the play not only mirrors but also mars his fortune. The elevation to 'Coriolanus' can always be revoked, the given name supplanted by new titles, such as 'traitor' and 'boy', that his enemies use to light the fuse of Martius' implacable rage. It is unclear why Aufidius asks the disguised Martius his name no fewer than six times (IV.5.56–67). But once in possession of the name, he twists it to his own purposes. Behind Martius' back, he addresses him intimately as 'Caius', the only person other than Volumnia to do so (IV.7.56). To his face, in the final scene, he strategically refuses to recognize his identity:

CORIOLANUS
  Traitor? How now?
AUFIDIUS   Ay, traitor, Martius!
CORIOLANUS   Martius?
AUFIDIUS
  Ay, Martius, Caius Martius! Dost thou think
  I'll grace thee with that robbery, thy stolen name
  Coriolanus in Corioles? (V.6.87–90)

He will not even allow Martius to swear by Mars, the god
of war whose name is embedded in 'Martius'. Deprived
of surname and the name of his achievements, he is
reduced to 'boy' (101), little Caius, the child who cries
and who is now a long way from home. Here, as
throughout *Coriolanus*, words hurt and speech is power.

'SOME HARLOT'S SPIRIT'

Shakespeare's Rome is a theatrical city. The art of politics, then as now, is to seduce and persuade a populace
into a certain set of beliefs and practices. The ideal seduc-
tion saves time and money by appealing to the public en
masse. Before the advent of mass media, this ideal
involved gathering people into the great public spaces of
mass sentiment: stadiums, churches, parks, squares – and
theatres. The existence of these spaces in the city is both
gift and curse to authority. If the government is popular
they are convenient sites for the widespread dissemina-
tion of more good news. If unpopular, they are equally
convenient meeting points, hubs for popular dissent.
Repressive governments will always limit the right to
congregate: mastery of these spaces is vital to power.

In his previous Roman plays Shakespeare had explored the overlaps between customs, politics and theatre. Cleopatra, a remarkable actress in her own right, worries that on being captured she will be exhibited in Rome and that a theatrical spectacle will be made of her suffering (*Antony and Cleopatra*, V.2.208–21). (Macduff threatens something similar to Macbeth: 'live to be the show and gaze o'the time', V.6.63.) In *Julius Caesar* Mark Antony uses Caesar's wounds as props in his brilliant, actorly performance that stirs up the plebeians against Caesar's assassins (III.2). In other plays, too, Shakespeare had drawn parallels between the actor and the politician, not least in the chameleon-like improvisations of Richard III. In *Coriolanus*, once again, public performance is central to Shakespeare's exploration of power. Moving from 'th'casque to th'cushion' (IV.7.43), from the battlefield back to the city, demands of Martius that he adapt to the public forums of political performance. Policy demands that he put himself in the market-place.

In order to win the consulship and achieve his mother's ambition, Martius must make a spectacle of himself. In a token display of humility he must undergo a ritualistic appearance in the market-place, wearing nothing but the '*gown of humility*' and imploring the general public for their 'voices', their votes (II.3). Theatrical ritual, as much as speaking politically, presents Martius with an ethical crisis. Because rituals, like proverbs, are widely agreed upon and predictable they become pre-scripted, pre-scribed theatrical events. Martius cannot see the value of such theatre. Temperamentally he prefers either the unscripted chaos of combat or the disruption of rituals. Menenius instructs Martius to 'fit' himself to custom, to match 'Your honour with your form', as if honour on its own were insufficient without theatrical reproduction.

Martius' response starts a train of theatrical analogies in the play: 'It is a part | That I shall blush in acting, and might well | Be taken from the people' (II.2.140–44). (The prospect of being evaluated by others tends to make Martius think of blushing: 'I will go wash; | And when my face is fair you shall perceive | Whether I blush or no' (I.9.67–9).) When in the market-place, Martius, in his theatrical costume, candidly shares with the Fourth Citizen a manifesto of hypocrisy:

> I will practise the insinuating nod ... That is, sir, I will counterfeit the bewitchment of some popular man and give it bountiful to the desirers. (II.3.98–101)

Is this not a description of the actor's art? And is it not a typically Shakespearian irony to have this deeply anti-theatrical character embodied by an actor, the 'popular man' who gives bountifully to his desiring audience? Brutus' great description (II.1.197–213) of how, on return from Corioles, ordinary people skip work, put aside their professions to gaze on celebrity is also highly relevant to the social practice of Globe theatregoing.

Martius fails in his first market-place performance. Although he formally passes the test, his unconvincing, bitterly sarcastic performance arouses suspicion among the people, and this suspicion is 'goaded onward' (II.3.262) by the Tribunes until their decision is reversed. The longest scene in the play, Act III, scene 1, shows the full extent of Rome's internal discord. Martius, relieved to be out of his costume, is nevertheless provoked into fresh rage by the Tribune's taunt that he is a traitor. In the stream of speech that follows, he compounds his already fraught position by explicitly articulating his anti-democratic beliefs. The upshot of the scene, and the punishment for Rome's errant son, is that he must perform again.

In returning to the market-place Martius again has to face a communal space almost directly antithetical to his personality. The market is a place of shifting value, of bartering, of shared transactions. Prices can go down as well as up. In the patrician mindset he has learnt from his mother, the people are 'things created | To buy and sell with groats' (III.2.9–10). The market-place is therefore the people's milieu. It will have to be the performance of his life. The ethical crisis has deepened for Martius. Not only is he still enraged at the Tribunes' slanders, but the need to perform is now perhaps a matter of exile or death. His mother and Menenius realize the severity of the situation and encourage him to curb his instincts and behave 'mildly' (139). Volumnia becomes the would-be playwright-director of the scene, handing him a prop and instructing him on the physical expression of mildness and humility:

> Go to them with this bonnet in thy hand;
> And thus far having stretched it – here be with them –
> Thy knee bussing [kissing] the stones – for in such
>   business
> Action is eloquence, and the eyes of th'ignorant
> More learnèd than the ears . . . (73–7)

He is to 'perform a part | Thou hast not done before' (109–10). This is profoundly confusing for Martius. Was it not his mother who taught him to be 'absolute', to despise the general public, and to assume that valour, not play-acting, is the chiefest virtue? The prospect of once again 'mountebanking' the people's loves (132) fills him with disgust. He is forced to think of himself not as the coherent, self-sufficient warrior, the indivisible 'thing of blood' (II.2.107), but rather as a composite, fragmented body, a compilation of everything he has been taught to hate:

> Away, my disposition, and possess me
> Some harlot's spirit! My throat of war be turned,
> Which choired with my drum, into a pipe
> Small as an eunuch or the virgin voice
> That babies lulls asleep! The smiles of knaves
> Tent in my cheeks, and schoolboys' tears take up
> The glasses of my sight! A beggar's tongue
> Make motion through my lips, and my armed knees,
> Who bowed but in my stirrup, bend like his
> That hath received an alms! I will not do't,
> Lest I surcease to honour mine own truth
> And by my body's action teach my mind
> A most inherent baseness. (III.2.111–23)

In the highly recommended Richard Burton audio recording of the role, for example, 'I will not do't' is an ear-splitting explosion. The speech is a crescendo of self-assertion, and it is hard not to find Martius admirable in this rigid rejection of hypocrisy. Yet, as she will do later to fatal effect, Volumnia talks him out of his position. It is one of the deep ironies of the play that Martius hates the people for their mutability – the way that they change their minds every minute (I.1.180) – but he himself has some spectacular changes of heart and mind, and this one sends him back to the market-place with an impossible role to play. A further unlikely affinity between Martius and the plebeians is that both are the objects of manipulation, a parallel process we see in the adjoining scenes at the beginning of the third act.

Modern politicians may strike poses of inflexibility but they always do accommodate, temporize, perform U-turns and accept the 'conditions' Aufidius finds so shameful (I.10.2–7). There is something disgusting about seeing Martius doing the same. Surely this creature will not capitulate to policy? But the pleasure (indeed the drama) in seeing him ultimately go through the theatrical ritual of Act III, scene 3 derives from how bad he is at it. No matter how repulsive his anti-democratic sentiments, the vertiginous collapse of his play-acting provides a theatrically thrilling effect. As the soaring 'incorrectness' of his political values bursts through the political façade, Martius seals his permanent exile from Rome. But his unwilling association with the market-place will not end here. At the opening of the play's final scene Aufidius sends a message to the 'lords o'th'city' to bid them 'repair to th'market-place' (V.6.1–3) where they and the people will hear Aufidius' justifications for the imminent assassination of Martius. It is terrible, but grimly appropriate, that this great warrior will die not on the battlefield, but at the hands of a man on his way to the theatre of the market-place.

'O, LET ME CLIP YE'

In such a relentlessly public world, what chance is there of privacy, or of sculpting and nurturing a personality through intimate personal interaction? In *Romeo and Juliet* the lovers find their own spaces of balcony, bedroom and tomb in which to escape the endless public strife of their families' feuds. Hamlet, if he cannot completely trust anyone save Horatio at Elsinore, at least has the privacy of the soliloquy in which to share, reflect and resolve. Duologue and soliloquy are the dramatic modes of intimacy but these modes are significantly rare in *Coriolanus*. The hero has only three moments in which he is alone onstage: II.3.111–23, IV.4.1–6 and 12–26. What Martius offers at these points has frustrated those readers and audience members who equate soliloquies with revelation of character. No privileged insight is offered into the tortured soul of the hero; rather, as in his blunt summary, 'My birthplace hate I, and my love's upon | This enemy town' (IV.4.23–4), Martius tells us little that we would not find out in time. As for the play's duologues, most are conducted in public spaces, and, as with those between Brutus and Sicinius, are more conspiratorial than emotionally intimate. We see Volumnia and her daughter-in-law in a domestic, presumably interior space, but their conversation is marked by contrast rather than harmony. If we define intimacy as the marriage of true minds in seclusion, there is only one moment of intimacy in the play and it is between two warriors.

The connection between love and war, sex and fighting, is announced early in the play. It is hard not to hear an erotic charge in Martius' 'O, they are at it!' (I.4.21) when he hears a distant alarum and this link is substantiated minutes later. When Martius enters caked in Volscian blood, Cominius asks whether he is covered with his own blood or that of the enemy. By way of response, Martius embraces him:

> O, let me clip ye
> In arms as sound as when I wooed, in heart
> As merry as when our nuptial day was done,
> And tapers burned to bedward! (I.6.29–32)

It is not unusual for fighting (or indeed anything else) to be compared to sex; it is, after all, a common point of reference and an easy source of analogies. Nevertheless, Martius' response is highly revealing. He compares himself to a bridegroom who has just married and is on his way to consummate the nuptial. He is, in other words, not tired or wounded as Cominius fears, but, in the least subtle sense, aroused. The bed that the tapers burn towards would be expected to be stained with the blood of his bride by the morning. Elsewhere in Shakespeare, both Claudio in *Measure for Measure* (III.1.87–8) and Antony in *Antony and Cleopatra* (IV.14.100–101) promise that, if they must die, they will 'encounter darkness as a bride, | And hug it in mine arms' or will be 'A bridegroom in my death, and run into't | As to a lover's bed'. But in *Coriolanus* the analogy is not referring to the death of the speaker; it is rather a testimony to his virility and thus his ability to keep on slaughtering. Killing other men is, for Martius, an erotic activity.

After the battle of Corioles, Cominius looks forward to relating Martius' prowess to a Roman audience of senators, patricians and ladies who 'shall be frighted | And, gladly quaked, hear more' (I.9.5–6). But it is not just women who are, in his suggestive paradox, 'gladly quaked' at the thought of war. Such a frisson needs also to be produced in men, who, after all, are the ones who usually have to fight in wars and therefore have most need to believe in its glamour. This is the point of Martius showing his scars in the market-place: 'I have wounds to show you, which shall be yours in private' (II.3.74–5), he tells the 'brace' of Citizens (60), although Martius somehow manages to avoid this demeaning peep-show. Significantly, Martius' one moment of self-exposure, in which he bares his throat to be cut (IV.5.98–100), is with his great rival Aufidius.

Long before their private meeting at Antium, Aufidius and Martius feel an affinity that borders on fidelity. They obsess each other. If Martius could not be himself, he tells us in the opening scene, he would be Aufidius. He sins in envying what he perceives – wrongly as it turns out – to be Aufidius' 'nobility' (I.1.228–30). Martius' customary disdain for report and his indifference to the opinion of others is suspended when it comes to Aufidius; witness his impatient cross-examining of Titus Lartius:

CORIOLANUS

Spoke he of me?

LARTIUS   He did, my lord.

CORIOLANUS   How? What? (III.1.12)

When Martius learns of his adversary's location in Antium he offers another of his self-fulfilling prophecies: 'I wish I had a cause to seek him there' (19). His banishment, his 'cause' to seek Aufidius, follows conveniently hot on the heels of this wish. Indeed, Martius' rather curious chirpiness in the scene following his market-place banishment might be the result not only of the natural relief anyone feels at the end of a complicated relationship like that between Martius and the people of Rome; it might also be a sprightliness born of the anticipation of seeking his rival.

In recent years many stage productions have sought to highlight what the director perceives to be the homosexual nature of Martius' and Aufidius' relationship. Certainly their scene together is one of few, if not the only moment in the play when the tension could be said to be sexual. The atmosphere is taut throughout Martius'

long speech in which he relates his banishment from Rome
and then offers either his life or his service to Aufidius.
We do not know how Aufidius will respond to this,
so the tension is eased, if not entirely dispelled, by
his apparent warmth: 'Let me twine | Mine arms about
that body ... Here I clip | The anvil of my sword'
(IV.5.109–13). 'Clip' is the word Martius had earlier used
with Cominius to describe their embrace: as a word that
can mean either to hug or to enfold, but also to cut, it is
perfectly suited to the love-hate ambivalence of the
warriors' embrace. For Aufidius, as for Martius before,
the embrace reminds him of an important heterosexual
moment in his civilian life:

> I loved the maid I married; never man
> Sighed truer breath. But that I see thee here,
> Thou noble thing, more dances my rapt heart
> Than when I first my wedded mistress saw
> Bestride my threshold. (117–21)

The association and confusion of marriage with warfare
forms a leitmotif in *Coriolanus*. The Roman deserter
Nicanor tells the Volscian Adrian that, following Martius'
banishment, Rome is ripe to be conquered: 'I have heard
it said the fittest time to corrupt a man's wife is when
she's fallen out with her husband' (IV.3.28–30). Two
scenes later it is Martius not Rome who is presented as
the corruptible wife. The Third Servingman reports that
inside the house, 'Our general himself makes a mistress
of him, sanctifies himself with's hand, and turns up the
white o'th'eye to his discourse' (IV.5.201–3). It is an
incongruous image: Martius as the female god of Aufidius'
idolatry. But then again we can't be sure what Aufidius
is playing at. A less naturally gifted warrior and more

talented actor than Martius, he is more than capable of
deception. If the Volsces were as internally turbulent as
the Romans – which they do not appear to be – he would
have no trouble in speaking them fair and mountebanking
their loves. He is at home in the market-place. Even his
most obviously sexual speech to Martius should not,
perhaps, be taken at face value:

> Thou hast beat me out
> Twelve several times, and I have nightly since
> Dreamt of encounters 'twixt thyself and me –
> We have been down together in my sleep,
> Unbuckling helms, fisting each other's throat –
> And waked half dead with nothing. (124–9)

Given that 'dying' was a Renaissance euphemism for an
orgasm, and 'nothing' (i.e. 'no-thing') slang for the female
genitals, might not Aufidius be implying that he wakes,
sexually dissatisfied, from these dreams of Martius only
to find his wife, and not his great rival, next to him in
bed? 'Thou noble thing' (119) is better than the female
no-thing. 'Nothing', as King Lear points out, 'will come
of nothing' (I.1.90). Perhaps. But then again, Aufidius is
by far the better dissembler of the two. This should be
considered before we too readily conflate Aufidius' dream
with the image of Oliver Reed and Alan Bates wrestling
naked in Ken Russell's film of *Women in Love*.

In one of his rare moments alone onstage, Martius
reflects on the impermanence of human relationships, of
the 'slippery turns' that transform friends into enemies,
and turn 'fellest foes, | Whose passions and whose plots
have broke their sleep', into 'dear friends' (IV.4.12, 18–21).
The way in which Martius and Aufidius conceptualize
war and their new-found friendship exemplifies such a

slippery linguistic turn, an almost Freudian confusion of
the martial with the marital. It is a displacement that
creates a paradoxical intimacy between enemies and that
helps the soldier forget the absence of women and the
claims of home.

'ONE ON'S FATHER'S MOODS'

It is unsurprising that words like 'Rome', 'power' and
'state' occur so frequently in this political tragedy. What
is more surprising is that the word 'home' is heard in
Coriolanus more frequently than in any other Shakespeare
play. Only two scenes are set in clearly domestic spaces:
Act I, scene 3, where it is not clear whether it is Volumnia
or Virgilia's house in which the women sew and discuss
Martius, and Act IV, scene 5, Aufidius' 'hearth' (26) which
hosts the bonding duet of the warriors. Before Aufidius
enters in the latter scene, one of the servingmen asks the
muffled Martius where he dwells:

CORIOLANUS Under the canopy.
THIRD SERVINGMAN Under the canopy?
CORIOLANUS Ay.
THIRD SERVINGMAN Where's that?
CORIOLANUS I'th'city of kites and crows. (40–44)

Martius does indeed spend most of the play under the
canopy, beneath the sky: he is fundamentally unhoused.
On his return from the Corioles, he tells his wife and
mother that he must meet the patricians 'Ere in our own
house I do shade my head' (II.1.187), but the restful,
recuperative moment seems infinitely delayed. Act III,
scene 2 may well be set in Martius' house, but the scene

is not restful, nor does Shakespeare think the location significant enough to make explicit. There is no shade in the 'city of kites and crows'.

When the idea of home is raised, it is notable that it is not often uttered in order to comfort or reassure. 'Go get you home, you fragments,' Martius tells the plebeians in the opening scene (220); at other points, 'home' is detached from physical reality and becomes associated with thorough rebuke, as when Brutus advises Sicinius, 'In this point charge him home' (III.3.1), or when Menenius praises Volumnia's scorn for the Tribunes: 'You have told them home' (IV.2.48). The concept becomes cankered through use. Shakespeare clearly wanted us to hear and think about the word, not least because it can only remind us of the architectural and social purpose of a home: to shelter a family.

Martius has a mother, wife and son. This may not sound remarkable but it makes him unique among Shakespeare's tragic heroes, none of whose onstage families span three generations. In the third scene of the play (a scene not found in his sources) Shakespeare, against the military, political and masculine strife of the surrounding scenes, counterpoises a domestic, entirely feminine setting. Yet there is little shade from conflict here. We have already heard the rumour that Martius fights to please his mother, and here she is. Volumnia immediately begins to relate to us (and presumably repeats to Virgilia) her role in making Martius the man he is: both she and Virgilia seem to have little life outside the man they have in common. Expanding Plutarch's verdict that after his father's death Volumnia's joy was 'the only thing that made [Martius] to love honour' (*Shakespeare's Plutarch*, p. 300), Shakespeare offers his most developed study of child-rearing and maternal influence.

The challenge in upbringing is for the parent to know when to cut the apron-strings and recognize their child as an adult. There is nothing remarkable about Martius and Virgilia sharing a house with his mother – many young Italian couples still do – but the emotional inter-dependency between mother and son seems too intense and overwrought to be healthy. As has been widely noted, almost the first thing we hear Volumnia say – 'If my son were my husband' (I.3.2) – more than hints at a subjunctive desire to be everything to her boy. When Volumnia castigates him, his first response is, 'Let go' (III.2.18). Primarily he is telling her to shut up, but more deeply it sounds like a plea for distance, for her to release him from her grip. Perhaps it was this moment Cole Porter had in mind when he wrote the following couplet for his song 'Brush Up Your Shakespeare': 'If she says your behavior is heinous | Kick her right in the "Coriolanus!"' Martius, however, finds it hard to dispatch his mother so efficiently.

Hers is the 'honoured mould' in which Martius' 'trunk was framed' (V.3.22–3). Her attitude to nurturing scorns our modern sensitivities about the sanctity of childhood. The 'embracements' between husband and wife in bed (I.3.4), as much as the beauty of Hecuba's breasts as she fed the infant Hector, cannot compare with the love-liness of the male body spitting forth blood on the battlefield (41–4). Martius has clearly taken her lessons to heart: his sometimes fallible memory retains her words. After his banishment, his attempt to cheer her up is struc-tured around memories of her indoctrination:

> You were used
> To say . . . You were used to load me
> With precepts that would make invincible

    The heart that conned them.
    ... you were wont to say ... (IV.1.3–16)

But no precepts can prepare her son for the no-win choice
he must make at the gates of Rome. The invincible heart
is a dangerous myth and an impossible aspiration. Aufidius
has only to call Martius 'boy' to make his heart 'Too great
for what contains it' (V.6.104).

    There has sometimes been a tendency to dehumanize
Volumnia, to blame her for Martius' severe shortcom-
ings, as if reading or seeing plays were a branch of social
work which seeks to apportion responsibility within
dysfunctional families. But has she not, like her son and
grandson, been 'bred in broils' (III.2.81), been born into
a culture of warfare and stark social antagonism? What
can be made clear in production, but less easily in reading,
is how much suffering this apparently impervious woman
goes through at the play's conclusion. For all her earlier
bravado might we not see a very different character –
pained, guilt-ridden – in the final procession? For all
her excited talk of Martius' wounds and 'bloody brow'
(I.3.35), she never really expected to have to bury her
son.

    We hear more about Martius' childhood than any of
Shakespeare's other protagonists'. To compound this
emphasis on childhood and socialization, we have the
presence of young Martius, the chip-off-the-old-block,
further living proof of the self-perpetuating nature of
family breeding. (None of the other tragic heroes since
Titus Andronicus have onstage sons.) Plutarch relates
that Martius and Virgilia had two children, but for reasons
probably both practical and thematic, Shakespeare, as he
does with the number of Consuls in Rome, halves the
number. He is interested in loneliness: like his father,

young Martius is an only child. Valeria offers us an abiding image of the boy before we meet him:

> I saw him run after a gilded butterfly, and when he caught it, he let it go again, and after it again, and over and over he comes and up again, catched it again; or whether his fall enraged him, or how 'twas, he did so set his teeth and tear it. O, I warrant, how he mammocked it! (I.3.61–6)

Here is the mini-Martius in action: the complete absorption in his task, the indifference to his spectators and the embodiment of an unselfconscious, all-engrossing will to destroy, to exert power and terror over other creatures. In *King Lear* Shakespeare used a comparable image to summarize nothing less than the cruel arbitrariness of human existence: 'As flies to wanton boys are we to the gods; | They kill us for their sport' (IV.1.36–7). Valeria's narrative about a wanton boy and a butterfly is nowhere near as compacted or despairing as that, partly because Valeria herself seems to find the story quite funny. But for us it offers a revealing glimpse into the home life of the hero. It is a home in which what is tender, ornamental or compassionate – a gilded butterfly or Virgilia's wish that her husband be unwounded – is 'mammocked'. Young Martius' encounter with the butterfly offers an allegory of an uneven contest. When it works in their favour the family find this amusing or exhilarating. But the wild boy will not always be on their side. Cominius reports after Martius' desertion to the Volsces that he is their 'god':

> ... they follow him
> Against us brats with no less confidence
> Than boys pursuing summer butterflies,
> Or butchers killing flies. (IV.6.93–6)

The Roman aristocracy, used to comparing itself to lions, foxes and ospreys, now plummets down the food chain to become butterflies and flies. They are 'brats' pursued by confident children; both sides are figured as infants. When the Volsces, led by Martius, attack Rome, it will be a massacre held in a school playground. Volumnia fails to make the connection between the behaviour of her grandson in the garden and the aggressive, all-consuming code of honour that will cleave her son in two. In her complacent approval of young Martius' behaviour, it is an irony unavailable to her that she will lose her Martius in just such an unevenly contested and senseless act of tearing to pieces.

'ASSIST'

How much of our lives do we live on our own and for ourselves, and how much do we live with and for others? Are our 'selves' distinguishable from those – parents, lovers, friends, enemies – who have shaped and influenced our experiences and personality? In the political spat between Menenius and the Tribunes at the opening of the second act, Brutus says that he and Sicinius are not 'alone' in blaming Martius for being proud. Menenius responds: 'I know you can do very little alone . . . Your abilities are too infant-like for doing much alone' (II.1.32–6). Acting alone is here a sign of maturity. We have just witnessed Martius acting alone in his solitary raid on Corioles, in the aftermath of which he utters the phrase 'Let him alone' twice (I.6.41, 73). On being lifted up by his soldiers, the word takes on another hue: 'O'me alone, make you a sword of me' (76). On his banishment the word is echoed and then evolved: 'I go alone, | Like to a lonely dragon that his fen | Makes feared and talked of more than seen' (IV.1.29–31). (Once again, Martius' self-image and subsequent behaviour are at odds: far from being a 'lonely dragon' in his exile, he will rush to find the company of Aufidius.) Loneliness, singularity, exclusivity and individuality: these are patrician concepts used to elevate themselves, through their most singular representative Martius, above the many.

While the myth that accrues around Martius emphasizes his solitariness, his adversary tends to act willingly with others. Aufidius is a collaborator. In the second scene of the play, when he tells his senators that next time he and Martius meet they will slug it out 'Till one can do no more', his senators greet the resolution with 'The gods assist you!' (I.2.36). In the event, it is '*certain Volsces*' that assist him, not the gods, during his hand-to-hand combat in Act I, scene 8. Realizing that he can never kill Martius 'True sword to sword', Aufidius determines to 'potch at him' more subtly (I.10.15). In the final scene he enlists the assistance of '*three or four Conspirators*' (V.6.8) – Macbeth, similarly, tells Banquo's murderers that he must 'make love' to their 'assistance' (III.1.123). The final word of *Coriolanus* is an invitation to others to help share the burden – physical and perhaps moral – of Martius' corpse: 'Assist' (V.6.156).

But there is a middle way between Martius' solitariness and Aufidius' crafty collaborations, just as there is a way of bridging the gap between the individual and society, the one and the many. It lies in those moments in *Coriolanus*, rare but more powerful for that, when human beings make real contact with each other. The capacity of the individual to place the needs of the bodies in front of him above abstract ideas of honour and revenge is most intensely dramatized in Martius' meeting

with his family at the gates of Rome (V.3). We have
heard from Cominius how Martius, no longer content
with his title 'Coriolanus', intends to earn a new one by
forging himself 'a name i'th'fire | Of burning Rome'
(V.1.14–15). Earlier, Martius rejected pleas to market
his identity, to recreate himself as a popular showman
and humble petitioner. He resisted the injunction, in
modern corporate jargon, to 'rebrand'. Now we see the
rebranding that really appeals to him, the flaying and
burning of Rome and the creation of a new name, etched
in the ashes of his birthplace. Cominius and Menenius,
both surrogate father figures for Martius, have failed to
divert him from this course of bloody revenge. The hand
that Martius offered in friendship to Menenius on his
banishment (IV.1.57) is now used to waft entreaties away
(V.1.67–8).

   When his family and Valeria approach him at the gates
of Rome something very strange happens to Martius. For
probably the first time in his life he begins to suspect that
he is 'not | Of stronger earth than others' (V.3.28–9).
He is anguished, doubt-ridden, dimly aware that the
inevitable choice he must make between his family and
his honour can only lead to his catastrophe. It is a remarkable scene and one in which he fears, like a 'dull actor',
he will cease to play the revenge character he has authored
for himself and forget his lines. In what follows, his
mother dominates, stage-managing a series of kneelings
and false exits while building up to the play's longest
speech, an aria of suffering, rebuke, pathos and anger
(131–82). It is impossible. His will buckles under the strain
of her words and the fantasy of autonomy collapses. In
this noisy world of blows, cuts and clips he signals his
surrender through the most original and eloquent action
available to him: he takes her hand and holds it in silence.

Martius invites Aufidius and the Volsces to watch his
meetings with Menenius and his family as if they were
theatre. Confident of his resolve, he will 'Hear naught
from Rome in private' (V.3.93), thus making a spectacle
of his reactions to the suitors. He assumes that there
will be nothing in his expression to read, no blushes,
smiles or tears. His performance, typically, surprises
him. On taking his mother's hand, he is suddenly and
sharply aware of one part of his audience and looks up
to see the gods laughing at 'this unnatural scene'
(184–6). But there is an audience closer to hand.
He asks Aufidius to empathize with his performance:
'Were you in my stead, would you have heard | A
mother less?' Aufidius' terse verdict to this spectacle of
supplication and capitulation: 'I was moved withal'
(193–5). Shakespeare knew about audience reaction as
an actor, a playwright and as a stakeholder. He felt it
palpably, not only in his nervous system and adrenalin,
but in his wallet too. And as a restless innovator he
experimented with ways of ending his plays. The end
of *Coriolanus* offers no easy resolutions. Even the
onstage audience of Volscian lords don't quite know
how to interpret what they have just seen. The First
Lord offers the standard platitudes about Martius' being
the 'most noble corse that ever herald | Did follow
to his urn', but, typically of this play, his verdict is
immediately complicated by the Second Lord, who
points to Martius' 'impatience' as justification for the
murder and concludes with the astonishingly pragmatic,
anti-heroic sentiment: 'Let's make the best of it'
(V.6.145–8).

Unlike Hamlet, Lear or Macbeth, Martius has no
moment of existential clarity before his death. There is no
sense that he has 'developed' or that he philosophically

accepts the imminence of death and the end of his journey. Quite the reverse: he dies as he lived, noisily, instinctively and violently. The wintry bleakness of the play's end bears closer resemblance to the downbeat pessimism of *Troilus and Cressida* than it does to the cathartic conclusions of the more famous tragedies. This was probably the last tragedy Shakespeare wrote and he seems to have reached a point of exhaustion with the form. In his last plays he would become obsessed with the motif of the parent–child reunion, a reunion that *almost* forms the climax of *Coriolanus*. He would also, taking his cue from Aufidius, seek assistance from others; Shakespeare's late, three-play collaboration with John Fletcher indicates that he was beginning to find play-wrighting a lonely business.

At the sight of Virgilia's tears on his return from Corioles, Martius exclaims: 'Ah, my dear, | Such eyes the widows in Corioles wear, | And mothers that lack sons' (II.1.170–72). At the end of *Coriolanus* it is unclear whether Martius' death has served any great political or metaphysical purpose. What is depressingly clear is that his death increases the world's stock of widowed wives and 'mothers that lack sons'. And who can blame the people of Corioles for their bloodthirstiness? In the chaos of noise before his death we hear from the relatives of Martius' victims: 'Tear him to pieces! – Do it presently! – He killed my son! – My daughter! – He killed my cousin Marcus! – He killed my father!' (V.6.121–3). Once again we are reminded of Phyrrus in *Hamlet*, 'horridly tricked | With blood of fathers, mothers, daughters, sons . . .' Has the cycle ended? That might depend on how much young Martius has taken to heart his father's last words to him: 'stick i'th'wars | Like a great sea-mark, standing every flaw | And saving those that eye thee!'

(V.3.73–5). It is only 'th'interpretation of full time' (69) that will show whether Martius, like his father, will carry noise before him and leave tears in his wake.

Paul Prescott

The Play in Performance

When the National Theatre produced *Coriolanus* in 1971, temper tantrums, personality clashes and crises of authority were not confined to the streets of Rome. While rehearsing Martius, Christopher Plummer complained that his part had been too heavily cut, that he needed a new costume and that he was beginning to doubt the interpretive vision of the German co-directors, Manfred Wekwerth and Joachim Tenschert. The pair had completed the adaptation that Brecht left unfinished at his death, and were, therefore, not politically unsympathetic to the people when it came to directing Shakespeare's original. When Plummer refused to take direction and cracked jokes at the directors' expense in front of the company, the rehearsal was cancelled, Plummer was invited to apologize and the whole project teetered on the verge of breakdown. Kenneth Tynan recorded in his diary: 'All this, of course, is a re-enactment of *Coriolanus* – Plummer versus the two people's Tribunes, too proud to bow his head and atone for his insults. He is crassly in the wrong, of course, but I fear in this case it will be the Tribunes and not Coriolanus, who are banished' (*Diaries*, pp. 34–5). Tynan's fears were misplaced. A company meeting was called and each actor voiced support for the 'tribune' directors. Plummer was sacked and replaced by Anthony Hopkins. Unhappy the production that needs star actors: Martius might be irreplaceable, but the actor playing him was not.

The challenges of staging *Coriolanus* seem to mimic the problems explored in the play: how should power be divided? How much should the needs of the 'star' individual be placed above those of the majority? What is Rome and to whom does it belong? What does it mean to represent others or one's self? Or to act a part? The banishment of Plummer from the National bears testimony to the precarious balances that must be struck in the theatre between the needs of different constituencies: star actors, supporting casts, supernumeraries, set and costume designers, and – a more recent constituent – the star director. (Anyone who doubts that theatre-making is a political process should read of the everyday squabbles and tensions so pungently described in Steven Berkoff's journal *Coriolanus in Deutschland*: in contrast to Wekwerth and Tenschert, Berkoff was forced to fire one of his Tribunes.) Throughout the eighteenth and nineteenth centuries the division of labour and power was widely agreed upon. Producing *Coriolanus* as an actor-manager meant detailed attention to one or two lead performances, the creation of elaborate, monumental scenery, and the marshalling of a cast of (often literally) hundreds to swell the Roman scene. This division of power inevitably reflected and perpetuated pervasive assumptions about the meaning of *Coriolanus*: that Shakespeare's intent was to show the singularity and indispensability of the great individual performer. But, as Plummer's fate illustrates, by the mid twentieth century the position of the Coriolanus actor had become assailable. Even without rebellion in the ranks of the cast there remains much in the text of *Coriolanus* to challenge and stretch the creative team undertaking its performance.

'AS IT WERE IN THE CAPITOL'

The nature of performance can be compressed into three words: as it were. Theatre invites the viewer to suspend disbelief, to engage with events as if they were happening in front of us, to enter an imaginative state of complicity. The title of John Osborne's adaptation of the play, *A Place Calling Itself Rome* (1971), points to this willing complicity between artist and audience: we agree that this is 'Rome' but that it is also here and now, wherever and whenever the performance is taking place. Over the centuries directors and designers have represented the Rome of *Coriolanus* in a variety of styles and locations. Perhaps the most popular option has been to recreate the Rome so economically evoked in the opening lines of T. S. Eliot's poem 'Coriolan':

Stone, bronze, stone, steel, stone, oakleaves, horses' heels
Over the paving.
And the flags. And the trumpets. And so many eagles.

John Philip Kemble's production at Covent Garden (in the repertoire from 1789 to 1817) – probably the most financially successful *Coriolanus* ever staged – owed much of its popularity to its grandiose Imperial Roman settings beneath which no opportunity was lost for pageantry and densely populated pomp. (Imperial Rome was chosen as a more picturesque alternative to the much older and more rugged city in which Martius dwelt.) Twentieth-century productions were generally more inclined towards analogy. The Rome of the fifth century BC becomes, *as it were*, Paris during the French Directoire, London during the Falklands War, Hitler's Berlin, Mussolini's Rome, or Japan in the twilight years of the Samurais. Choice of historical setting will inevitably affect the depiction of the Volsces. How much should the two cultures, Roman and Volscian, be contrasted? It has been argued that, as Antium was only twelve miles from Rome, the ironic similarities between the tribes should be stressed. But geography was not Shakespeare's strong point, and that small distance has not deterred directors keen to dramatize the clash between different nationalities or even races.

As the detailed illusionistic sets typical of nineteenth-century productions have given way to more abstracted settings, so costumes and props assume a greater importance in conjuring up the fictive world of the play. *Coriolanus* is full of images of synecdoche, a rhetorical device whereby a detail represents the whole, or vice versa; thus the plebeians are described in terms of cobbled shoes, tongues, breaths, voices and unclean teeth and other fragments that suggest a complete, if diseased, body. Similarly, theatre design often depends – as it did on Shakespeare's stage – on the audience reading a part for the whole. Thus props such as stools and sewing kits will represent the whole of a domestic interior, or the laying of cushions will evoke the Capitol. The props needed to stage the play are few and lie easily within the resources of even the most impoverished theatre company. This economy can charge certain properties with significance. For example, might the two stools on which Volumnia and Valeria sit in Act I, scene 3 reappear four acts later at the gates of Rome? Act V, scene 3 opens with the stage direction '*Enter Coriolanus and Aufidius with others. They sit*'. The last direction is ambiguous, but probably refers to the two warriors. Might the stools not be spatially arranged so as to echo the earlier scene and to suggest a male counterpoint to the now deserted domestic sphere?

Choice of costume will largely be defined by period and location. The text explicitly requires costume changes at key points, the most obvious of which is Martius' reappearance in Act II, scene 3 in the '*gown of humility*' (38). The decline in the aristocracy's fortunes must also be shown. When the Tribunes see Menenius in Act IV, scene 6, Brutus' question 'Is this Menenius?' (10) hints at some change, most likely a deterioration, in his appearance. Similarly, when Martius' family and Valeria come to plead for Rome, Volumnia points up a costume change: 'Should we be silent and not speak, our raiment | And state of bodies would bewray what life | We have led since thy exile' (V.3.94–6). Perhaps this is why she seems to introduce Valeria and young Martius as if Martius might not even recognize them (63, 68). The visual landscape of a production – its structures, materials, textures, costumes – will, before a word is spoken, 'bewray' the life of Rome and the world in which the tragedy will unfold.

'*ENTER MARTIUS, CURSING*'

As with many of Shakespeare's plays one of the main challenges for the director is to cast the title role. Laurence Olivier described him as 'a very straight-forward, reactionary, son of a so-and-so' (Burton, *Great Acting*, p. 21), and it is true that, compared with some of Shakespeare's other tragic protagonists, the part can appear uncomplicated. Yet, while Martius likes to think of himself as 'constant' (I.1.237), the role actually demands a degree of versatility. The ability to sneer, swagger, flare the

nostrils and to convey a palpable sense of danger are
prerequisites. Incandescent fury, 'soaring insolence'
(II.1.246) and an inability to self-censor must also be
within the actor's range. Like a sufferer of Tourette's
Syndrome, Martius is often unable to curb his language,
and this must be made spontaneous in performance. But
there must also be the knack of awful stillness, restraint
and grim irony. Martius' unlikeability has been a recur-
rent theme of the play's critical history. But on stage a
form of attraction and collusion between Martius and the
audience can be mined through humour, as Olivier,
Burton and Alan Howard all, in their different ways,
proved. There is a comic streak to the hothead's irritated
promise to conduct himself 'mildly' in the market-place
(III.2.142) and his subsequent struggle to live up to the
word. Laughter sometimes comes unexpectedly in the
theatre: simply by stressing the second word in 'There's
some among you have beheld me fighting' (III.1.223),
Greg Hicks's Martius sardonically highlighted the military cowardice of those who were now baying for his
blood back in the safety of Rome (Royal Shakespeare
Company, 2002). And it was, after all, the humorous,
mechanical inflexibility of the character that prompted
George Bernard Shaw to claim that *Coriolanus* was 'the
greatest of all Shakespeare's comedies' (*On Shakespeare*,
p. 225).

It is also clear that the actor needs a distinctive voice;
Cominius, among others, praises its singularity: 'The
shepherd knows not thunder from a tabor | More than
I know the sound of Martius' tongue | From every
meaner man' (I.6.25–7). Martius describes his own voice
(in a characteristic metonym) as 'My throat of war'
(III.2.112). It must be precise and supple enough to pick
through the intricate arguments of III.1.91–161, yet also

powerful enough to 'choir' with the drum on the field of
battle (III.2.113). Possession of a big voice is more vital
than possession of a statuesque or imposing body.
Physically, much will depend on how other characters
react to Martius. An audience will largely sense Martius'
danger and potential to inflict pain from the cowed or
nervous responses of others. In stage combat the golden
rule is that the person being struck is in control; thus, it
is up to the actor playing Aufidius' first servingman to
give us the impression of Martius' strength – 'What an
arm he has! He turned me about with his finger and his
thumb as one would set up a top' (IV.5.155–7) – rather
than Martius himself, who will actually do very little.

The actor must also decide who this 'lonely dragon'
(IV.1.30) loves and in what way. Each of the key personal
relationships in the play must be examined and explored.
How do his emotions divide between mother, wife, son
and arch-rival? Edmund Kean's insightful interpretation
of the part in 1820 stressed the boyish and near-hysterical
insecurity of the warrior. Kean, unlike Kemble, showed
the psychological fissures in the warrior's stature and
many actors in the more hero-sceptical twentieth century
followed his lead. Age may determine interpretation. It
cannot have helped Henry Irving's performance that,
when he finally played the role, he was sixty-three
years old and certainly could not have been the son
of Ellen Terry's Volumnia: Aufidius' taunt, 'boy', was
more implausible than impertinent. Conversely, Toby
Stephens's twenty-four year old was an all-too-plausible
boy of tears, a public-school Napoleon for whom the
apron-strings were still taut.

'CITIZENS STEAL AWAY'

Coriolanus contains a number of what are called 'permissive' stage directions: '*Enter two Senators, with others, on the walls of Corioles*' (I.4.12), '*Enter seven or eight Citizens*' (II.3.0), '*Enter Coriolanus, with Nobles*' (III.2). These directions acknowledge the unpredictability and contingency of the theatrical process. The number of '*others*' and '*Nobles*', and most importantly, the size of the plebeian groups, will vary depending on the human and spatial resources of the company. Deborah Warner's two starkly contrasting productions of the play, the first (1986) an intimate affair with twelve pyjama-clad actors, the second (1993) employing the enormous resources of the Salzburg Festival – stallions and all – demonstrate the defining effects of space and money on interpretation. Tim Supple's 1992 Chichester Festival production invited over fifty local volunteers to become the people of Rome and thus the residents of Chichester, although not renowned for their bolshevism, provided the revolutionary resistance to Kenneth Branagh's Martius.

'*Citizens steal away*' (I.1.248), like the later stage directional descriptions of the people as a '*rabble*', has given some left-wing commentators cause for alarm. Stealing away reeks too much of Menenius' description of the people as 'passing cowardly' (I.1.201), as well as implicitly making the clichéd connection between the working class and criminality. How, then, should a director and costume designer cast this crowd? Actors nowadays, despite the enduring precariousness of their profession, often look far from lean and hungry in these scenes. Ruffled hair, sackcloth shirt and a strategic smudge of dirt on the face will not do if the plebeians' cause is to be taken seriously. Then again, how real is the threat posed by their improvised weapons? Do they know how to use them? Given the amount of citizens who have presumably been conscripted in the ongoing internecine conflicts, they should appear – despite Martius' verdict – as if they know how to fight. Should the soldiers we see in the battle of Corioli be recognizably drawn from the pool of citizens we have met in the play's opening scene? It would make sense. How should they move through the stage space? As one of Brecht's collaborators astutely queried: 'They can go in rags, but does that mean they have to go raggedly?' (Brecht, *On Theatre*, p. 257). Costume need not dictate character, but in fact can act in contrast to it.

Performance requires the orchestration of bodies in and through space. Shakespeare left more clues than average in the stage directions and dialogue of *Coriolanus* for how actors should enter the stage and for when they should kneel, sit, rise, embrace or weep. Martius' description of the entrance of his family (V.3.22–4) makes it quite clear, for example, how Shakespeare envisioned that procession, including the specific request that young Martius should be holding the hand not of his mother but of his grandmother. Perhaps Shakespeare wanted to foreshadow visually the great later image of Volumnia holding hands with another Martius. The text is full of such hints. But, as with the way in which the plebeians are choreographed and characterized, many key features of the play invite interpretation and reinvention. A textual crux can open up performance opportunities. In the Folio – the only authoritative text we have for *Coriolanus* – Martius says, 'Oh me alone, make you a sword of me:' and subsequent editors have experimented with different ways of punctuating this extraordinary sentence. Some have even redistributed it to the newly inspired soldiers, who are now eager to offer their services to Martius. Most likely it is Martius himself who is expressing something. But what? In this edition, it is an enraptured response to their taking him up in their arms (see Commentary, note to I.6.76). But if interpreted as a command, or as an expression of surprise or protest, this will affect the physical, theatrical nature of this rare instance of integration. Similarly, there is no binding guideline as to how the great mother and son reunion of Act V, scene 3 should be staged. How long does he pause before he takes her hand? Does she offer it to him or does he grab it, overwhelmed finally by instinct and nature, as she tries to depart? How long does he hold it silent before he speaks? Nicol Williamson (RSC, 1973) is reported to have stood silent for a minute before taking his mother's hand, and then paused for a remarkable ninety seconds before the terrible apostrophe, 'O mother, mother!' (183).

'AUFIDIUS STANDS ON HIM'

Central to any production of *Coriolanus* is the staging of violence. The 200-line sequence of five scenes (I.4–8) comprises one of the most sustained stage battles in Shakespeare. (While the scene division in this edition exists to help the reader, the scenes should be run on in the mind's eye without pause.) The events of the battle of Corioli will reverberate throughout the rest of the play as characters describe and debate their significance, from Cominius' eulogy, via Martius' claim that he was not supported by his troops (III.1.125–7; a claim which forgets I.6.80–85), to his final nostalgic boast, 'Alone I did it' (V.6.117). It is not obvious how such fight directions as '*The Romans are beat back to their trenches*' (I.4.29) would have been staged in Shakespeare's theatres. The modern director has an arsenal of sound, lighting and special effects at her disposal through which to create the topography and atmosphere of battle. But, as theatre cannot compete with the realism of cinema in the depiction of warfare, many directors openly embrace theatricality by making the fights more balletic than ballistic. The final battle sequence at Corioles brings Martius and Aufidius face to face. How sensuous is this strife? How physically entwined are the actors? Is it a more or less formal duel or a messy playground wrestle? Much can happen within the simple stage direction '*they fight*': Greg Hicks's Martius dominated and had the chance to finish Aufidius off, but he paused, as if – to paraphrase Oscar Wilde – each man cannot quite kill the thing he loves.

How should Martius die? The script describes it thus: '*The Conspirators draw their swords, and kill Martius, who falls*' (V.6.131). One of the most famous deaths in theatre history more or less followed this suggestion. At Stratford in 1959 Laurence Olivier soared up a flight of steps to a twelve-foot platform in order to vent his spleen. Having thrown away his sword in despair and disgust, he was impaled by the conspirators and then, breathtakingly, fell from the platform, only to be caught at the ankles by his assassins. Suspended head-down like the slaughtered Mussolini, he received Aufidius' final, superfluous stab to the stomach. As indelible as that image has proved, other options can and have been taken in performance. Might not Martius be ripped apart by the people of Corioles/Antium after his suicidal invitation: 'Cut me to pieces, Volsces. Men and lads, | Stain all your edges on me' (112–13). Death at the hands of an anonymous Volscian crowd would, through association, appear as an ultimate victory for the Roman masses – the same actors will probably be used – and might evoke the sacrificial scapegoating of Cinna the Poet in *Julius Caesar* or the shameful mass slaughter of Hector by Achilles' Myrmidons in *Troilus and Cressida*. Alternatively, might the death be an intimate moment between the two great adversaries? In the BBC production, Martius and Aufidius half embrace, half wrestle over a sword, the significance of which becomes increasingly phallic the longer they wrestle, until Martius administers his own *coup de grâce*. Does this violent intimacy extend beyond death, as it did in the 2002 RSC production, when Aufidius fulfilled his grotesque desire to wash his 'fierce hand' (I.10.27) in Martius' heart? How does Aufidius stand on Martius (V.6.131)? What motivates his final lines of ostensible regret: genuine remorse or political expediency? The delivery of the play's closing lines, together with the manner of removing Martius' corpse in the '*dead march*' leave, *as it were*, a taste in the mouth of the audience. Deciding on the degree of bitterness of that taste is the final challenge faced by the director and actors of the play.

Every new performance of *Coriolanus* involves a direct confrontation between a 400-year-old text and the moment of performance, a confrontation no less volatile than the class and tribal warfare chronicled in the action. Each production must establish an attitude to the politics of the play and the politics of the time. The latter can sometimes be so unstable that even an unremarkable production can spark riots. The Comédie-Française in Paris was shut down by police for a month in 1934 after a new production of *Coriolanus* became the focal point for right-wing, and ultimately riotous, protests against the scandal-ridden left-wing Daladier government. Two years earlier the Nazis had banned a new radio translation of the play and banished its author, and then, in a move typical of the slippery world of the 1930s, reworked the play as an educational warning to the Hitler Youth of the dangers of democracy and weak leadership. We should be grateful that the recent reception of the play has not been so colourful – extreme response is usually a symptom that something is rotten in the state. But then again, states by their nature incline towards rottenness, absolute power tends to corrupt absolutely, and *Coriolanus* will continue to resonate in any land in which the will of the people clashes with the desires of a military-political elite. When asked by a colleague whether he thought their pro-plebeian interpretation 'can be read in the play', Brecht wisely responded: 'Read in it and read into it' (*On Theatre*, p. 264). To read or perform *Coriolanus* is to be forced into activity, to be provoked into politics, to both read and unavoidably read meaning into this difficult, uncompromising and controversial play.

Paul Prescott

Further Reading

The two most useful, interesting and substantial editions of *Coriolanus* are Philip Brockbank's Arden (1975) and R. B. Parker's Oxford Shakespeare (1994). The latter is particularly rich and impressive in its examination of the play's 'Shakespearian' context, 'Shakespeare's developing, and darkening, concept of political life'. Parker notes that the early history plays were ideologically orthodox, the crucial change in attitude coming with *King John*, which he dates to 1594, between the two tetralogies. There is an increasing scepticism about war heroes – beginning with Talbot in *Henry VI, Part I* and intensifying through Hotspur, Henry V, Hector, Achilles, Othello, Macbeth and the 'Roman' side of Mark Antony. Parker invites us to compare Menenius and Coriolanus with Falstaff and Hal; and Coriolanus and Aufidius with Hector and Achilles in *Troilus and Cressida*. But the deepest 'sources' for the play, Parker argues, are *Hamlet* and *King Lear*.

While not exhibiting the revulsion of Dr Johnson and Coleridge, much modern criticism approaches the play gingerly, as the characters approach Coriolanus. Two anthologies reflect this nervousness: B. A. Brockman's *Casebook* (1977) and James Philips's less substantial *Twentieth-Century Interpretations* (1970). Brockman talks of this 'masterful but forbidding play' and notes how many productions 'have taken advantage of its susceptibility to doctrinaire manipulations'. J. L. Simmons in *Shakespeare's Pagan World: The Roman Tragedies* (1973) describes the play as 'magnificently perverse and ironic'; but what he calls cosmic irony has to rely too heavily on 'the absence of [Christian] revelation and the real hope of glory'. Janet Adelman's absorbing book, *Suffocating Mothers: Fantasies of Maternal Origin in Shakespeare's Plays, 'Hamlet' to 'The Tempest'* (1992), sees Coriolanus as reduced finally and pathetically to a boy with a triumphant mother in Rome. Adrian Poole in his Harvester New Critical Introduction (1988) calls it 'this great, brutal play' and describes Coriolanus himself as 'this hypnotic, infuriating, calamitous person'. His close reading often leads him into the fanciful and speculative.

Fancifulness about *Coriolanus* comes in many guises. Parker, for instance, suggests that much left-wing criticism of the play overstates its case, as do the twentieth-century denigrators (especially the feminists) of Volumnia as a virago and Coriolanus as a mindless juggernaut. The play itself, he says, is perversely even-handed: 'The contradictory values held by patricians and plebians, by Martius, Volumnia, Menenius, Aufidius and the Tribunes, are so evenly balanced that they seem to cancel each other out.' Bruce King's exemplary discussion of *Coriolanus* in The Critics Debate series (1989) assesses much critical commentary in similar fashion, noting that it seldom seems 'solidly grounded in much textual evidence'. His sober conclusion is worth pondering: 'If interpretation is a form of fiction-making, at least we can try to be accurate and humble. If our maps of reality are bound to be wrong, they benefit by being made with an awareness that the critical methods we employ are themselves sources of distortion while being necessary. That's life in the post-modern age.'

There are many helpful works on the play's Roman background and context – catering, as it happens, to our postmodern sensitivity to the reality of other cultures. Reuben A. Brower, in his *Hero & Saint: Shakespeare and the Graeco-Roman Heroic Tradition* (1971), highlights the resemblances between the Shakespearian heroic and the Graeco-Roman, noting that Coriolanus is most like Achilles, especially 'in his willingness to push the heroic to the limit until he destroys his own society along with his enemy's'. Vivian Thomas's *Shakespeare's Roman Worlds* (1989) explores the play's Roman values: service to the state, constancy, fortitude, valour, friendship, love of family, respect for the gods. Thomas also closely studies Shakespeare's handling of his sources, as does David C. Green in *Plutarch Revisited: A Study of Shakespeare's Last Roman Tragedies and Their Source* (1979), in which he notes that Shakespeare's treatment of Plutarch in *Antony and Cleopatra* and *Coriolanus* is superior to that in *Julius Caesar*. Robert Miola's *Shakespeare's Rome* (1983) investigates the city behind *The Rape of Lucrece*, *Titus Andronicus*, *Antony and Cleopatra*, *Coriolanus* and (interestingly) *Cymbeline*. A slightly different viewpoint is provided in Paul Cantor's *Shakespeare's Rome: Republic & Empire* (1976), which explores what *Antony and Cleopatra* and *Coriolanus* tell us about Shakespeare's conception of Rome rather than the real Rome behind the play. C. C. Huffman's *'Coriolanus' in Context* (1971) explores the Jacobean rather than the Ancient Roman context and is disappointingly restrictive: in it, as Bruce King notes, 'James becomes a master myth, which explains everything'. A book that masterfully combines both worlds, without explaining everything, is

Charles Wells's *The Wide Arch: Roman Values in Shakespeare* (1992), in which he points out that the power struggles between York and Lancaster were seen by the Elizabethans as a parallel to the civil wars of Caesar and Pompey, Octavius and Antony, and the flowering of Elizabeth as the flowering of Rome. The Romans were routinely compared with Frobisher, Sidney, Grenville, Essex and Blount.

Good introductions are provided by Derek Traversi's *Shakespeare: The Roman Plays* (1963); Alexander Leggatt's *Shakespeare's Political Drama: The History Plays and the Roman Plays* (1988); Annabel Patterson's *Shakespeare and the Popular Voice* (1989), which suggests that we are reading against the grain of the play to see it as a deliberately anti-democratic work; and Maurice Charney's *Shakespeare's Roman Plays: The Function of Imagery in the Drama* (1963), which studies *Julius Caesar*, *Antony and Cleopatra* and *Coriolanus* as 'poetry of the theater'. Introductory books working at a more simplistic level are Leigh Holt's *From Man to Dragon: A Study of Shakespeare's 'Coriolanus'* (1976) and Marion Smith's *Casque to Cushion: A Study of Othello and Coriolanus* (1979), which would have been improved had the plays not been treated as virtually discrete entities. David Daniell's gossipy *'Coriolanus' in Europe* (1980) follows Terry Hands's 1979 RSC production on its tour of major European cities.

Michael Taylor, 1995

Works cited in the Introduction and The Play in Performance:

Jonathan Bate (ed.), *The Romantics on Shakespeare* (1992).

Bertolt Brecht, *Brecht on Theatre: The Development of an Aesthetic*, ed. and trans. John Willett (1964).

Hal Burton (ed.), *Great Acting* (1967).

Paul A. Jorgensen, *Shakespeare's Military World* (1956).

Plato, *The Republic*, trans. Desmond Lee, 2nd edn (1974).

[North's] Plutarch, *Shakespeare's Plutarch*, ed. T. J. B. Spencer (1964).

George Bernard Shaw, *Shaw on Shakespeare*, ed. Edwin Wilson (1969).

Kenneth Tynan, *The Diaries of Kenneth Tynan*, ed. John Lahr (2001).

Paul Prescott, 2005

THE TRAGEDY OF
CORIOLANUS

The Characters in the Play

Caius MARTIUS, afterwards Caius Martius Coriolanus
Titus LARTIUS ⎱ Roman generals against the Volsces
COMINIUS ⎰
MENENIUS Agrippa, friend of Coriolanus
SICINIUS Velutus ⎱ Tribunes of the People, opposed
Junius BRUTUS ⎰ to Coriolanus
A crowd of Roman CITIZENS
A Roman HERALD
Nicanor, a ROMAN in the pay of the Volsces

VOLUMNIA, mother of Coriolanus
VIRGILIA, wife of Coriolanus
BOY, young Martius, son of Coriolanus
VALERIA, friend of Virgilia
A GENTLEWOMAN attending on Virgilia

Tullus AUFIDIUS, General of the Volsces
A LIEUTENANT under Aufidius
CONSPIRATORS with Aufidius
Adrian, a VOLSCE
A CITIZEN of Antium
Volscian WATCH

Roman and Volscian SENATORS

PATRICIANS
OFFICERS
AEDILES
A Roman LIEUTENANT
SOLDIERS
MESSENGERS
Volscian LORDS
SERVINGMEN of Aufidius

Volscian citizens, lictors, and other attendants

Enter a company of mutinous Citizens, with staves,
clubs, and other weapons

FIRST CITIZEN Before we proceed any further, hear me
speak.

ALL Speak, speak.

FIRST CITIZEN You are all resolved rather to die than to
famish?

ALL Resolved, resolved.

FIRST CITIZEN First, you know Caius Martius is chief
enemy to the people?

ALL We know't, we know't.

FIRST CITIZEN Let us kill him, and we'll have corn at 10
our own price. Is't a verdict?

ALL No more talking on't. Let it be done. Away, away!

SECOND CITIZEN One word, good citizens.

FIRST CITIZEN We are accounted poor citizens, the patricians good. What authority surfeits on would relieve
us. If they would yield us but the superfluity while it
were wholesome, we might guess they relieved us
humanely. But they think we are too dear. The leanness
that afflicts us, the object of our misery, is as an inventory to particularize their abundance. Our sufferance is a 20
gain to them. Let us revenge this with our pikes ere we

become rakes. For the gods know I speak this in hunger
for bread, not in thirst for revenge.

SECOND CITIZEN Would you proceed especially against
Caius Martius?

FIRST CITIZEN Against him first. He's a very dog to the
commonalty.

SECOND CITIZEN Consider you what services he has
done for his country?

30 FIRST CITIZEN Very well, and could be content to give
him good report for't, but that he pays himself with being
proud.

SECOND CITIZEN Nay, but speak not maliciously.

FIRST CITIZEN I say unto you, what he hath done
famously he did it to that end. Though soft-conscienced
men can be content to say it was for his country, he did
it to please his mother and to be partly proud, which he
is, even to the altitude of his virtue.

SECOND CITIZEN What he cannot help in his nature you
40 account a vice in him. You must in no way say he is
covetous.

FIRST CITIZEN If I must not, I need not be barren of
accusations. He hath faults, with surplus, to tire in repetition.

Shouts within

What shouts are these? The other side o'th'city is risen.
Why stay we prating here? To th'Capitol!

ALL Come, come.

FIRST CITIZEN Soft, who comes here?

Enter Menenius Agrippa

SECOND CITIZEN Worthy Menenius Agrippa, one that
50 hath always loved the people.

FIRST CITIZEN He's one honest enough. Would all the
rest were so!

MENENIUS

What work's, my countrymen, in hand? Where go you
With bats and clubs? The matter? Speak, I pray you.

FIRST CITIZEN Our business is not unknown to th'
Senate. They have had inkling this fortnight what we
intend to do, which now we'll show 'em in deeds. They
say poor suitors have strong breaths. They shall know
we have strong arms too.

MENENIUS

Why, masters, my good friends, mine honest neighbours,   60
Will you undo yourselves?

FIRST CITIZEN

We cannot, sir, we are undone already.

MENENIUS

I tell you, friends, most charitable care
Have the patricians of you. For your wants,
Your suffering in this dearth, you may as well
Strike at the heaven with your staves as lift them
Against the Roman state, whose course will on
The way it takes, cracking ten thousand curbs
Of more strong link asunder than can ever
Appear in your impediment. For the dearth,   70
The gods, not the patricians, make it, and
Your knees to them, not arms, must help. Alack,
You are transported by calamity
Thither where more attends you, and you slander
The helms o'th'state, who care for you like fathers,
When you curse them as enemies.

FIRST CITIZEN Care for us? True indeed! They ne'er
cared for us yet. Suffer us to famish, and their store-
houses crammed with grain; make edicts for usury, to
support usurers; repeal daily any wholesome act estab-   80
lished against the rich, and provide more piercing
statutes daily to chain up and restrain the poor. If the

wars eat us not up, they will; and there's all the love they
bear us.

MENENIUS

Either you must
Confess yourselves wondrous malicious,
Or be accused of folly. I shall tell you
A pretty tale. It may be you have heard it,
But, since it serves my purpose, I will venture
90   To stale't a little more.

FIRST CITIZEN Well, I'll hear it, sir. Yet you must not
think to fob off our disgrace with a tale. But, an't please
you, deliver.

MENENIUS

There was a time when all the body's members
Rebelled against the belly, thus accused it:
That only like a gulf it did remain
I'th'midst o'th'body, idle and unactive,
Still cupboarding the viand, never bearing
Like labour with the rest, where th'other instruments
100   Did see and hear, devise, instruct, walk, feel,
And, mutually participate, did minister
Unto the appetite and affection common
Of the whole body. The belly answered –

FIRST CITIZEN

Well, sir, what answer made the belly?

MENENIUS

Sir, I shall tell you. With a kind of smile,
Which ne'er came from the lungs, but even thus –
For look you, I may make the belly smile
As well as speak – it tauntingly replied
To th'discontented members, the mutinous parts
110   That envied his receipt; even so most fitly
As you malign our senators for that
They are not such as you.

FIRST CITIZEN   Your belly's answer — What?
  The kingly crownèd head, the vigilant eye,
  The counsellor heart, the arm our soldier,
  Our steed the leg, the tongue our trumpeter,
  With other muniments and petty helps
  In this our fabric, if that they —
MENENIUS   What then?
  'Fore me, this fellow speaks! What then? What
        then?
FIRST CITIZEN
  Should by the cormorant belly be restrained
  Who is the sink o'th'body —
MENENIUS   Well, what then?   120
FIRST CITIZEN
  The former agents, if they did complain,
  What could the belly answer?
MENENIUS   I will tell you.
  If you'll bestow a small — of what you have little —
  Patience awhile, you'st hear the belly's answer.
FIRST CITIZEN
  Y'are long about it.
MENENIUS   Note me this, good friend —
  Your most grave belly was deliberate,
  Not rash like his accusers, and thus answered.
  'True is it, my incorporate friends,' quoth he,
  'That I receive the general food at first
  Which you do live upon; and fit it is,   130
  Because I am the storehouse and the shop
  Of the whole body. But, if you do remember,
  I send it through the rivers of your blood
  Even to the court, the heart, to th'seat o'th'brain;
  And, through the cranks and offices of man,
  The strongest nerves and small inferior veins
  From me receive that natural competency

Whereby they live. And though that all at once' –
You, my good friends, this says the belly, mark me –

FIRST CITIZEN

140   Ay, sir, well, well.

MENENIUS   'Though all at once cannot
See what I do deliver out to each,
Yet I can make my audit up, that all
From me do back receive the flour of all,
And leave me but the bran.' What say you to't?

FIRST CITIZEN

It was an answer. How apply you this?

MENENIUS

The senators of Rome are this good belly,
And you the mutinous members. For examine
Their counsels and their cares, digest things rightly
Touching the weal o'th'common, you shall find

150   No public benefit which you receive
But it proceeds or comes from them to you,
And no way from yourselves. What do you think,
You, the great toe of this assembly?

FIRST CITIZEN

I the great toe? Why the great toe?

MENENIUS

For that being one o'th'lowest, basest, poorest
Of this most wise rebellion, thou goest foremost.
Thou rascal, that art worst in blood to run,
Lead'st first to win some vantage.
But make you ready your stiff bats and clubs.

160   Rome and her rats are at the point of battle;
The one side must have bale.

    Enter Caius Martius

                    Hail, noble Martius!

MARTIUS

Thanks. What's the matter, you dissentious rogues,

That rubbing the poor itch of your opinion
Make yourselves scabs?
FIRST CITIZEN   We have ever your good word.
MARTIUS
He that will give good words to thee will flatter
Beneath abhorring. What would you have, you curs,
That like nor peace nor war? The one affrights you,
The other makes you proud. He that trusts to you,
Where he should find you lions, finds you hares;
Where foxes, geese. You are no surer, no,   170
Than is the coal of fire upon the ice
Or hailstone in the sun. Your virtue is
To make him worthy whose offence subdues him
And curse that justice did it. Who deserves greatness
Deserves your hate; and your affections are
A sick man's appetite, who desires most that
Which would increase his evil. He that depends
Upon your favours swims with fins of lead
And hews down oaks with rushes. Hang ye! Trust ye?
With every minute you do change a mind   180
And call him noble that was now your hate,
Him vile that was your garland. What's the matter
That in these several places of the city
You cry against the noble Senate, who,
Under the gods, keep you in awe, which else
Would feed on one another? What's their seeking?
MENENIUS
For corn at their own rates, whereof they say
The city is well stored.
MARTIUS   Hang 'em! They say?
They'll sit by th'fire and presume to know
What's done i'th'Capitol, who's like to rise,   190
Who thrives and who declines; side factions and give out
Conjectural marriages, making parties strong

And feebling such as stand not in their liking
Below their cobbled shoes. They say there's grain
   enough!
Would the nobility lay aside their ruth
And let me use my sword, I'd make a quarry
With thousands of these quartered slaves as high
As I could pick my lance.

MENENIUS

Nay, these are almost thoroughly persuaded,
200   For though abundantly they lack discretion,
Yet are they passing cowardly. But, I beseech you,
What says the other troop?

MARTIUS   They are dissolved. Hang 'em!
They said they were an-hungry, sighed forth proverbs –
That hunger broke stone walls, that dogs must eat,
That meat was made for mouths, that the gods sent not
Corn for the rich men only. With these shreds
They vented their complainings; which being answered
And a petition granted them – a strange one,
To break the heart of generosity
210   And make bold power look pale – they threw their caps
As they would hang them on the horns o'th'moon,
Shouting their emulation.

MENENIUS   What is granted them?

MARTIUS

Five tribunes to defend their vulgar wisdoms,
Of their own choice. One's Junius Brutus, one
Sicinius Velutus, and – I know not. 'Sdeath!
The rabble should have first unroofed the city
Ere so prevailed with me. It will in time
Win upon power and throw forth greater themes
For insurrection's arguing.

MENENIUS   This is strange.

MARTIUS

Go get you home, you fragments.   220

Enter a Messenger, hastily

MESSENGER

Where's Caius Martius?

MARTIUS   Here. What's the matter?

MESSENGER

The news is, sir, the Volsces are in arms.

MARTIUS

I am glad on't. Then we shall ha' means to vent

Our musty superfluity. See, our best elders.

Enter Cominius, Titus Lartius, with other Senators;
Junius Brutus and Sicinius Velutus

FIRST SENATOR

Martius, 'tis true that you have lately told us:

The Volsces are in arms.

MARTIUS   They have a leader,

Tullus Aufidius, that will put you to't.

I sin in envying his nobility,

And were I anything but what I am,

I would wish me only he.

COMINIUS   You have fought together.   230

MARTIUS

Were half to half the world by th'ears and he

Upon my party, I'd revolt, to make

Only my wars with him. He is a lion

That I am proud to hunt.

FIRST SENATOR   Then, worthy Martius,

Attend upon Cominius to these wars.

COMINIUS

It is your former promise.

MARTIUS   Sir, it is,

And I am constant. Titus Lartius, thou

Shalt see me once more strike at Tullus' face.

What, art thou stiff? Stand'st out?

LARTIUS   No, Caius Martius,

240   I'll lean upon one crutch and fight with t'other
Ere stay behind this business.

MENENIUS   O, true bred!

FIRST SENATOR
Your company to th'Capitol, where I know
Our greatest friends attend us.

LARTIUS (to Cominius)   Lead you on.
(To Martius) Follow Cominius. We must follow you.
Right worthy you priority.

COMINIUS   Noble Martius!

FIRST SENATOR (to the Citizens)
Hence to your homes, be gone.

MARTIUS   Nay, let them follow.
The Volsces have much corn. Take these rats thither
To gnaw their garners. (Citizens steal away) Worshipful
    mutineers,
Your valour puts well forth. Pray follow.
    Exeunt Patricians. Sicinius and Brutus stay behind

SICINIUS
250   Was ever man so proud as is this Martius?

BRUTUS
He has no equal.

SICINIUS
When we were chosen tribunes for the people –

BRUTUS
Marked you his lip and eyes?

SICINIUS   Nay, but his taunts.

BRUTUS
Being moved, he will not spare to gird the gods.

SICINIUS
Bemock the modest moon.

BRUTUS
The present wars devour him; he is grown
Too proud to be so valiant.

SICINIUS   Such a nature,
Tickled with good success, disdains the shadow
Which he treads on at noon. But I do wonder
His insolence can brook to be commanded   260
Under Cominius.

BRUTUS   Fame, at the which he aims –
In whom already he's well graced – cannot
Better be held nor more attained than by
A place below the first; for what miscarries
Shall be the general's fault, though he perform
To th'utmost of a man, and giddy censure
Will then cry out of Martius, 'O, if he
Had borne the business!'

SICINIUS   Besides, if things go well,
Opinion, that so sticks on Martius, shall
Of his demerits rob Cominius.

BRUTUS   Come.   270
Half all Cominius' honours are to Martius,
Though Martius earned them not; and all his faults
To Martius shall be honours, though indeed
In aught he merit not.

SICINIUS   Let's hence and hear
How the dispatch is made, and in what fashion,
More than his singularity, he goes
Upon this present action.

BRUTUS   Let's along.   *Exeunt*

Enter Tullus Aufidius, with Senators of Corioles   I.2
FIRST SENATOR
So, your opinion is, Aufidius,

That they of Rome are entered in our counsels
And know how we proceed.

AUFIDIUS   Is it not yours?
What ever have been thought on in this state
That could be brought to bodily act ere Rome
Had circumvention? 'Tis not four days gone
Since I heard thence. These are the words – I think
I have the letter here; yes, here it is:

They have pressed a power, but it is not known
10   *Whether for east or west. The dearth is great,*
The people mutinous. And it is rumoured,
Cominius, Martius your old enemy,
Who is of Rome worse hated than of you,
And Titus Lartius, a most valiant Roman,
These three lead on this preparation
Whither 'tis bent. Most likely 'tis for you.
Consider of it.

FIRST SENATOR Our army's in the field.
We never yet made doubt but Rome was ready
To answer us.

AUFIDIUS   Nor did you think it folly
20   To keep your great pretences veiled till when
They needs must show themselves, which in the hatching,
It seemed, appeared to Rome. By the discovery
We shall be shortened in our aim, which was
To take in many towns ere almost Rome
Should know we were afoot.

SECOND SENATOR   Noble Aufidius,
Take your commission, hie you to your bands.
Let us alone to guard Corioles.
If they set down before's, for the remove
Bring up your army. But, I think, you'll find

Th' have not prepared for us.

AUFIDIUS   O, doubt not that.   30
　　I speak from certainties. Nay more,
　　Some parcels of their power are forth already,
　　And only hitherward. I leave your honours.
　　If we and Caius Martius chance to meet,
　　'Tis sworn between us we shall ever strike
　　Till one can do no more.

ALL   The gods assist you!

AUFIDIUS
　　And keep your honours safe!

FIRST SENATOR   Farewell.

SECOND SENATOR   Farewell.

ALL Farewell.   *Exeunt*

Enter Volumnia and Virgilia, mother and wife to   **I.3**
　　Martius. They set them down on two low stools and sew

VOLUMNIA I pray you, daughter, sing, or express yourself
　　in a more comfortable sort. If my son were my husband,
　　I should freelier rejoice in that absence wherein he won
　　honour than in the embracements of his bed where he
　　would show most love. When yet he was but tender-
　　bodied and the only son of my womb, when youth with
　　comeliness plucked all gaze his way, when for a day of
　　kings' entreaties a mother should not sell him an hour
　　from her beholding, I, considering how honour would
　　become such a person – that it was no better than pic-   10
　　ture-like to hang by th'wall, if renown made it not stir –
　　was pleased to let him seek danger where he was like to
　　find fame. To a cruel war I sent him, from whence he
　　returned his brows bound with oak. I tell thee, daughter,
　　I sprang not more in joy at first hearing he was a man-
　　child than now in first seeing he had proved himself a
　　man.

VIRGILIA But had he died in the business, madam, how
then?

20 VOLUMNIA Then his good report should have been my
son; I therein would have found issue. Hear me profess
sincerely, had I a dozen sons, each in my love alike, and
none less dear than thine and my good Martius, I had
rather had eleven die nobly for their country than one
voluptuously surfeit out of action.

Enter a Gentlewoman

GENTLEWOMAN Madam, the Lady Valeria is come to
visit you.

VIRGILIA
Beseech you, give me leave to retire myself.

VOLUMNIA
Indeed you shall not.

30 Methinks I hear hither your husband's drum;
See him pluck Aufidius down by th'hair;
As children from a bear, the Volsces shunning him.
Methinks I see him stamp thus, and call thus:
'Come on, you cowards! You were got in fear,
Though you were born in Rome.' His bloody brow
With his mailed hand then wiping, forth he goes,
Like to a harvest-man that's tasked to mow
Or all or lose his hire.

VIRGILIA
His bloody brow? O Jupiter, no blood!

VOLUMNIA
40 Away, you fool! It more becomes a man
Than gilt his trophy. The breasts of Hecuba,
When she did suckle Hector, looked not lovelier
Than Hector's forehead when it spit forth blood
At Grecian sword, contemning. Tell Valeria
We are fit to bid her welcome.   *Exit Gentlewoman*

VIRGILIA

Heavens bless my lord from fell Aufidius!

VOLUMNIA

He'll beat Aufidius' head below his knee

And tread upon his neck.

Enter Valeria, with an Usher and a Gentlewoman

VALERIA My ladies both, good day to you.

VOLUMNIA Sweet madam!   50

VIRGILIA I am glad to see your ladyship.

VALERIA How do you both? You are manifest housekeepers. What are you sewing here? A fine spot, in good faith.
How does your little son?

VIRGILIA I thank your ladyship. Well, good madam.

VOLUMNIA He had rather see the swords and hear a drum
than look upon his schoolmaster.

VALERIA O'my word, the father's son! I'll swear 'tis a
very pretty boy. O'my troth, I looked upon him o'Wed-
nesday half an hour together. 'Has such a confirmed   60
countenance! I saw him run after a gilded butterfly, and
when he caught it, he let it go again, and after it again,
and over and over he comes and up again, catched it
again; or whether his fall enraged him, or how 'twas, he
did so set his teeth and tear it. O, I warrant, how he
mammocked it!

VOLUMNIA One on's father's moods.

VALERIA Indeed, la, 'tis a noble child.

VIRGILIA A crack, madam.

VALERIA Come, lay aside your stitchery. I must have you   70
play the idle housewife with me this afternoon.

VIRGILIA No, good madam, I will not out of doors.

VALERIA Not out of doors?

VOLUMNIA She shall, she shall.

VIRGILIA Indeed, no, by your patience. I'll not over the
threshold till my lord return from the wars.

VALERIA Fie, you confine yourself most unreasonably.
   Come, you must go visit the good lady that lies in.

VIRGILIA I will wish her speedy strength and visit her
80   with my prayers, but I cannot go thither.

VOLUMNIA Why, I pray you?

VIRGILIA 'Tis not to save labour, nor that I want love.

VALERIA You would be another Penelope. Yet they say
   all the yarn she spun in Ulysses' absence did but fill
   Ithaca full of moths. Come, I would your cambric were
   sensible as your finger, that you might leave pricking it
   for pity. Come, you shall go with us.

VIRGILIA No, good madam, pardon me, indeed I will not
   forth.

90 VALERIA In truth, la, go with me, and I'll tell you excellent news of your husband.

VIRGILIA O, good madam, there can be none yet.

VALERIA Verily I do not jest with you. There came news
   from him last night.

VIRGILIA Indeed, madam?

VALERIA In earnest, it's true. I heard a senator speak it.
   Thus it is: the Volsces have an army forth, against whom
   Cominius the general is gone with one part of our
   Roman power. Your lord and Titus Lartius are set
100   down before their city Corioles. They nothing doubt
   prevailing and to make it brief wars. This is true, on
   mine honour, and so, I pray, go with us.

VIRGILIA Give me excuse, good madam, I will obey you
   in everything hereafter.

VOLUMNIA Let her alone, lady. As she is now, she will
   but disease our better mirth.

VALERIA In troth, I think she would. Fare you well, then.
   Come, good sweet lady. Prithee, Virgilia, turn thy
   solemnness out o'door and go along with us.

VIRGILIA No, at a word, madam. Indeed I must not. I   110
wish you much mirth.
VALERIA Well then, farewell.   *Exeunt*

Enter Martius, Titus Lartius, with Drum and   I.4
Colours, with Captains and Soldiers, as before the
city Corioles. To them a Messenger

MARTIUS
Yonder comes news. A wager they have met.
LARTIUS
My horse to yours, no.
MARTIUS   'Tis done.
LARTIUS   Agreed.
MARTIUS
Say, has our general met the enemy?
MESSENGER
They lie in view, but have not spoke as yet.
LARTIUS
So, the good horse is mine.
MARTIUS   I'll buy him of you.
LARTIUS
No, I'll nor sell nor give him. Lend you him I will
For half a hundred years. (*To the Trumpeter*) Summon
    the town.
MARTIUS
How far off lie these armies?
MESSENGER   Within this mile and half.
MARTIUS
Then shall we hear their 'larum, and they ours.
Now Mars, I prithee, make us quick in work,   10
That we with smoking swords may march from hence
To help our fielded friends! Come, blow thy blast.
    They sound a parley

Enter two Senators, with others, on the walls of
Corioles

Tullus Aufidius, is he within your walls?

FIRST SENATOR

No, nor a man that fears you less than he:
That's lesser than a little. (*Drum afar off*) Hark, our
    drums
Are bringing forth our youth. We'll break our walls
Rather than they shall pound us up. Our gates,
Which yet seem shut, we have but pinned with rushes;
They'll open of themselves. (*Alarum far off*) Hark
    you, far off!

20   There is Aufidius. List what work he makes
Amongst your cloven army.

MARTIUS   O, they are at it!

LARTIUS

Their noise be our instruction. Ladders, ho!

Enter the army of the Volsces

MARTIUS

They fear us not, but issue forth their city.
Now put your shields before your hearts, and fight
With hearts more proof than shields. Advance, brave
    Titus.
They do disdain us much beyond our thoughts,
Which makes me sweat with wrath. Come on, my
    fellows.
He that retires, I'll take him for a Volsce,
And he shall feel mine edge.

Alarum. The Romans are beat back to their trenches.
Enter Martius, cursing

MARTIUS

30   All the contagion of the south light on you,
You shames of Rome! You herd of – Boils and plagues
Plaster you o'er, that you may be abhorred

Farther than seen, and one infect another
Against the wind a mile! You souls of geese
That bear the shapes of men, how have you run
From slaves that apes would beat! Pluto and hell!
All hurt behind! Backs red, and faces pale
With flight and agued fear! Mend and charge home,
Or, by the fires of heaven, I'll leave the foe
And make my wars on you. Look to't. Come on!   40
If you'll stand fast, we'll beat them to their wives,
As they us to our trenches. Follow's!

    Another alarum. The Volsces fly, and Martius follows
    them to the gates, and is shut in

So, now the gates are ope. Now prove good seconds.
'Tis for the followers fortune widens them,
Not for the fliers. Mark me, and do the like.

    He enters the gates

FIRST SOLDIER Fool-hardiness, not I.
SECOND SOLDIER Nor I.
FIRST SOLDIER See, they have shut him in.
ALL To th'pot, I warrant him.

    Alarum continues
    Enter Titus Lartius

LARTIUS
What is become of Martius?
ALL   Slain, sir, doubtless.   50
FIRST SOLDIER
Following the fliers at the very heels,
With them he enters, who upon the sudden
Clapped to their gates. He is himself alone,
To answer all the city.
LARTIUS   O noble fellow!
Who sensibly outdares his senseless sword,
And when it bows stand'st up. Thou art lost, Martius.
A carbuncle entire, as big as thou art,

Were not so rich a jewel. Thou wast a soldier
Even to Cato's wish, not fierce and terrible
60   Only in strokes, but with thy grim looks and
The thunder-like percussion of thy sounds
Thou mad'st thine enemies shake, as if the world
Were feverous and did tremble.
    Enter Martius, bleeding, assaulted by the enemy
FIRST SOLDIER   Look, sir.
LARTIUS   O, 'tis Martius!
Let's fetch him off, or make remain alike.
    They fight, and all enter the city

I.5   *Enter certain Romans, with spoils*
FIRST ROMAN This will I carry to Rome.
SECOND ROMAN And I this.
THIRD ROMAN A murrain on't! I took this for silver.
    Alarum continues still afar off
    Enter Martius and Titus Lartius, with a Trumpeter
MARTIUS
See here these movers that do prize their hours
At a cracked drachma. Cushions, leaden spoons,
Irons of a doit, doublets that hangmen would
Bury with those that wore them, these base slaves,
Ere yet the fight be done, pack up. Down with them!
                              Exeunt spoilers
And hark, what noise the general makes! To him!
10   There is the man of my soul's hate, Aufidius,
Piercing our Romans. Then, valiant Titus, take
Convenient numbers to make good the city,
Whilst I, with those that have the spirit, will haste
To help Cominius.
LARTIUS   Worthy sir, thou bleed'st.
Thy exercise hath been too violent

For a second course of fight.

MARTIUS   Sir, praise me not.
My work hath not yet warmed me. Fare you well.
The blood I drop is rather physical
Than dangerous to me. To Aufidius thus
I will appear and fight.

LARTIUS   Now the fair goddess Fortune   20
Fall deep in love with thee, and her great charms
Misguide thy opposers' swords! Bold gentleman,
Prosperity be thy page!

MARTIUS   Thy friend no less
Than those she placeth highest. So farewell.

LARTIUS
Thou worthiest Martius.   *Exit Martius*
Go sound thy trumpet in the market-place.
Call thither all the officers o'th'town,
Where they shall know our mind. Away!   *Exeunt*

Enter Cominius, as it were in retire, with Soldiers   1.6

COMINIUS
Breathe you, my friends. Well fought! We are come off
Like Romans, neither foolish in our stands
Nor cowardly in retire. Believe me, sirs,
We shall be charged again. Whiles we have struck,
By interims and conveying gusts we have heard
The charges of our friends. The Roman gods
Lead their successes as we wish our own,
That both our powers, with smiling fronts encountering,
May give you thankful sacrifice!
    Enter a Messenger
                                                  Thy news?

MESSENGER
The citizens of Corioles have issued   10

And given to Lartius and to Martius battle.
I saw our party to their trenches driven,
And then I came away.

COMINIUS   Though thou speak'st truth,
Methinks thou speak'st not well. How long is't since?

MESSENGER
Above an hour, my lord.

COMINIUS
'Tis not a mile; briefly we heard their drums.
How couldst thou in a mile confound an hour,
And bring thy news so late?

MESSENGER   Spies of the Volsces
Held me in chase, that I was forced to wheel
Three or four miles about, else had I, sir,
Half an hour since brought my report.

      Enter Martius

COMINIUS   Who's yonder
That does appear as he were flayed? O gods!
He has the stamp of Martius, and I have
Before-time seen him thus.

MARTIUS (*shouts*)   Come I too late?

COMINIUS
The shepherd knows not thunder from a tabor
More than I know the sound of Martius' tongue
From every meaner man.

MARTIUS   Come I too late?

COMINIUS
Ay, if you come not in the blood of others,
But mantled in your own.

MARTIUS   O, let me clip ye
In arms as sound as when I wooed, in heart
As merry as when our nuptial day was done,
And tapers burned to bedward!

COMINIUS   Flower of warriors,

How is't with Titus Lartius?

MARTIUS

As with a man busied about decrees:
Condemning some to death and some to exile,
Ransoming him or pitying, threatening th'other;
Holding Corioles in the name of Rome
Even like a fawning greyhound in the leash,
To let him slip at will.

COMINIUS   Where is that slave
Which told me they had beat you to your trenches?   40
Where is he? Call him hither.

MARTIUS   Let him alone.
He did inform the truth – but for our gentlemen.
The common file – a plague! Tribunes for them! –
The mouse ne'er shunned the cat as they did budge
From rascals worse than they.

COMINIUS   But how prevailed you?

MARTIUS

Will the time serve to tell? I do not think.
Where is the enemy? Are you lords o'th'field?
If not, why cease you till you are so?

COMINIUS   Martius,
We have at disadvantage fought, and did
Retire to win our purpose.   50

MARTIUS

How lies their battle? Know you on which side
They have placed their men of trust?

COMINIUS   As I guess, Martius,
Their bands i'th'vaward are the Antiates,
Of their best trust; o'er them Aufidius,
Their very heart of hope.

MARTIUS   I do beseech you
By all the battles wherein we have fought,
By th'blood we have shed together, by th'vows

We have made to endure friends, that you directly
Set me against Aufidius and his Antiates,
And that you not delay the present, but,
Filling the air with swords advanced and darts,
We prove this very hour.

COMINIUS   Though I could wish
You were conducted to a gentle bath
And balms applied to you, yet dare I never
Deny your asking. Take your choice of those
That best can aid your action.

MARTIUS   Those are they
That most are willing. If any such be here –
As it were sin to doubt – that love this painting
Wherein you see me smeared; if any fear
Lesser his person than an ill report;
If any think brave death outweighs bad life
And that his country's dearer than himself;
Let him alone, or so many so minded,
Wave thus to express his disposition,
And follow Martius.

They all shout and wave their swords, take him up in
their arms, and cast up their caps

O'me alone, make you a sword of me.
If these shows be not outward, which of you
But is four Volsces? None of you but is
Able to bear against the great Aufidius
A shield as hard as his. A certain number,
Though thanks to all, must I select from all. The rest
Shall bear the business in some other fight,
As cause will be obeyed. Please you to march;
And I shall quickly draw out my command,
Which men are best inclined.

COMINIUS   March on, my fellows.
Make good this ostentation, and you shall
Divide in all with us.   *Exeunt*

Titus Lartius, having set a guard upon Corioles,   I.7
going with Drum and Trumpet toward Cominius and
Caius Martius, enters with a Lieutenant, other
Soldiers, and a Scout

LARTIUS

So, let the ports be guarded. Keep your duties
As I have set them down. If I do send, dispatch
Those centuries to our aid. The rest will serve
For a short holding. If we lose the field,
We cannot keep the town.

LIEUTENANT   Fear not our care, sir.

LARTIUS

Hence, and shut your gates upon's.
Our guider, come; to th'Roman camp conduct us.

                                                    Exeunt

Alarum, as in battle. Enter Martius and Aufidius at   I.8
several doors

MARTIUS

I'll fight with none but thee, for I do hate thee
Worse than a promise-breaker.

AUFIDIUS   We hate alike.
Not Afric owns a serpent I abhor
More than thy fame and envy. Fix thy foot.

MARTIUS

Let the first budger die the other's slave,
And the gods doom him after.

AUFIDIUS   If I fly, Martius,
Holloa me like a hare.

MARTIUS   Within these three hours, Tullus,
Alone I fought in your Corioles walls,
And made what work I pleased. 'Tis not my blood
Wherein thou seest me masked. For thy revenge   10

Wrench up thy power to th'highest.

AUFIDIUS   Wert thou the Hector

That was the whip of your bragged progeny,

Thou shouldst not scape me here.

Here they fight, and certain Volsces come in the aid
of Aufidius. Martius fights till they be driven in
breathless

Officious and not valiant, you have shamed me

In your condemnèd seconds.   *Exeunt*

I.9   *Flourish. Alarum. A retreat is sounded. Enter, at one*
door, Cominius, with the Romans; at another door,
Martius, with his arm in a scarf

COMINIUS

If I should tell thee o'er this thy day's work,

Thou't not believe thy deeds. But I'll report it

Where senators shall mingle tears with smiles;

Where great patricians shall attend and shrug,

I'th'end admire; where ladies shall be frighted

And, gladly quaked, hear more; where the dull tribunes,

That with the fusty plebeians hate thine honours,

Shall say against their hearts 'We thank the gods

Our Rome hath such a soldier.'

10   Yet cam'st thou to a morsel of this feast,

Having fully dined before.

Enter Titus Lartius, with his power, from the pursuit

LARTIUS   O general,

Here is the steed, we the caparison.

Hadst thou beheld –

MARTIUS   Pray now, no more. My mother,

Who has a charter to extol her blood,

When she does praise me grieves me. I have done

As you have done – that's what I can; induced

As you have been – that's for my country.
He that has but effected his good will
Hath overta'en mine act.

COMINIUS   You shall not be
The grave of your deserving. Rome must know   20
The value of her own. 'Twere a concealment
Worse than a theft, no less than a traducement,
To hide your doings and to silence that
Which, to the spire and top of praises vouched,
Would seem but modest. Therefore, I beseech you –
In sign of what you are, not to reward
What you have done – before our army hear me.

MARTIUS
I have some wounds upon me, and they smart
To hear themselves remembered.

COMINIUS   Should they not,
Well might they fester 'gainst ingratitude   30
And tent themselves with death. Of all the horses –
Whereof we have ta'en good and good store – of all
The treasure in this field achieved and city,
We render you the tenth, to be ta'en forth
Before the common distribution at
Your only choice.

MARTIUS   I thank you, general,
But cannot make my heart consent to take
A bribe to pay my sword. I do refuse it,
And stand upon my common part with those
That have beheld the doing.   40

     A long flourish. They all cry 'Martius! Martius!',
     cast up their caps and lances. Cominius and Lartius
     stand bare

MARTIUS
May these same instruments which you profane
Never sound more! When drums and trumpets shall

I'th'field prove flatterers, let courts and cities be
Made all of false-faced soothing. When steel grows
Soft as the parasite's silk, let him be made
An overture for th'wars. No more, I say.
For that I have not washed my nose that bled,
Or foiled some debile wretch, which without note
Here's many else have done, you shout me forth
50   In acclamations hyperbolical,
As if I loved my little should be dieted
In praises sauced with lies.

COMINIUS   Too modest are you,
More cruel to your good report than grateful
To us that give you truly. By your patience,
If 'gainst yourself you be incensed, we'll put you –
Like one that means his proper harm – in manacles,
Then reason safely with you. Therefore be it known,
As to us, to all the world, that Caius Martius
Wears this war's garland; in token of the which,
60   My noble steed, known to the camp, I give him,
With all his trim belonging; and from this time,
For what he did before Corioles, call him
With all th'applause and clamour of the host,
Caius Martius Coriolanus.
Bear th'addition nobly ever!

Flourish. Trumpets sound, and drums

ALL
Caius Martius Coriolanus!

CORIOLANUS
I will go wash;
And when my face is fair you shall perceive
Whether I blush or no. Howbeit, I thank you.
70   I mean to stride your steed, and at all times
To undercrest your good addition

To th'fairness of my power.

COMINIUS   So, to our tent,
Where, ere we do repose us, we will write
To Rome of our success. You, Titus Lartius,
Must to Corioles back. Send us to Rome
The best, with whom we may articulate
For their own good and ours.

LARTIUS   I shall, my lord.

CORIOLANUS
The gods begin to mock me. I, that now
Refused most princely gifts, am bound to beg
Of my lord general.

COMINIUS   Take 't, 'tis yours. What is 't?   80

CORIOLANUS
I sometime lay here in Corioles
At a poor man's house; he used me kindly.
He cried to me; I saw him prisoner;
But then Aufidius was within my view,
And wrath o'erwhelmed my pity. I request you
To give my poor host freedom.

COMINIUS   O, well begged!
Were he the butcher of my son, he should
Be free as is the wind. Deliver him, Titus.

LARTIUS
Martius, his name?

CORIOLANUS   By Jupiter, forgot!
I am weary; yea, my memory is tired.   90
Have we no wine here?

COMINIUS   Go we to our tent.
The blood upon your visage dries, 'tis time
It should be looked to. Come.   *Exeunt*

I.10   *A flourish. Cornets. Enter Tullus Aufidius, bloody,*
            with two or three Soldiers

AUFIDIUS
    The town is ta'en.
FIRST SOLDIER
    'Twill be delivered back on good condition.
AUFIDIUS
    Condition?
    I would I were a Roman, for I cannot,
    Being a Volsce, be that I am. Condition?
    What good condition can a treaty find
    I'th'part that is at mercy? Five times, Martius,
    I have fought with thee; so often hast thou beat me;
    And wouldst do so, I think, should we encounter
10 As often as we eat. By th'elements,
    If e'er again I meet him beard to beard,
    He's mine or I am his. Mine emulation
    Hath not that honour in't it had; for where
    I thought to crush him in an equal force,
    True sword to sword, I'll potch at him some way
    Or wrath or craft may get him.
FIRST SOLDIER   He's the devil.
AUFIDIUS
    Bolder, though not so subtle. My valour's poisoned
    With only suffering stain by him; for him
    Shall fly out of itself. Nor sleep nor sanctuary,
20 Being naked, sick, nor fane nor Capitol,
    The prayers of priests nor times of sacrifice,
    Embarquements all of fury, shall lift up
    Their rotten privilege and custom 'gainst
    My hate to Martius. Where I find him, were it
    At home upon my brother's guard, even there,
    Against the hospitable canon, would I
    Wash my fierce hand in's heart. Go you to th'city.

Learn how 'tis held, and what they are that must
Be hostages for Rome.

FIRST SOLDIER   Will not you go?

AUFIDIUS

I am attended at the cypress grove. I pray you –   30
'Tis south the city mills – bring me word thither
How the world goes, that to the pace of it
I may spur on my journey.

FIRST SOLDIER   I shall, sir.   *Exeunt*

*

Enter Menenius, with the two Tribunes of the People,   II.1
Sicinius and Brutus

MENENIUS The augurer tells me we shall have news tonight.

BRUTUS Good or bad?

MENENIUS Not according to the prayer of the people, for
they love not Martius.

SICINIUS Nature teaches beasts to know their friends.

MENENIUS Pray you, who does the wolf love?

SICINIUS The lamb.

MENENIUS Ay, to devour him, as the hungry plebeians
would the noble Martius.

BRUTUS He's a lamb indeed, that baas like a bear.

MENENIUS He's a bear indeed, that lives like a lamb. You   10
two are old men; tell me one thing that I shall ask you.

BOTH Well, sir?

MENENIUS In what enormity is Martius poor in that you
two have not in abundance?

BRUTUS He's poor in no one fault, but stored with all.

SICINIUS Especially in pride.

BRUTUS And topping all others in boasting.

20 MENENIUS This is strange now. Do you two know how
      you are censured here in the city – I mean of us o'th'
      right-hand file? Do you?

   BOTH Why, how are we censured?

   MENENIUS Because you talk of pride now – will you not
      be angry?

   BOTH Well, well, sir, well?

   MENENIUS Why, 'tis no great matter, for a very little
      thief of occasion will rob you of a great deal of patience.
      Give your dispositions the reins and be angry at your
30   pleasures – at the least, if you take it as a pleasure to you
      in being so. You blame Martius for being proud?

   BRUTUS We do it not alone, sir.

   MENENIUS I know you can do very little alone, for your
      helps are many, or else your actions would grow wond-
      rous single. Your abilities are too infant-like for doing
      much alone. You talk of pride. O that you could turn
      your eyes toward the napes of your necks, and make but
      an interior survey of your good selves! O that you could!

   BOTH What then, sir?

40 MENENIUS Why, then you should discover a brace of un-
      meriting, proud, violent, testy magistrates – alias fools –
      as any in Rome.

   SICINIUS Menenius, you are known well enough too.

   MENENIUS I am known to be a humorous patrician, and
      one that loves a cup of hot wine with not a drop of allay-
      ing Tiber in't; said to be something imperfect in favour-
      ing the first complaint, hasty and tinder-like upon too
      trivial motion; one that converses more with the but-
      tock of the night than with the forehead of the morning.
50   What I think I utter, and spend my malice in my breath.
      Meeting two such wealsmen as you are – I cannot call
      you Lycurguses – if the drink you give me touch my
      palate adversely, I make a crooked face at it. I cannot

say your worships have delivered the matter well, when
I find the ass in compound with the major part of your
syllables. And though I must be content to bear with
those that say you are reverend grave men, yet they lie
deadly that tell you have good faces. If you see this in the
map of my microcosm, follows it that I am known well
enough too? What harm can your bisson conspectuities   60
glean out of this character, if I be known well enough too?

BRUTUS Come, sir, come, we know you well enough.

MENENIUS You know neither me, yourselves, nor any
thing. You are ambitious for poor knaves' caps and legs.
You wear out a good wholesome forenoon in hearing a
cause between an orange-wife and a faucet-seller, and
then rejourn the controversy of threepence to a second
day of audience. When you are hearing a matter between
party and party, if you chance to be pinched with the
colic, you make faces like mummers, set up the bloody   70
flag against all patience, and, in roaring for a chamber-
pot, dismiss the controversy bleeding, the more en-
tangled by your hearing. All the peace you make in their
cause is calling both the parties knaves. You are a pair of
strange ones.

BRUTUS Come, come, you are well understood to be a perfecter giber for the table than a necessary bencher in the
Capitol.

MENENIUS Our very priests must become mockers, if they
shall encounter such ridiculous subjects as you are.   80
When you speak best unto the purpose, it is not worth
the wagging of your beards; and your beards deserve not
so honourable a grave as to stuff a botcher's cushion or to
be entombed in an ass's pack-saddle. Yet you must be
saying Martius is proud; who, in a cheap estimation, is
worth all your predecessors since Deucalion, though
peradventure some of the best of 'em were hereditary

hangmen. Good-e'en to your worships. More of your
conversation would infect my brain, being the herdsmen
90   of the beastly plebeians. I will be bold to take my leave
of you.

Brutus and Sicinius stand aside
Enter Volumnia, Virgilia, and Valeria

How now, my as fair as noble ladies – and the moon,
were she earthly, no nobler – whither do you follow your
eyes so fast?

VOLUMNIA Honourable Menenius, my boy Martius
approaches. For the love of Juno, let's go.

MENENIUS Ha? Martius coming home?

VOLUMNIA Ay, worthy Menenius, and with most prosperous approbation.

100   MENENIUS Take my cap, Jupiter, and I thank thee. Hoo!
Martius coming home?

VIRGILIA *and* VALERIA Nay, 'tis true.

VOLUMNIA Look, here's a letter from him. The state hath
another, his wife another, and I think there's one at home
for you.

MENENIUS I will make my very house reel tonight. A
letter for me?

VIRGILIA Yes, certain, there's a letter for you, I saw't.

MENENIUS A letter for me! It gives me an estate of seven
110   years' health, in which time I will make a lip at the physician. The most sovereign prescription in Galen is but
empiricutic and, to this preservative, of no better report
than a horse-drench. Is he not wounded? He was wont
to come home wounded.

VIRGILIA O, no, no, no.

VOLUMNIA O, he is wounded, I thank the gods for't.

MENENIUS So do I too – if it be not too much. Brings 'a
victory in his pocket, the wounds become him.

VOLUMNIA On's brows, Menenius. He comes the third
120   time home with the oaken garland.

MENENIUS Has he disciplined Aufidius soundly?

VOLUMNIA Titus Lartius writes they fought together, but Aufidius got off.

MENENIUS And 'twas time for him too, I'll warrant him that. An he had stayed by him, I would not have been so fidiused for all the chests in Corioles and the gold that's in them. Is the Senate possessed of this?

VOLUMNIA Good ladies, let's go. Yes, yes, yes! The Senate has letters from the general, wherein he gives my son the whole name of the war. He hath in this action outdone his former deeds doubly.   130

VALERIA In troth, there's wondrous things spoke of him.

MENENIUS Wondrous? Ay, I warrant you, and not without his true purchasing.

VIRGILIA The gods grant them true.

VOLUMNIA True? Pow waw!

MENENIUS True? I'll be sworn they are true. Where is he wounded? (*To the Tribunes*) God save your good worships! Martius is coming home. He has more cause to be proud. – Where is he wounded?   140

VOLUMNIA I'th'shoulder and i'th'left arm. There will be large cicatrices to show the people, when he shall stand for his place. He received in the repulse of Tarquin seven hurts i'th'body.

MENENIUS One i'th'neck and two i'th'thigh – there's nine that I know.

VOLUMNIA He had before this last expedition twenty-five wounds upon him.

MENENIUS Now it's twenty-seven. Every gash was an enemy's grave. (*A shout and flourish*) Hark, the trumpets.   150

VOLUMNIA These are the ushers of Martius. Before him he carries noise, and behind him he leaves tears.
Death, that dark spirit, in's nervy arm doth lie,
Which, being advanced, declines, and then men die.

*A sennet. Trumpets sound. Enter Cominius the
General and Titus Lartius; between them,
Coriolanus, crowned with an oaken garland; with
Captains and Soldiers and a Herald*

HERALD

Know, Rome, that all alone Martius did fight
Within Corioles gates, where he hath won,
With fame, a name to Caius Martius; these
In honour follows 'Coriolanus'.
Welcome to Rome, renownèd Coriolanus!
    Sound flourish

ALL

160 Welcome to Rome, renownèd Coriolanus!

CORIOLANUS

No more of this; it does offend my heart.
Pray now, no more.

COMINIUS   Look, sir, your mother!

CORIOLANUS   O,

You have, I know, petitioned all the gods
For my prosperity!
    He kneels

VOLUMNIA   Nay, my good soldier, up,

My gentle Martius, worthy Caius, and
By deed-achieving honour newly named –
What is it? – Coriolanus must I call thee? –
But, O, thy wife!

CORIOLANUS   My gracious silence, hail!

Wouldst thou have laughed had I come coffined home,
170 That weep'st to see me triumph? Ah, my dear,
Such eyes the widows in Corioles wear,
And mothers that lack sons.

MENENIUS   Now the gods crown thee!

CORIOLANUS

And live you yet? (*To Valeria*) O my sweet lady, pardon.

VOLUMNIA

    I know not where to turn. O, welcome home.

    And welcome, general, and y'are welcome all.

MENENIUS

    A hundred thousand welcomes. I could weep

    And I could laugh, I am light and heavy. Welcome.

    A curse begin at very root on's heart

    That is not glad to see thee. You are three

    That Rome should dote on. Yet, by the faith of men,   180

    We have some old crab-trees here at home that will not

    Be grafted to your relish. Yet welcome, warriors.

    We call a nettle but a nettle and

    The faults of fools but folly.

COMINIUS   Ever right.

CORIOLANUS

    Menenius, ever, ever.

HERALD

    Give way there, and go on.

CORIOLANUS (*to Volumnia and Virgilia*)

                     Your hand, and yours.

    Ere in our own house I do shade my head,

    The good patricians must be visited,

    From whom I have received not only greetings,

    But with them change of honours.

VOLUMNIA   I have lived   190

    To see inherited my very wishes

    And the buildings of my fancy. Only

    There's one thing wanting, which I doubt not but

    Our Rome will cast upon thee.

CORIOLANUS   Know, good mother,

    I had rather be their servant in my way

    Than sway with them in theirs.

COMINIUS   On, to the Capitol.

         Flourish. Cornets. Exeunt in state, as before.

Brutus and Sicinius come forward

BRUTUS
    All tongues speak of him and the blearèd sights
    Are spectacled to see him. Your prattling nurse
    Into a rapture lets her baby cry
200   While she chats him. The kitchen malkin pins
    Her richest lockram 'bout her reechy neck,
    Clambering the walls to eye him. Stalls, bulks, windows
    Are smothered up, leads filled, and ridges horsed
    With variable complexions, all agreeing
    In earnestness to see him. Seld-shown flamens
    Do press among the popular throngs and puff
    To win a vulgar station. Our veiled dames
    Commit the war of white and damask in
    Their nicely gawded cheeks to th'wanton spoil
210   Of Phoebus' burning kisses. Such a pother
    As if that whatsoever god who leads him
    Were slily crept into his human powers
    And gave him graceful posture.

SICINIUS   On the sudden
    I warrant him consul.

BRUTUS   Then our office may
    During his power go sleep.

SICINIUS
    He cannot temperately transport his honours
    From where he should begin and end, but will
    Lose those he hath won.

BRUTUS   In that there's comfort.

SICINIUS   Doubt not
    The commoners, for whom we stand, but they
220   Upon their ancient malice will forget
    With the least cause these his new honours, which
    That he will give them make I as little question
    As he is proud to do't.

BRUTUS   I heard him swear,
  Were he to stand for consul, never would he
  Appear i'th'market-place nor on him put
  The napless vesture of humility,
  Nor showing, as the manner is, his wounds
  To th'people, beg their stinking breaths.
SICINIUS   'Tis right.
BRUTUS
  It was his word. O, he would miss it rather
  Than carry it but by the suit of the gentry to him   230
  And the desire of the nobles.
SICINIUS   I wish no better
  Than have him hold that purpose and to put it
  In execution.
BRUTUS   'Tis most like he will.
SICINIUS
  It shall be to him then as our good wills,
  A sure destruction.
BRUTUS   So it must fall out
  To him, or our authority's for an end.
  We must suggest the people in what hatred
  He still hath held them; that to's power he would
  Have made them mules, silenced their pleaders and
  Dispropertied their freedoms, holding them   240
  In human action and capacity
  Of no more soul nor fitness for the world
  Than camels in the war, who have their provand
  Only for bearing burdens, and sore blows
  For sinking under them.
SICINIUS   This, as you say, suggested
  At some time when his soaring insolence
  Shall teach the people – which time shall not want,
  If he be put upon't, and that's as easy
  As to set dogs on sheep – will be his fire

250   To kindle their dry stubble; and their blaze
        Shall darken him for ever.

            Enter a Messenger

BRUTUS   What's the matter?

MESSENGER
        You are sent for to the Capitol. 'Tis thought
        That Martius shall be consul.
        I have seen the dumb men throng to see him and
        The blind to hear him speak. Matrons flung gloves,
        Ladies and maids their scarfs and handkerchers,
        Upon him as he passed. The nobles bended
        As to Jove's statue, and the commons made
        A shower and thunder with their caps and shouts.
260   I never saw the like.

BRUTUS   Let's to the Capitol,
        And carry with us ears and eyes for th'time,
        But hearts for the event.

SICINIUS   Have with you.   *Exeunt*

II.2   *Enter two Officers, to lay cushions, as it were in the*
            Capitol

        FIRST OFFICER Come, come, they are almost here. How
            many stand for consulships?

        SECOND OFFICER Three, they say; but 'tis thought of
            everyone Coriolanus will carry it.

        FIRST OFFICER That's a brave fellow, but he's vengeance
            proud and loves not the common people.

        SECOND OFFICER Faith, there hath been many great men
            that have flattered the people, who ne'er loved them; and
            there be many that they have loved, they know not
10   wherefore. So that, if they love they know not why, they
            hate upon no better a ground. Therefore, for Coriolanus
            neither to care whether they love or hate him manifests

the true knowledge he has in their disposition, and out of
his noble carelessness lets them plainly see't.

FIRST OFFICER If he did not care whether he had their
love or no, he waved indifferently 'twixt doing them
neither good nor harm. But he seeks their hate with
greater devotion than they can render it him, and leaves
nothing undone that may fully discover him their opposite. Now to seem to affect the malice and displeasure of   20
the people is as bad as that which he dislikes – to flatter
them for their love.

SECOND OFFICER He hath deserved worthily of his country; and his ascent is not by such easy degrees as those
who, having been supple and courteous to the people,
bonneted, without any further deed to have them at all,
into their estimation and report. But he hath so planted
his honours in their eyes and his actions in their hearts
that for their tongues to be silent and not confess so much
were a kind of ingrateful injury. To report otherwise   30
were a malice that, giving itself the lie, would pluck
reproof and rebuke from every ear that heard it.

FIRST OFFICER No more of him, he's a worthy man.
Make way, they are coming.

*A sennet. Enter the Patricians and the Tribunes of
the People, Lictors before them; Coriolanus, Menenius,
Cominius the Consul. Sicinius and Brutus take their
places by themselves*

MENENIUS

Having determined of the Volsces and
To send for Titus Lartius, it remains,
As the main point of this our after-meeting,
To gratify his noble service that
Hath thus stood for his country. Therefore please you,
Most reverend and grave elders, to desire   40
The present consul and last general

In our well-found successes to report
A little of that worthy work performed
By Caius Martius Coriolanus, whom
We met here both to thank and to remember
With honours like himself.

FIRST SENATOR   Speak, good Cominius.
Leave nothing out for length, and make us think
Rather our state's defective for requital
Than we to stretch it out. (*To the Tribunes*) Masters
    o'th'people,
50 We do request your kindest ears, and after,
Your loving motion toward the common body
To yield what passes here.

SICINIUS   We are convented
Upon a pleasing treaty, and have hearts
Inclinable to honour and advance
The theme of our assembly.

BRUTUS   Which the rather
We shall be blessed to do, if he remember
A kinder value of the people than
He hath hereto prized them at.

MENENIUS   That's off, that's off!
I would you rather had been silent. Please you
60 To hear Cominius speak?

BRUTUS   Most willingly.
But yet my caution was more pertinent
Than the rebuke you give it.

MENENIUS   He loves your people;
But tie him not to be their bedfellow.
Worthy Cominius, speak.
    Coriolanus rises, and offers to go away
                             Nay, keep your place.

FIRST SENATOR
Sit, Coriolanus, never shame to hear

What you have nobly done.

CORIOLANUS   Your honours' pardon.
I had rather have my wounds to heal again
Than hear say how I got them.

BRUTUS   Sir, I hope
My words disbenched you not.

CORIOLANUS   No, sir. Yet oft,
When blows have made me stay, I fled from words.   70
You soothed not, therefore hurt not. But your people,
I love them as they weigh –

MENENIUS   Pray now, sit down.

CORIOLANUS
I had rather have one scratch my head i'th'sun
When the alarum were struck than idly sit
To hear my nothings monstered.   *Exit Coriolanus*

MENENIUS   · Masters of the people,
Your multiplying spawn how can he flatter –
That's thousand to one good one – when you now see
He had rather venture all his limbs for honour
Than one on's ears to hear it. Proceed, Cominius.

COMINIUS
I shall lack voice. The deeds of Coriolanus   80
Should not be uttered feebly. It is held
That valour is the chiefest virtue and
Most dignifies the haver. If it be,
The man I speak of cannot in the world
Be singly counterpoised. At sixteen years,
When Tarquin made a head for Rome, he fought
Beyond the mark of others. Our then dictator,
Whom with all praise I point at, saw him fight
When with his Amazonian chin he drove
The bristled lips before him. He bestrid   90
An o'erpressed Roman and i'th'Consul's view
Slew three opposers. Tarquin's self he met,

And struck him on his knee. In that day's feats,
When he might act the woman in the scene,
He proved best man i'th'field, and for his meed
Was brow-bound with the oak. His pupil age
Man-entered thus, he waxèd like a sea,
And in the brunt of seventeen battles since
He lurched all swords of the garland. For this last,
100 Before and in Corioles, let me say
I cannot speak him home. He stopped the fliers,
And by his rare example made the coward
Turn terror into sport. As weeds before
A vessel under sail, so men obeyed
And fell below his stem. His sword, death's stamp,
Where it did mark, it took from face to foot.
He was a thing of blood, whose every motion
Was timed with dying cries. Alone he entered
The mortal gate of th'city, which he painted
110 With shunless destiny; aidless came off,
And with a sudden reinforcement struck
Corioles like a planet. Now all's his,
When by and by the din of war 'gan pierce
His ready sense, then straight his doubled spirit
Requickened what in flesh was fatigate,
And to the battle came he, where he did
Run reeking o'er the lives of men, as if
'Twere a perpetual spoil; and till we called
Both field and city ours he never stood
120 To ease his breast with panting.

MENENIUS   Worthy man!

FIRST SENATOR
He cannot but with measure fit the honours
Which we devise him.

COMINIUS   Our spoils he kicked at,
And looked upon things precious as they were

The common muck of the world. He covets less
Than misery itself would give, rewards
His deeds with doing them, and is content
To spend the time to end it.

MENENIUS   He's right noble.
Let him be called for.

FIRST SENATOR   Call Coriolanus.

Enter Coriolanus

OFFICER
He doth appear.

MENENIUS
The Senate, Coriolanus, are well pleased   130
To make thee consul.

CORIOLANUS   I do owe them still
My life and services.

MENENIUS   It then remains
That you do speak to the people.

CORIOLANUS   I do beseech you
Let me o'erleap that custom, for I cannot
Put on the gown, stand naked, and entreat them
For my wounds' sake to give their suffrage. Please you
That I may pass this doing.

SICINIUS   Sir, the people
Must have their voices, neither will they bate
One jot of ceremony.

MENENIUS   Put them not to't.
Pray you go fit you to the custom and   140
Take to you, as your predecessors have,
Your honour with your form.

CORIOLANUS   It is a part
That I shall blush in acting, and might well
Be taken from the people.

BRUTUS (*to Sicinius*)   Mark you that?

CORIOLANUS
  To brag unto them 'Thus I did, and thus!',
  Show them th'unaching scars which I should hide,
  As if I had received them for the hire
  Of their breath only!

MENENIUS   Do not stand upon't.
  We recommend to you, Tribunes of the People,
150 Our purpose to them; and to our noble Consul
  Wish we all joy and honour.

SENATORS
  To Coriolanus come all joy and honour!

                  Flourish. Cornets. Then exeunt.
  Sicinius and Brutus stay behind

BRUTUS
  You see how he intends to use the people.

SICINIUS
  May they perceive's intent! He will require them
  As if he did contemn what he requested
  Should be in them to give.

BRUTUS   Come, we'll inform them
  Of our proceedings here. On th'market-place
  I know they do attend us.   *Exeunt*

II.3   *Enter seven or eight Citizens*

FIRST CITIZEN Once, if he do require our voices, we
  ought not to deny him.

SECOND CITIZEN We may, sir, if we will.

THIRD CITIZEN We have power in ourselves to do it, but
  it is a power that we have no power to do. For if he show
  us his wounds and tell us his deeds, we are to put our
  tongues into those wounds and speak for them. So, if he
  tell us his noble deeds, we must also tell him our noble
  acceptance of them. Ingratitude is monstrous, and for

the multitude to be ingrateful were to make a monster of   10
the multitude; of the which we being members should
bring ourselves to be monstrous members.

FIRST CITIZEN And to make us no better thought of a
little help will serve; for once we stood up about the
corn, he himself stuck not to call us the many-headed
multitude.

THIRD CITIZEN We have been called so of many; not
that our heads are some brown, some black, some abram,
some bald, but that our wits are so diversely coloured.
And truly I think if all our wits were to issue out of one   20
skull, they would fly east, west, north, south, and their
consent of one direct way should be at once to all the
points o'th'compass.

SECOND CITIZEN Think you so? Which way do you
judge my wit would fly?

THIRD CITIZEN Nay, your wit will not so soon out as
another man's will – 'tis strongly wedged up in a blockhead; but if it were at liberty 'twould sure southward.

SECOND CITIZEN Why that way?

THIRD CITIZEN To lose itself in a fog, where being three   30
parts melted away with rotten dews, the fourth would
return for conscience' sake to help to get thee a wife.

SECOND CITIZEN You are never without your tricks. You
may, you may!

THIRD CITIZEN Are you all resolved to give your voices?
But that's no matter, the greater part carries it. I say, if
he would incline to the people, there was never a worthier
man.

    Enter Coriolanus in a gown of humility, with
    Menenius

Here he comes, and in the gown of humility. Mark his
behaviour. We are not to stay all together, but to come   40
by him where he stands, by ones, by twos, and by threes.

He's to make his requests by particulars, wherein every
one of us has a single honour, in giving him our own
voices with our own tongues. Therefore follow me, and
I'll direct you how you shall go by him.

ALL Content, content.   *Exeunt Citizens*

MENENIUS
    O sir, you are not right. Have you not known
    The worthiest men have done't?

CORIOLANUS   What must I say? –
    'I pray, sir' – Plague upon't! I cannot bring
50 My tongue to such a pace. 'Look, sir, my wounds!
    I got them in my country's service, when
    Some certain of your brethren roared and ran
    From th'noise of our own drums.'

MENENIUS   O me, the gods!
    You must not speak of that. You must desire them
    To think upon you.

CORIOLANUS   Think upon me? Hang 'em!
    I would they would forget me, like the virtues
    Which our divines lose by 'em.

MENENIUS   You'll mar all.
    I'll leave you. Pray you speak to 'em, I pray you,
    In wholesome manner.   *Exit*

        Enter three of the Citizens

CORIOLANUS   Bid them wash their faces
60 And keep their teeth clean. So, here comes a brace.
    You know the cause, sir, of my standing here.

THIRD CITIZEN
    We do, sir. Tell us what hath brought you to't.

CORIOLANUS Mine own desert.

SECOND CITIZEN Your own desert?

CORIOLANUS Ay, but not mine own desire.

THIRD CITIZEN How not your own desire?

CORIOLANUS No, sir, 'twas never my desire yet to trouble
    the poor with begging.

THIRD CITIZEN You must think, if we give you anything, we hope to gain by you.   70

CORIOLANUS Well then, I pray, your price o'th'consulship?

FIRST CITIZEN The price is to ask it kindly.

CORIOLANUS Kindly, sir, I pray let me ha't. I have wounds to show you, which shall be yours in private. (*To the Second Citizen*) Your good voice, sir. What say you?

SECOND CITIZEN You shall ha't, worthy sir.

CORIOLANUS A match, sir. There's in all two worthy voices begged. I have your alms. Adieu.   80

THIRD CITIZEN But this is something odd.

SECOND CITIZEN An 'twere to give again — but 'tis no matter.   *Exeunt*

Enter two other Citizens

CORIOLANUS Pray you now, if it may stand with the tune of your voices that I may be consul, I have here the customary gown.

FOURTH CITIZEN You have deserved nobly of your country, and you have not deserved nobly.

CORIOLANUS Your enigma?

FOURTH CITIZEN You have been a scourge to her   90
enemies, you have been a rod to her friends. You have not indeed loved the common people.

CORIOLANUS You should account me the more virtuous that I have not been common in my love. I will, sir, flatter my sworn brother, the people, to earn a dearer estimation of them. 'Tis a condition they account gentle; and since the wisdom of their choice is rather to have my hat than my heart, I will practise the insinuating nod and be off to them most counterfeitly. That is, sir, I will counterfeit the bewitchment of some popular man and   100
give it bountiful to the desirers. Therefore, beseech you

I may be consul.

FIFTH CITIZEN We hope to find you our friend, and
therefore give you our voices heartily.

FOURTH CITIZEN You have received many wounds for
your country.

CORIOLANUS I will not seal your knowledge with showing
them. I will make much of your voices and so trouble
you no farther.

110 BOTH The gods give you joy, sir, heartily!   *Exeunt*

CORIOLANUS

Most sweet voices!
Better it is to die, better to starve,
Than crave the hire which first we do deserve.
Why in this wolvish toge should I stand here
To beg of Hob and Dick that does appear
Their needless vouches? Custom calls me to't.
What custom wills, in all things should we do't,
The dust on antique time would lie unswept
And mountainous error be too highly heaped
120 For truth to o'erpeer. Rather than fool it so,
Let the high office and the honour go
To one that would do thus. I am half through;
The one part suffered, the other will I do.

    Enter three Citizens more

Here come more voices.
Your voices! For your voices I have fought,
Watched for your voices; for your voices bear
Of wounds two dozen odd. Battles thrice six
I have seen and heard of; for your voices have
Done many things, some less, some more. Your voices!
130 Indeed, I would be consul.

SIXTH CITIZEN He has done nobly, and cannot go without any honest man's voice.

SEVENTH CITIZEN Therefore let him be consul. The

gods give him joy and make him good friend to the
people!

ALL

Amen, amen. God save thee, noble Consul!

Exeunt Citizens

CORIOLANUS Worthy voices.

Enter Menenius, with Brutus and Sicinius

MENENIUS

You have stood your limitation, and the Tribunes
Endue you with the people's voice. Remains
That in th'official marks invested you   140
Anon do meet the Senate.

CORIOLANUS   Is this done?

SICINIUS

The custom of request you have discharged.
The people do admit you, and are summoned
To meet anon upon your approbation.

CORIOLANUS

Where? At the Senate House?

SICINIUS   There, Coriolanus.

CORIOLANUS

May I change these garments?

SICINIUS   You may, sir.

CORIOLANUS

That I'll straight do and, knowing myself again,
Repair to th'Senate House.

MENENIUS

I'll keep you company. (*To the Tribunes*) Will you along?

BRUTUS

We stay here for the people.

SICINIUS   Fare you well.   150

Exeunt Coriolanus and Menenius

He has it now, and by his looks methinks
'Tis warm at's heart.

BRUTUS   With a proud heart he wore
  His humble weeds. Will you dismiss the people?
    Enter the Plebeians
SICINIUS
  How now, my masters, have you chose this man?
FIRST CITIZEN
  He has our voices, sir.
BRUTUS
  We pray the gods he may deserve your loves.
SECOND CITIZEN
  Amen, sir. To my poor unworthy notice,
  He mocked us when he begged our voices.
THIRD CITIZEN   Certainly,
  He flouted us downright.
FIRST CITIZEN
160 No, 'tis his kind of speech – he did not mock us.
SECOND CITIZEN
  Not one amongst us, save yourself, but says
  He used us scornfully. He should have showed us
  His marks of merit, wounds received for's country.
SICINIUS
  Why, so he did, I am sure.
ALL   No, no! No man saw 'em.
THIRD CITIZEN
  He said he had wounds which he could show in private,
  And with his hat, thus waving it in scorn,
  'I would be consul,' says he. 'Aged custom
  But by your voices will not so permit me;
  Your voices therefore.' When we granted that,
170 Here was 'I thank you for your voices. Thank you,
  Your most sweet voices. Now you have left your voices,
  I have no further with you.' Was not this mockery?
SICINIUS
  Why either were you ignorant to see't,

Or, seeing it, of such childish friendliness
To yield your voices?

BRUTUS   Could you not have told him –
As you were lessoned – when he had no power,
But was a petty servant to the state,
He was your enemy, ever spake against
Your liberties and the charters that you bear
I'th'body of the weal; and now, arriving   180
A place of potency and sway o'th'state,
If he should still malignantly remain
Fast foe to th'plebeii, your voices might
Be curses to yourselves? You should have said
That as his worthy deeds did claim no less
Than what he stood for, so his gracious nature
Would think upon you for your voices and
Translate his malice towards you into love,
Standing your friendly lord.

SICINIUS   Thus to have said,
As you were fore-advised, had touched his spirit   190
And tried his inclination; from him plucked
Either his gracious promise, which you might,
As cause had called you up, have held him to;
Or else it would have galled his surly nature,
Which easily endures not article
Tying him to aught. So putting him to rage,
You should have ta'en th'advantage of his choler
And passed him unelected.

BRUTUS   Did you perceive
He did solicit you in free contempt
When he did need your loves, and do you think   200
That his contempt shall not be bruising to you
When he hath power to crush? Why, had your bodies
No heart among you? Or had you tongues to cry
Against the rectorship of judgement?

SICINIUS   Have you
Ere now denied the asker, and now again,
Of him that did not ask but mock, bestow
Your sued-for tongues?

THIRD CITIZEN
He's not confirmed; we may deny him yet.

SECOND CITIZEN
And will deny him.
210   I'll have five hundred voices of that sound.

FIRST CITIZEN
I twice five hundred, and their friends to piece 'em.

BRUTUS
Get you hence instantly, and tell those friends
They have chose a consul that will from them take
Their liberties, make them of no more voice
Than dogs that are as often beat for barking
As therefore kept to do so.

SICINIUS   Let them assemble,
And on a safer judgement all revoke
Your ignorant election. Enforce his pride
And his old hate unto you. Besides, forget not
220   With what contempt he wore the humble weed,
How in his suit he scorned you; but your loves,
Thinking upon his services, took from you
Th'apprehension of his present portance,
Which most gibingly, ungravely, he did fashion
After the inveterate hate he bears you.

BRUTUS   Lay
A fault on us, your Tribunes, that we laboured,
No impediment between, but that you must
Cast your election on him.

SICINIUS   Say you chose him
More after our commandment than as guided
230   By your own true affections, and that your minds,

Pre-occupied with what you rather must do
Than what you should, made you against the grain
To voice him consul. Lay the fault on us.

BRUTUS

Ay, spare us not. Say we read lectures to you,
How youngly he began to serve his country,
How long continued, and what stock he springs of –
The noble house o'th'Martians, from whence came
That Ancus Martius, Numa's daughter's son,
Who after great Hostilius here was king.
Of the same house Publius and Quintus were,   240
That our best water brought by conduits hither;
And Censorinus, nobly namèd so,
Twice being by the people chosen censor,
Was his great ancestor.

SICINIUS   One thus descended,
That hath beside well in his person wrought
To be set high in place, we did commend
To your remembrances. But you have found,
Scaling his present bearing with his past,
That he's your fixèd enemy, and revoke
Your sudden approbation.

BRUTUS   Say you ne'er had done't –   250
Harp on that still – but by our putting on.
And presently, when you have drawn your number,
Repair to th'Capitol.

ALL   We will so. Almost all
Repent in their election.   *Exeunt Plebeians*

BRUTUS   Let them go on.
This mutiny were better put in hazard
Than stay, past doubt, for greater.
If, as his nature is, he fall in rage
With their refusal, both observe and answer
The vantage of his anger.

SICINIUS   To th'Capitol, come.
260   We will be there before the stream o'th'people;
       And this shall seem, as partly 'tis, their own,
       Which we have goaded onward.   *Exeunt*

                              *

III.I   *Cornets. Enter Coriolanus, Menenius, all the Gentry,*
            Cominius, Titus Lartius, and other Senators

CORIOLANUS
    Tullus Aufidius then had made new head?

LARTIUS
    He had, my lord, and that it was which caused
    Our swifter composition.

CORIOLANUS
    So then the Volsces stand but as at first,
    Ready, when time shall prompt them, to make road
    Upon's again.

COMINIUS   They are worn, lord Consul, so
    That we shall hardly in our ages see
    Their banners wave again.

CORIOLANUS   Saw you Aufidius?

LARTIUS
    On safeguard he came to me, and did curse
10 Against the Volsces, for they had so vilely
    Yielded the town. He is retired to Antium.

CORIOLANUS
    Spoke he of me?

LARTIUS   He did, my lord.

CORIOLANUS   How? What?

LARTIUS
    How often he had met you, sword to sword;
    That of all things upon the earth he hated

Your person most; that he would pawn his fortunes
To hopeless restitution, so he might
Be called your vanquisher.

CORIOLANUS   At Antium lives he?

LARTIUS
At Antium.

CORIOLANUS
I wish I had a cause to seek him there,
To oppose his hatred fully. Welcome home.   20
    Enter Sicinius and Brutus
Behold, these are the Tribunes of the People,
The tongues o'th'common mouth. I do despise them,
For they do prank them in authority
Against all noble sufferance.

SICINIUS   Pass no further.

CORIOLANUS
Ha? What is that?

BRUTUS
It will be dangerous to go on. No further.

CORIOLANUS
What makes this change?

MENENIUS
The matter?

COMINIUS
Hath he not passed the noble and the common?

BRUTUS
Cominius, no.

CORIOLANUS   Have I had children's voices?   30

FIRST SENATOR
Tribunes, give way. He shall to th'market-place.

BRUTUS
The people are incensed against him.

SICINIUS   Stop,
Or all will fall in broil.

CORIOLANUS   Are these your herd?
Must these have voices, that can yield them now
And straight disclaim their tongues? What are your
       offices?
You being their mouths, why rule you not their teeth?
Have you not set them on?

MENENIUS   Be calm, be calm.

CORIOLANUS
It is a purposed thing, and grows by plot,
To curb the will of the nobility.
40   Suffer't, and live with such as cannot rule
Nor ever will be ruled.

BRUTUS   Call't not a plot.
The people cry you mocked them; and of late,
When corn was given them gratis, you repined,
Scandalled the suppliants for the people, called them
Time-pleasers, flatterers, foes to nobleness.

CORIOLANUS
Why, this was known before.

BRUTUS   Not to them all.

CORIOLANUS
Have you informed them sithence?

BRUTUS   How? I inform them!

COMINIUS
You are like to do such business.

BRUTUS   Not unlike
Each way to better yours.

CORIOLANUS
50   Why then should I be consul? By yond clouds,
Let me deserve so ill as you, and make me
Your fellow tribune.

SICINIUS   You show too much of that
For which the people stir. If you will pass
To where you are bound, you must enquire your way,

Which you are out of, with a gentler spirit,
Or never be so noble as a consul,
Nor yoke with him for tribune.

MENENIUS   Let's be calm.

COMINIUS
The people are abused. Set on. This paltering
Becomes not Rome, nor has Coriolanus
Deserved this so dishonoured rub, laid falsely   60
I'th'plain way of his merit.

CORIOLANUS   Tell me of corn!
This was my speech, and I will speak't again –

MENENIUS
Not now, not now.

FIRST SENATOR   Not in this heat, sir, now.

CORIOLANUS
Now, as I live I will.
My nobler friends, I crave their pardons. For
The mutable, rank-scented meiny, let them
Regard me as I do not flatter, and
Therein behold themselves. I say again,
In soothing them we nourish 'gainst our Senate
The cockle of rebellion, insolence, sedition,   70
Which we ourselves have ploughed for, sowed, and
     scattered
By mingling them with us, the honoured number,
Who lack not virtue, no, nor power, but that
Which they have given to beggars.

MENENIUS   Well, no more.

FIRST SENATOR
No more words, we beseech you.

CORIOLANUS   How? No more?
As for my country I have shed my blood,
Not fearing outward force, so shall my lungs
Coin words till their decay against those measles

Which we disdain should tetter us, yet sought
80   The very way to catch them.

BRUTUS   You speak o'th'people
   As if you were a god to punish, not
   A man of their infirmity.

SICINIUS   'Twere well
   We let the people know't.

MENENIUS   What, what? His choler?

CORIOLANUS
   Choler!
   Were I as patient as the midnight sleep,
   By Jove, 'twould be my mind.

SICINIUS   It is a mind
   That shall remain a poison where it is,
   Not poison any further.

CORIOLANUS   Shall remain!
   Hear you this Triton of the minnows? Mark you
90   His absolute 'shall'?

COMINIUS   'Twas from the canon.

CORIOLANUS   'Shall'!
   O good but most unwise patricians! Why,
   You grave but reckless Senators, have you thus
   Given Hydra here to choose an officer
   That with his peremptory 'shall', being but
   The horn and noise o'th'monster's, wants not spirit
   To say he'll turn your current in a ditch
   And make your channel his? If he have power,
   Then vail your ignorance; if none, awake
   Your dangerous lenity. If you are learned,
100   Be not as common fools; if you are not,
   Let them have cushions by you. You are plebeians
   If they be senators; and they are no less
   When, both your voices blended, the great'st taste
   Most palates theirs. They choose their magistrate;

And such a one as he, who puts his 'shall',
His popular 'shall', against a graver bench
Than ever frowned in Greece. By Jove himself,
It makes the consuls base! And my soul aches
To know, when two authorities are up,
Neither supreme, how soon confusion   110
May enter 'twixt the gap of both and take
The one by th'other.

COMINIUS   Well, on to th'market-place.

CORIOLANUS
Whoever gave that counsel to give forth
The corn o'th'storehouse gratis, as 'twas used
Sometime in Greece –

MENENIUS   Well, well, no more of that.

CORIOLANUS
Though there the people had more absolute power –
I say they nourished disobedience, fed
The ruin of the state.

BRUTUS   Why shall the people give
One that speaks thus their voice?

CORIOLANUS   I'll give my reasons,
More worthier than their voices. They know the corn   120
Was not our recompense, resting well assured
They ne'er did service for't. Being pressed to th'war,
Even when the navel of the state was touched,
They would not thread the gates. This kind of service
Did not deserve corn gratis. Being i'th'war,
Their mutinies and revolts, wherein they showed
Most valour, spoke not for them. Th'accusation
Which they have often made against the Senate,
All cause unborn, could never be the native
Of our so frank donation. Well, what then?   130
How shall this bosom multiplied digest
The Senate's courtesy? Let deeds express

What's like to be their words: 'We did request it;
We are the greater poll, and in true fear
They gave us our demands.' Thus we debase
The nature of our seats, and make the rabble
Call our cares fears; which will in time
Break ope the locks o'th'Senate and bring in
The crows to peck the eagles.

MENENIUS   Come, enough.

BRUTUS

140 Enough, with over measure.

CORIOLANUS   No, take more.
What may be sworn by, both divine and human,
Seal what I end withal! This double worship,
Where one part does disdain with cause, the other
Insult without all reason; where gentry, title, wisdom,
Cannot conclude but by the yea and no
Of general ignorance – it must omit
Real necessities, and give way the while
To unstable slightness. Purpose so barred, it follows
Nothing is done to purpose. Therefore, beseech you –
150 You that will be less fearful than discreet,
That love the fundamental part of state
More than you doubt the change on't, that prefer
A noble life before a long, and wish
To jump a body with a dangerous physic
That's sure of death without it – at once pluck out
The multitudinous tongue, let them not lick
The sweet which is their poison. Your dishonour
Mangles true judgement, and bereaves the state
Of that integrity which should become't,
160 Not having the power to do the good it would
For th'ill which doth control't.

BRUTUS   'Has said enough.

SICINIUS

    'Has spoken like a traitor and shall answer
    As traitors do.

CORIOLANUS   Thou wretch, despite o'erwhelm thee!
    What should the people do with these bald Tribunes,
    On whom depending, their obedience fails
    To th'greater bench? In a rebellion,
    When what's not meet, but what must be, was law,
    Then were they chosen. In a better hour
    Let what is meet be said it must be meet,
    And throw their power i'th'dust.   170

BRUTUS

    Manifest treason!

SICINIUS   This a Consul? No.

BRUTUS

    The Aediles, ho!

    Enter an Aedile

              Let him be apprehended.

SICINIUS

    Go call the people, (*exit Aedile*) in whose name myself
    Attach thee as a traitorous innovator,
    A foe to th'public weal. Obey, I charge thee,
    And follow to thine answer.

CORIOLANUS   Hence, old goat!

PATRICIANS

    We'll surety him.

COMINIUS   Aged sir, hands off.

CORIOLANUS

    Hence, rotten thing! or I shall shake thy bones
    Out of thy garments.

SICINIUS   Help, ye citizens!

    Enter a rabble of Plebeians, with the Aediles

MENENIUS

    On both sides more respect.   180

SICINIUS

Here's he that would take from you all your power.

BRUTUS Seize him, Aediles!

PLEBEIANS Down with him, down with him!

SECOND SENATOR Weapons, weapons, weapons!

They all bustle about Coriolanus

ALL (*shouting confusedly*)

Tribunes! Patricians! Citizens! What ho!

Sicinius! Brutus! Coriolanus! Citizens!

MENENIUS

Peace, peace, peace! Stay, hold, peace!

What is about to be? I am out of breath.

Confusion's near. I cannot speak. You Tribunes

190   To th'People – Coriolanus, patience! –

Speak, good Sicinius.

SICINIUS   Hear me, people. Peace!

PLEBEIANS

Let's hear our Tribune. Peace! Speak, speak, speak.

SICINIUS

You are at point to lose your liberties.

Martius would have all from you, Martius,

Whom late you have named for consul.

MENENIUS   Fie, fie, fie!

This is the way to kindle, not to quench.

FIRST SENATOR

To unbuild the city and to lay all flat.

SICINIUS

What is the city but the people?

PLEBEIANS   True,

The people are the city.

BRUTUS

200   By the consent of all we were established

The people's magistrates.

PLEBEIANS   You so remain.

MENENIUS
And so are like to do.

COMINIUS
That is the way to lay the city flat,
To bring the roof to the foundation,
And bury all which yet distinctly ranges
In heaps and piles of ruin.

SICINIUS   This deserves death.

BRUTUS
Or let us stand to our authority,
Or let us lose it. We do here pronounce,
Upon the part o'th'people, in whose power
We were elected theirs, Martius is worthy   210
Of present death.

SICINIUS   Therefore lay hold of him;
Bear him to th'rock Tarpeian, and from thence
Into destruction cast him.

BRUTUS   Aediles, seize him.

PLEBEIANS
Yield, Martius, yield.

MENENIUS   Hear me one word.
Beseech you, Tribunes, hear me but a word.

AEDILES
Peace, peace!

MENENIUS (to Brutus)
Be that you seem, truly your country's friend,
And temperately proceed to what you would
Thus violently redress.

BRUTUS   Sir, those cold ways,
That seem like prudent helps, are very poisonous   220
Where the disease is violent. Lay hands upon him
And bear him to the rock.

     Coriolanus draws his sword

CORIOLANUS   No, I'll die here.

There's some among you have beheld me fighting;
Come, try upon yourselves what you have seen me.

MENENIUS
Down with that sword! Tribunes, withdraw awhile.

BRUTUS
Lay hands upon him.

MENENIUS   Help Martius, help,
You that be noble, help him, young and old!

PLEBEIANS Down with him, down with him!

In this mutiny the Tribunes, the Aediles, and the
people are beat in

MENENIUS
Go, get you to your house! Be gone, away!
230   All will be naught else.

SECOND SENATOR   Get you gone.

CORIOLANUS   Stand fast!
We have as many friends as enemies.

MENENIUS
Shall it be put to that?

FIRST SENATOR   The gods forbid!
I prithee, noble friend, home to thy house;
Leave us to cure this cause.

MENENIUS   For 'tis a sore upon us
You cannot tent yourself. Be gone, beseech you.

COMINIUS
Come, sir, along with us.

CORIOLANUS
I would they were barbarians, as they are,
Though in Rome littered; not Romans, as they are not,
Though calved i'th'porch o'th'Capitol.

MENENIUS   Be gone.
240   Put not your worthy rage into your tongue.
One time will owe another.

CORIOLANUS   On fair ground

I could beat forty of them.

MENENIUS   I could myself
Take up a brace o'th'best of them; yea, the two
    Tribunes.

COMINIUS
But now 'tis odds beyond arithmetic,
And manhood is called foolery when it stands
Against a falling fabric. Will you hence
Before the tag return, whose rage doth rend
Like interrupted waters, and o'erbear
What they are used to bear?

MENENIUS   Pray you be gone.
I'll try whether my old wit be in request   250
With those that have but little. This must be patched
With cloth of any colour.

COMINIUS   Nay, come away.
                Exeunt Coriolanus and Cominius

PATRICIAN
This man has marred his fortune.

MENENIUS
His nature is too noble for the world.
He would not flatter Neptune for his trident,
Or Jove for's power to thunder. His heart's his mouth.
What his breast forges, that his tongue must vent,
And, being angry, does forget that ever
He heard the name of death.
    A noise within
Here's goodly work!

PATRICIAN   I would they were a-bed!   260

MENENIUS
I would they were in Tiber! What the vengeance,
Could he not speak 'em fair?
    Enter Brutus and Sicinius, with the rabble again

SICINIUS   Where is this viper

That would depopulate the city and
Be every man himself?

MENENIUS   You worthy Tribunes —

SICINIUS

He shall be thrown down the Tarpeian rock
With rigorous hands. He hath resisted law,
And therefore law shall scorn him further trial
Than the severity of the public power,
Which he so sets at naught.

FIRST CITIZEN   He shall well know
270   The noble Tribunes are the people's mouths,
And we their hands.

PLEBEIANS   He shall, sure on't.

MENENIUS   Sir, sir —

SICINIUS

Peace!

MENENIUS

Do not cry havoc, where you should but hunt
With modest warrant.

SICINIUS   Sir, how comes't that you
Have holp to make this rescue?

MENENIUS   Hear me speak.
As I do know the Consul's worthiness,
So can I name his faults.

SICINIUS   Consul! What Consul?

MENENIUS

The Consul Coriolanus.

BRUTUS   He Consul!

PLEBEIANS No, no, no, no, no.

MENENIUS
280   If, by the Tribunes' leave and yours, good people,
I may be heard, I would crave a word or two,
The which shall turn you to no further harm
Than so much loss of time.

SICINIUS   Speak briefly then,
   For we are peremptory to dispatch
   This viperous traitor. To eject him hence
   Were but our danger, and to keep him here
   Our certain death. Therefore it is decreed
   He dies tonight.
MENENIUS   Now the good gods forbid
   That our renownèd Rome, whose gratitude
   Towards her deservèd children is enrolled   290
   In Jove's own book, like an unnatural dam
   Should now eat up her own!
SICINIUS
   He's a disease that must be cut away.
MENENIUS
   O, he's a limb that has but a disease –
   Mortal, to cut it off; to cure it, easy.
   What has he done to Rome that's worthy death?
   Killing our enemies, the blood he hath lost –
   Which I dare vouch is more than that he hath
   By many an ounce – he dropped it for his country;
   And what is left, to lose it by his country   300
   Were to us all that do't and suffer it
   A brand to th'end o'th'world.
SICINIUS   This is clean kam.
BRUTUS
   Merely awry. When he did love his country,
   It honoured him.
SICINIUS   The service of the foot,
   Being once gangrened, is not then respected
   For what before it was.
BRUTUS   We'll hear no more.
   Pursue him to his house and pluck him thence,
   Lest his infection, being of catching nature,
   Spread further.

MENENIUS   One word more, one word!
310   This tiger-footed rage, when it shall find
       The harm of unscanned swiftness, will too late
       Tie leaden pounds to's heels. Proceed by process,
       Lest parties — as he is beloved — break out
       And sack great Rome with Romans.
BRUTUS   If it were so —
SICINIUS
       What do ye talk?
       Have we not had a taste of his obedience?
       Our Aediles smote? Ourselves resisted? Come!
MENENIUS
       Consider this. He has been bred i'th'wars
       Since 'a could draw a sword, and is ill schooled
320   In bolted language. Meal and bran together
       He throws without distinction. Give me leave,
       I'll go to him and undertake to bring him
       Where he shall answer by a lawful form,
       In peace, to his utmost peril.
FIRST SENATOR   Noble Tribunes,
       It is the humane way. The other course
       Will prove too bloody, and the end of it
       Unknown to the beginning.
SICINIUS   Noble Menenius,
       Be you then as the people's officer.
       Masters, lay down your weapons.
BRUTUS   Go not home.
SICINIUS
330   Meet on the market-place. We'll attend you there;
       Where, if you bring not Martius, we'll proceed
       In our first way.
MENENIUS   I'll bring him to you.
       (*To the Senators*) Let me desire your company. He must
       come,

Or what is worst will follow.

FIRST SENATOR   Pray you let's to him.

Exeunt

Enter Coriolanus, with Nobles   III.2

CORIOLANUS

Let them pull all about mine ears, present me
Death on the wheel or at wild horses' heels,
Or pile ten hills on the Tarpeian rock,
That the precipitation might down stretch
Below the beam of sight, yet will I still
Be thus to them.

NOBLE   You do the nobler.

CORIOLANUS

I muse my mother
Does not approve me further, who was wont
To call them woollen vassals, things created
To buy and sell with groats, to show bare heads   10
In congregations, to yawn, be still and wonder,
When one but of my ordinance stood up
To speak of peace or war.

Enter Volumnia

                    I talk of you:
Why did you wish me milder? Would you have me
False to my nature? Rather say I play
The man I am.

VOLUMNIA   O, sir, sir, sir,
I would have had you put your power well on
Before you had worn it out.

CORIOLANUS   Let go.

VOLUMNIA

You might have been enough the man you are
With striving less to be so. Lesser had been   20

The crossings of your dispositions, if
You had not showed them how ye were disposed
Ere they lacked power to cross you.

CORIOLANUS   Let them hang!

VOLUMNIA

Ay, and burn too!

Enter Menenius, with the Senators

MENENIUS

Come, come, you have been too rough, something too
    rough.
You must return and mend it.

FIRST SENATOR   There's no remedy,
Unless, by not so doing, our good city
Cleave in the midst and perish.

VOLUMNIA   Pray be counselled.
I have a heart as little apt as yours,
30   But yet a brain that leads my use of anger
To better vantage.

MENENIUS   Well said, noble woman!
Before he should thus stoop to th'heart, but that
The violent fit o'th'time craves it as physic
For the whole state, I would put mine armour on,
Which I can scarcely bear.

CORIOLANUS   What must I do?

MENENIUS

Return to th'Tribunes.

CORIOLANUS   Well, what then? What then?

MENENIUS

Repent what you have spoke.

CORIOLANUS

For them! I cannot do it to the gods.
Must I then do't to them?

VOLUMNIA   You are too absolute,
40   Though therein you can never be too noble.

But when extremities speak, I have heard you say,
Honour and policy, like unsevered friends,
I'th'war do grow together. Grant that, and tell me
In peace what each of them by th'other lose
That they combine not there.

CORIOLANUS   Tush, tush!

MENENIUS   A good demand.

VOLUMNIA
If it be honour in your wars to seem
The same you are not, which for your best ends
You adopt your policy, how is it less or worse
That it shall hold companionship in peace
With honour as in war, since that to both   50
It stands in like request?

CORIOLANUS   Why force you this?

VOLUMNIA
Because that now it lies you on to speak
To th'people, not by your own instruction,
Nor by th'matter which your heart prompts you,
But with such words that are but roted in
Your tongue, though but bastards and syllables
Of no allowance to your bosom's truth.
Now this no more dishonours you at all
Than to take in a town with gentle words,
Which else would put you to your fortune and   60
The hazard of much blood.
I would dissemble with my nature where
My fortunes and my friends at stake required
I should do so in honour. I am in this
Your wife, your son, these Senators, the nobles;
And you will rather show our general louts
How you can frown, than spend a fawn upon 'em
For the inheritance of their loves and safeguard
Of what that want might ruin.

MENENIUS   Noble lady!
70   – Come, go with us, speak fair. You may salve so,
      Not what is dangerous present, but the loss
      Of what is past.
VOLUMNIA   I prithee now, my son,
      Go to them with this bonnet in thy hand;
      And thus far having stretched it – here be with them –
      Thy knee bussing the stones – for in such business
      Action is eloquence, and the eyes of th'ignorant
      More learnèd than the ears – waving thy head,
      With often thus correcting thy stout heart,
      Now humble as the ripest mulberry
80   That will not hold the handling, say to them
      Thou art their soldier, and being bred in broils
      Hast not the soft way which, thou dost confess,
      Were fit for thee to use as they to claim,
      In asking their good loves; but thou wilt frame
      Thyself, forsooth, hereafter theirs, so far
      As thou hast power and person.
MENENIUS   This but done
      Even as she speaks, why, their hearts were yours.
      For they have pardons, being asked, as free
      As words to little purpose.
VOLUMNIA   Prithee now,
90   Go, and be ruled; although I know thou hadst rather
      Follow thine enemy in a fiery gulf
      Than flatter him in a bower.
        Enter Cominius
                              Here is Cominius.
COMINIUS
      I have been i'th'market-place; and, sir, 'tis fit
      You make strong party, or defend yourself
      By calmness or by absence. All's in anger.
MENENIUS
      Only fair speech.

COMINIUS   I think 'twill serve, if he
  Can thereto frame his spirit.
VOLUMNIA   He must, and will.
  Prithee now, say you will, and go about it.
CORIOLANUS
  Must I go show them my unbarbed sconce? Must I
  With my base tongue give to my noble heart   100
  A lie that it must bear? Well, I will do't.
  Yet, were there but this single plot to lose,
  This mould of Martius, they to dust should grind it
  And throw't against the wind. To th'market-place!
  You have put me now to such a part which never
  I shall discharge to th'life.
COMINIUS   Come, come, we'll prompt you.
VOLUMNIA
  I prithee now, sweet son, as thou hast said
  My praises made thee first a soldier, so,
  To have my praise for this, perform a part
  Thou hast not done before.
CORIOLANUS   Well, I must do't.   110
  Away, my disposition, and possess me
  Some harlot's spirit! My throat of war be turned,
  Which choired with my drum, into a pipe
  Small as an eunuch or the virgin voice
  That babies lulls asleep! The smiles of knaves
  Tent in my cheeks, and schoolboys' tears take up
  The glasses of my sight! A beggar's tongue
  Make motion through my lips, and my armed knees,
  Who bowed but in my stirrup, bend like his
  That hath received an alms! I will not do't,   120
  Lest I surcease to honour mine own truth
  And by my body's action teach my mind
  A most inherent baseness.
VOLUMNIA   At thy choice, then.

To beg of thee, it is my more dishonour
Than thou of them. Come all to ruin. Let
Thy mother rather feel thy pride than fear
Thy dangerous stoutness, for I mock at death
With as big heart as thou. Do as thou list.
Thy valiantness was mine, thou suck'dst it from me,
130   But owe thy pride thyself.

CORIOLANUS   Pray be content.
Mother, I am going to the market-place.
Chide me no more. I'll mountebank their loves,
Cog their hearts from them, and come home beloved
Of all the trades in Rome. Look, I am going.
Commend me to my wife. I'll return consul,
Or never trust to what my tongue can do
I'th'way of flattery further.

VOLUMNIA   Do your will. *Exit Volumnia*

COMINIUS
Away! The Tribunes do attend you. Arm yourself
To answer mildly; for they are prepared
140   With accusations, as I hear, more strong
Than are upon you yet.

CORIOLANUS
The word is 'mildly'. Pray you let us go.
Let them accuse me by invention, I
Will answer in mine honour.

MENENIUS   Ay, but mildly.

CORIOLANUS
Well, mildly be it then – mildly.   *Exeunt*

III.3   *Enter Sicinius and Brutus*

BRUTUS
In this point charge him home, that he affects
Tyrannical power. If he evade us there,

Enforce him with his envy to the people,
And that the spoil got on the Antiates
Was ne'er distributed.

    Enter an Aedile

                         What, will he come?

AEDILE
He's coming.

BRUTUS   How accompanied?

AEDILE
With old Menenius and those senators
That always favoured him.

SICINIUS   Have you a catalogue
Of all the voices that we have procured,
Set down by th'poll?

AEDILE   I have; 'tis ready.   10

SICINIUS
Have you collected them by tribes?

AEDILE   I have.

SICINIUS
Assemble presently the people hither.
And when they hear me say 'It shall be so
I'th'right and strength o'th'commons' be it either
For death, for fine, or banishment, then let them,
If I say 'Fine', cry 'Fine!', if 'Death', cry 'Death!'
Insisting on the old prerogative
And power i'th'truth o'th'cause.

AEDILE   I shall inform them.

BRUTUS
And when such time they have begun to cry,
Let them not cease, but with a din confused   20
Enforce the present execution
Of what we chance to sentence.

AEDILE   Very well.

SICINIUS

    Make them be strong, and ready for this hint
    When we shall hap to give't them.

BRUTUS   Go about it.

                                          Exit Aedile

    Put him to choler straight. He hath been used
    Ever to conquer and to have his worth
    Of contradiction. Being once chafed, he cannot
    Be reined again to temperance, then he speaks
    What's in his heart, and that is there which looks
30   With us to break his neck.

     Enter Coriolanus, Menenius, and Cominius, with others

SICINIUS   Well, here he comes.

MENENIUS

    Calmly, I do beseech you.

CORIOLANUS

    Ay, as an hostler, that for th'poorest piece
    Will bear the knave by th'volume. (*Aloud*) Th'honoured
       gods
    Keep Rome in safety and the chairs of justice
    Supplied with worthy men! Plant love among's!
    Throng our large temples with the shows of peace,
    And not our streets with war!

FIRST SENATOR   Amen, amen.

MENENIUS

    A noble wish.

     Enter the Aedile, with the Plebeians

SICINIUS

    Draw near, ye people.

AEDILE

40   List to your Tribunes. Audience! Peace, I say!

CORIOLANUS

    First, hear me speak.

BOTH TRIBUNES   Well, say. Peace ho!

CORIOLANUS
   Shall I be charged no further than this present?
   Must all determine here?
SICINIUS   I do demand
   If you submit you to the people's voices,
   Allow their officers, and are content
   To suffer lawful censure for such faults
   As shall be proved upon you?
CORIOLANUS   I am content.
MENENIUS
   Lo, citizens, he says he is content.
   The warlike service he has done, consider. Think
   Upon the wounds his body bears, which show   50
   Like graves i'th'holy churchyard.
CORIOLANUS   Scratches with briers,
   Scars to move laughter only.
MENENIUS   Consider further,
   That when he speaks not like a citizen,
   You find him like a soldier. Do not take
   His rougher accents for malicious sounds,
   But, as I say, such as become a soldier
   Rather than envy you.
COMINIUS   Well, well, no more.
CORIOLANUS
   What is the matter
   That being passed for consul with full voice,
   I am so dishonoured that the very hour   60
   You take it off again?
SICINIUS   Answer to us.
CORIOLANUS
   Say, then. 'Tis true, I ought so.
SICINIUS
   We charge you that you have contrived to take
   From Rome all seasoned office and to wind

Yourself into a power tyrannical,
For which you are a traitor to the people.

CORIOLANUS
How – traitor?

MENENIUS   Nay, temperately! Your promise.

CORIOLANUS
The fires i'th'lowest hell fold in the people!
Call me their traitor, thou injurious Tribune!
70   Within thine eyes sat twenty thousand deaths,
In thy hands clutched as many millions, in
Thy lying tongue both numbers, I would say
'Thou liest' unto thee with a voice as free
As I do pray the gods.

SICINIUS   Mark you this, people?

PLEBEIANS
To th'rock, to th'rock with him!

SICINIUS   Peace!
We need not put new matter to his charge.
What you have seen him do and heard him speak,
Beating your officers, cursing yourselves,
Opposing laws with strokes, and here defying
80   Those whose great power must try him – even this,
So criminal and in such capital kind,
Deserves th'extremest death.

BRUTUS   But since he hath
Served well for Rome –

CORIOLANUS   What do you prate of service?

BRUTUS
I talk of that that know it.

CORIOLANUS
You!

MENENIUS
Is this the promise that you made your mother?

COMINIUS
    Know, I pray you —
CORIOLANUS   I'll know no further.
    Let them pronounce the steep Tarpeian death,
    Vagabond exile, flaying, pent to linger
    But with a grain a day, I would not buy   90
    Their mercy at the price of one fair word,
    Nor check my courage for what they can give,
    To have't with saying 'Good morrow'.
SICINIUS   For that he has —
    As much as in him lies — from time to time
    Envied against the people, seeking means
    To pluck away their power, as now at last
    Given hostile strokes, and that not in the presence
    Of dreaded justice, but on the ministers
    That doth distribute it — in the name o'th'people
    And in the power of us the Tribunes, we,   100
    Even from this instant, banish him our city,
    In peril of precipitation
    From off the rock Tarpeian, never more
    To enter our Rome gates. I'th'people's name,
    I say it shall be so.
PLEBEIANS
    It shall be so, it shall be so! Let him away!
    He's banished, and it shall be so.
COMINIUS
    Hear me, my masters and my common friends —
SICINIUS
    He's sentenced. No more hearing.
COMINIUS   Let me speak.
    I have been Consul, and can show for Rome   110
    Her enemies' marks upon me. I do love
    My country's good with a respect more tender,
    More holy and profound, than mine own life,

My dear wife's estimate, her womb's increase
And treasure of my loins. Then if I would
Speak that –

SICINIUS   We know your drift. Speak what?

BRUTUS

There's no more to be said, but he is banished
As enemy to the people and his country.
It shall be so.

PLEBEIANS   It shall be so, it shall be so!

CORIOLANUS

120   You common cry of curs, whose breath I hate
As reek o'th'rotten fens, whose loves I prize
As the dead carcasses of unburied men
That do corrupt my air – I banish you.
And here remain with your uncertainty!
Let every feeble rumour shake your hearts;
Your enemies, with nodding of their plumes,
Fan you into despair! Have the power still
To banish your defenders, till at length
Your ignorance – which finds not till it feels,
130   Making but reservation of yourselves
Still your own foes – deliver you
As most abated captives to some nation
That won you without blows! Despising
For you the city, thus I turn my back.
There is a world elsewhere.   *Exeunt Coriolanus,*
                    Cominius, Menenius, with the other Patricians

AEDILE

The people's enemy is gone, is gone!

PLEBEIANS

Our enemy is banished, he is gone! Hoo-oo!
    They all shout, and throw up their caps

SICINIUS

Go see him out at gates, and follow him

As he hath followed you, with all despite;
Give him deserved vexation. Let a guard   140
Attend us through the city.

PLEBEIANS
Come, come, let's see him out at gates, come!
The gods preserve our noble Tribunes! Come! *Exeunt*

*

Enter Coriolanus, Volumnia, Virgilia, Menenius,   IV.I
Cominius, with the young Nobility of Rome

CORIOLANUS
Come, leave your tears. A brief farewell. The beast
With many heads butts me away. Nay, mother,
Where is your ancient courage? You were used
To say extremities was the trier of spirits;
That common chances common men could bear;
That when the sea was calm all boats alike
Showed mastership in floating; fortune's blows
When most struck home, being gentle wounded craves
A noble cunning. You were used to load me
With precepts that would make invincible   10
The heart that conned them.

VIRGILIA
O heavens! O heavens!

CORIOLANUS   Nay, I prithee, woman –

VOLUMNIA
Now the red pestilence strike all trades in Rome,
And occupations perish!

CORIOLANUS   What, what, what!
I shall be loved when I am lacked. Nay, mother,
Resume that spirit when you were wont to say,
If you had been the wife of Hercules,

Six of his labours you'd have done, and saved
Your husband so much sweat. Cominius,
20 Droop not. Adieu. Farewell, my wife, my mother.
I'll do well yet. Thou old and true Menenius,
Thy tears are salter than a younger man's
And venomous to thine eyes. My sometime general,
I have seen thee stern, and thou hast oft beheld
Heart-hardening spectacles. Tell these sad women
'Tis fond to wail inevitable strokes,
As 'tis to laugh at 'em. My mother, you wot well
My hazards still have been your solace, and
Believe't not lightly – though I go alone,
30 Like to a lonely dragon that his fen
Makes feared and talked of more than seen – your son
Will or exceed the common or be caught
With cautelous baits and practice.
VOLUMNIA   My first son,
Whither wilt thou go? Take good Cominius
With thee awhile. Determine on some course
More than a wild exposture to each chance
That starts i'th'way before thee.
VIRGILIA   O the gods!
COMINIUS
I'll follow thee a month, devise with thee
Where thou shalt rest, that thou mayst hear of us
40 And we of thee. So, if the time thrust forth
A cause for thy repeal, we shall not send
O'er the vast world to seek a single man,
And lose advantage, which doth ever cool
I'th'absence of the needer.
CORIOLANUS   Fare ye well.
Thou hast years upon thee, and thou art too full
Of the wars' surfeits to go rove with one
That's yet unbruised. Bring me but out at gate.

Come, my sweet wife, my dearest mother, and
My friends of noble touch; when I am forth,
Bid me farewell, and smile. I pray you come.   50
While I remain above the ground you shall
Hear from me still, and never of me aught
But what is like me formerly.

MENENIUS   That's worthily
As any ear can hear. Come, let's not weep.
If I could shake off but one seven years
From these old arms and legs, by the good gods,
I'd with thee every foot.

CORIOLANUS   Give me thy hand.
Come.   *Exeunt*

Enter the two Tribunes, Sicinius and Brutus, with the   IV.2
Aedile

SICINIUS
Bid them all home. He's gone, and we'll no further.
The nobility are vexed, whom we see have sided
In his behalf.

BRUTUS   Now we have shown our power,
Let us seem humbler after it is done
Than when it was a-doing.

SICINIUS   Bid them home.
Say their great enemy is gone, and they
Stand in their ancient strength.

BRUTUS   Dismiss them home.
                                              Exit Aedile
Here comes his mother.
        Enter Volumnia, Virgilia, and Menenius
SICINIUS   Let's not meet her.
BRUTUS   Why?

SICINIUS
    They say she's mad.
BRUTUS
10   They have ta'en note of us. Keep on your way.
VOLUMNIA
    O, y'are well met. Th'hoarded plague o'th'gods
    Requite your love!
MENENIUS   Peace, peace, be not so loud.
VOLUMNIA
    If that I could for weeping, you should hear –
    Nay, and you shall hear some. (*To Brutus*) Will you be
        gone?
VIRGILIA (*to Sicinius*)
    You shall stay too. I would I had the power
    To say so to my husband.
SICINIUS   Are you mankind?
VOLUMNIA
    Ay, fool, is that a shame? Note but this, fool:
    Was not a man my father? Hadst thou foxship
    To banish him that struck more blows for Rome
20   Than thou hast spoken words?
SICINIUS   O blessed heavens!
VOLUMNIA
    More noble blows than ever thou wise words,
    And for Rome's good. I'll tell thee what – yet go.
    Nay, but thou shalt stay too. I would my son
    Were in Arabia, and thy tribe before him,
    His good sword in his hand.
SICINIUS   What then?
VIRGILIA   What then!
    He'd make an end of thy posterity.
VOLUMNIA
    Bastards and all.
    Good man, the wounds that he does bear for Rome!

MENENIUS
  Come, come, peace.
SICINIUS
  I would he had continued to his country   30
  As he began, and not unknit himself
  The noble knot he made.
BRUTUS   I would he had.
VOLUMNIA
  'I would he had'! 'Twas you incensed the rabble –
  Cats that can judge as fitly of his worth
  As I can of those mysteries which heaven
  Will not have earth to know.
BRUTUS   Pray, let's go.
VOLUMNIA
  Now, pray, sir, get you gone.
  You have done a brave deed. Ere you go, hear this:
  As far as doth the Capitol exceed
  The meanest house in Rome, so far my son –   40
  This lady's husband here, this, do you see? –
  Whom you have banished does exceed you all.
BRUTUS
  Well, well, we'll leave you.
SICINIUS   Why stay we to be baited
  With one that wants her wits?   *Exeunt Tribunes*
VOLUMNIA   Take my prayers with you.
  I would the gods had nothing else to do
  But to confirm my curses. Could I meet 'em
  But once a day, it would unclog my heart
  Of what lies heavy to't.
MENENIUS   You have told them home,
  And, by my troth, you have cause. You'll sup with me?
VOLUMNIA
  Anger's my meat. I sup upon myself,   50
  And so shall starve with feeding. (*To Virgilia*) Come,
    let's go.

Leave this faint puling and lament as I do,
In anger, Juno-like. Come, come, come.

Exeunt Volumnia and Virgilia

MENENIUS
Fie, fie, fie.   *Exit*

IV.3   *Enter a Roman and a Volsce*

ROMAN I know you well, sir, and you know me. Your
    name, I think, is Adrian.
VOLSCE It is so, sir. Truly, I have forgot you.
ROMAN I am a Roman; and my services are, as you are,
    against 'em. Know you me yet?
VOLSCE Nicanor, no?
ROMAN The same, sir.
VOLSCE You had more beard when I last saw you, but your
    favour is well approved by your tongue. What's the news
10 in Rome? I have a note from the Volscian state to find
    you out there. You have well saved me a day's journey.
ROMAN There hath been in Rome strange insurrections:
    the people against the senators, patricians and nobles.
VOLSCE Hath been? Is it ended then? Our state thinks not
    so. They are in a most warlike preparation, and hope to
    come upon them in the heat of their division.
ROMAN The main blaze of it is past, but a small thing
    would make it flame again. For the nobles receive so to
    heart the banishment of that worthy Coriolanus that
20 they are in a ripe aptness to take all power from the
    people and to pluck from them their tribunes for ever.
    This lies glowing, I can tell you, and is almost mature
    for the violent breaking out.
VOLSCE Coriolanus banished?
ROMAN Banished, sir.
VOLSCE You will be welcome with this intelligence,
    Nicanor.

ROMAN The day serves well for them now. I have heard it
    said the fittest time to corrupt a man's wife is when she's
    fallen out with her husband. Your noble Tullus Aufidius   30
    will appear well in these wars, his great opposer, Corio-
    lanus, being now in no request of his country.

VOLSCE He cannot choose. I am most fortunate thus
    accidentally to encounter you. You have ended my busi-
    ness, and I will merrily accompany you home.

ROMAN I shall between this and supper tell you most
    strange things from Rome, all tending to the good of
    their adversaries. Have you an army ready, say you?

VOLSCE A most royal one. The centurions and their
    charges distinctly billeted, already in th'entertainment,   40
    and to be on foot at an hour's warning.

ROMAN I am joyful to hear of their readiness, and am the
    man, I think, that shall set them in present action. So,
    sir, heartily well met, and most glad of your company.

VOLSCE You take my part from me, sir. I have the most
    cause to be glad of yours.

ROMAN Well, let us go together.   *Exeunt*

Enter Coriolanus in mean apparel, disguised and   **IV.4**
    muffled

CORIOLANUS
    A goodly city is this Antium. City,
    'Tis I that made thy widows. Many an heir
    Of these fair edifices 'fore my wars
    Have I heard groan and drop. Then know me not,
    Lest that thy wives with spits and boys with stones
    In puny battle slay me.
        Enter a Citizen
                            Save you, sir.
CITIZEN
    And you.

CORIOLANUS Direct me, if it be your will,
   Where great Aufidius lies. Is he in Antium?
CITIZEN
   He is, and feasts the nobles of the state
10   At his house this night.
CORIOLANUS   Which is his house, beseech you?
CITIZEN
   This here before you.
CORIOLANUS   Thank you, sir. Farewell.
                                                         Exit Citizen
   O world, thy slippery turns! Friends now fast sworn,
   Whose double bosoms seems to wear one heart,
   Whose hours, whose bed, whose meal and exercise
   Are still together, who twin, as 'twere, in love
   Unseparable, shall within this hour,
   On a dissension of a doit, break out
   To bitterest enmity. So fellest foes,
   Whose passions and whose plots have broke their sleep
20   To take the one the other, by some chance,
   Some trick not worth an egg, shall grow dear friends
   And interjoin their issues. So with me.
   My birthplace hate I, and my love's upon
   This enemy town. I'll enter. If he slay me,
   He does fair justice. If he give me way,
   I'll do his country service.   *Exit*

IV.5   *Music plays. Enter a Servingman*
   FIRST SERVINGMAN Wine, wine, wine! What service is
      here? I think our fellows are asleep.   *Exit*
         Enter another Servingman
   SECOND SERVINGMAN Where's Cotus? My master calls
      for him. Cotus!   *Exit*
         Enter Coriolanus

CORIOLANUS
  A goodly house. The feast smells well, but I
  Appear not like a guest.
    Enter the First Servingman
FIRST SERVINGMAN What would you have, friend?
  Whence are you? Here's no place for you. Pray go to the
  door.   *Exit*
CORIOLANUS
  I have deserved no better entertainment   10
  In being Coriolanus.
    Enter Second Servingman
SECOND SERVINGMAN Whence are you, sir? Has the
  porter his eyes in his head that he gives entrance to such
  companions? Pray get you out.
CORIOLANUS Away!
SECOND SERVINGMAN Away? Get you away.
CORIOLANUS Now th'art troublesome.
SECOND SERVINGMAN Are you so brave? I'll have you
  talked with anon.
    Enter Third Servingman. The First meets him
THIRD SERVINGMAN What fellow's this?   20
FIRST SERVINGMAN A strange one as ever I looked on.
  I cannot get him out o'th'house. Prithee call my master
  to him.
THIRD SERVINGMAN What have you to do here, fellow?
  Pray you avoid the house.
CORIOLANUS
  Let me but stand – I will not hurt your hearth.
THIRD SERVINGMAN What are you?
CORIOLANUS A gentleman.
THIRD SERVINGMAN A marvellous poor one.
CORIOLANUS True, so I am.   30
THIRD SERVINGMAN Pray you, poor gentleman, take up

some other station. Here's no place for you. Pray you
avoid. Come.

CORIOLANUS Follow your function, go and batten on
cold bits.

He pushes him away from him

THIRD SERVINGMAN What, you will not? Prithee tell
my master what a strange guest he has here.

SECOND SERVINGMAN And I shall.

Exit Second Servingman

THIRD SERVINGMAN Where dwell'st thou?

40 CORIOLANUS Under the canopy.

THIRD SERVINGMAN Under the canopy?

CORIOLANUS Ay.

THIRD SERVINGMAN Where's that?

CORIOLANUS I'th'city of kites and crows.

THIRD SERVINGMAN I'th'city of kites and crows? What
an ass it is! Then thou dwell'st with daws too?

CORIOLANUS No, I serve not thy master.

THIRD SERVINGMAN How, sir? Do you meddle with my
master?

50 CORIOLANUS Ay, 'tis an honester service than to meddle
with thy mistress. Thou prat'st and prat'st. Serve with
thy trencher. Hence!

He beats him away from the stage
Enter Aufidius with the Second Servingman

AUFIDIUS Where is this fellow?

SECOND SERVINGMAN Here, sir. I'd have beaten him
like a dog, but for disturbing the lords within.

Servingmen stand aside

AUFIDIUS

Whence com'st thou? What wouldst thou? Thy name?
Why speak'st not? Speak, man. What's thy name?

CORIOLANUS *(unmuffling)*   If, Tullus,
Not yet thou know'st me, and, seeing me, dost not

Think me for the man I am, necessity
Commands me name myself.

AUFIDIUS   What is thy name?   60

CORIOLANUS

A name unmusical to the Volscians' ears,
And harsh in sound to thine.

AUFIDIUS   Say, what's thy name?
Thou hast a grim appearance, and thy face
Bears a command in't. Though thy tackle's torn,
Thou show'st a noble vessel. What's thy name?

CORIOLANUS

Prepare thy brow to frown. Know'st thou me yet?

AUFIDIUS

I know thee not. Thy name?

CORIOLANUS

My name is Caius Martius, who hath done
To thee particularly and to all the Volsces
Great hurt and mischief; thereto witness may   70
My surname, Coriolanus. The painful service,
The extreme dangers, and the drops of blood
Shed for my thankless country, are requited
But with that surname – a good memory
And witness of the malice and displeasure
Which thou shouldst bear me. Only that name remains.
The cruelty and envy of the people,
Permitted by our dastard nobles, who
Have all forsook me, hath devoured the rest,
And suffered me by th'voice of slaves to be   80
Whooped out of Rome. Now this extremity
Hath brought me to thy hearth, not out of hope –
Mistake me not – to save my life; for if
I had feared death, of all men i'th'world
I would have 'voided thee; but in mere spite,
To be full quit of those my banishers,

Stand I before thee here. Then if thou hast
A heart of wreak in thee, that wilt revenge
Thine own particular wrongs and stop those maims
90   Of shame seen through thy country, speed thee straight
And make my misery serve thy turn. So use it
That my revengeful services may prove
As benefits to thee. For I will fight
Against my cankered country with the spleen
Of all the under fiends. But if so be
Thou dar'st not this, and that to prove more fortunes
Th' art tired, then, in a word, I also am
Longer to live most weary, and present
My throat to thee and to thy ancient malice;
100   Which not to cut would show thee but a fool,
Since I have ever followed thee with hate,
Drawn tuns of blood out of thy country's breast,
And cannot live but by thy shame, unless
It be to do thee service.

AUFIDIUS   O Martius, Martius!
Each word thou hast spoke hath weeded from my heart
A root of ancient envy. If Jupiter
Should from yond cloud speak divine things,
And say ''Tis true', I'd not believe them more
Than thee, all-noble Martius. Let me twine
110   Mine arms about that body, whereagainst
My grainèd ash an hundred times hath broke
And scarred the moon with splinters. Here I clip
The anvil of my sword, and do contest
As hotly and as nobly with thy love
As ever in ambitious strength I did
Contend against thy valour. Know thou first,
I loved the maid I married; never man
Sighed truer breath. But that I see thee here,
Thou noble thing, more dances my rapt heart

Than when I first my wedded mistress saw   120
Bestride my threshold. Why, thou Mars, I tell thee
We have a power on foot, and I had purpose
Once more to hew thy target from thy brawn,
Or lose mine arm for't. Thou hast beat me out
Twelve several times, and I have nightly since
Dreamt of encounters 'twixt thyself and me –
We have been down together in my sleep,
Unbuckling helms, fisting each other's throat –
And waked half dead with nothing. Worthy Martius,
Had we no other quarrel else to Rome but that   130
Thou art thence banished, we would muster all
From twelve to seventy, and pouring war
Into the bowels of ungrateful Rome,
Like a bold flood o'erbear't. O, come, go in,
And take our friendly senators by th'hands,
Who now are here, taking their leaves of me
Who am prepared against your territories,
Though not for Rome itself.

CORIOLANUS   You bless me, gods!

AUFIDIUS
Therefore, most absolute sir, if thou wilt have
The leading of thine own revenges, take   140
Th'one half of my commission, and set down –
As best thou art experienced, since thou know'st
Thy country's strength and weakness – thine own ways,
Whether to knock against the gates of Rome,
Or rudely visit them in parts remote
To fright them ere destroy. But come in.
Let me commend thee first to those that shall
Say yea to thy desires. A thousand welcomes!
And more a friend than e'er an enemy;
Yet, Martius, that was much. Your hand. Most welcome!   150

                                          Exeunt

First and Second Servingmen come forward

FIRST SERVINGMAN Here's a strange alteration!

SECOND SERVINGMAN By my hand, I had thought to
have strucken him with a cudgel, and yet my mind gave
me his clothes made a false report of him.

FIRST SERVINGMAN What an arm he has! He turned me
about with his finger and his thumb as one would set up
a top.

SECOND SERVINGMAN Nay, I knew by his face that
there was something in him. He had, sir, a kind of face,
160 methought – I cannot tell how to term it.

FIRST SERVINGMAN He had so, looking as it were –
Would I were hanged, but I thought there was more in
him than I could think.

SECOND SERVINGMAN So did I, I'll be sworn. He is
simply the rarest man i'th'world.

FIRST SERVINGMAN I think he is. But a greater soldier
than he you wot one.

SECOND SERVINGMAN Who, my master?

FIRST SERVINGMAN Nay, it's no matter for that.

170 SECOND SERVINGMAN Worth six on him.

FIRST SERVINGMAN Nay, not so neither. But I take him
to be the greater soldier.

SECOND SERVINGMAN Faith, look you, one cannot tell
how to say that. For the defence of a town our general
is excellent.

FIRST SERVINGMAN Ay, and for an assault too.

Enter the Third Servingman

THIRD SERVINGMAN O slaves, I can tell you news –
news, you rascals!

BOTH What, what, what? Let's partake.

180 THIRD SERVINGMAN I would not be a Roman, of all
nations. I had as lief be a condemned man.

BOTH Wherefore? Wherefore?

THIRD SERVINGMAN Why, here's he that was wont to
thwack our general, Caius Martius.

FIRST SERVINGMAN Why do you say 'thwack our
general'?

THIRD SERVINGMAN I do not say 'thwack our general',
but he was always good enough for him.

SECOND SERVINGMAN Come, we are fellows and friends.
He was ever too hard for him, I have heard him say so   190
himself.

FIRST SERVINGMAN He was too hard for him, directly
to say the truth on't. Before Corioles he scotched him
and notched him like a carbonado.

SECOND SERVINGMAN An he had been cannibally given,
he might have boiled and eaten him too.

FIRST SERVINGMAN But more of thy news!

THIRD SERVINGMAN Why, he is so made on here within
as if he were son and heir to Mars; set at upper end
o'th'table; no question asked him by any of the senators   200
but they stand bald before him. Our general himself
makes a mistress of him, sanctifies himself with's hand,
and turns up the white o'th'eye to his discourse. But the
bottom of the news is, our general is cut i'th'middle and
but one half of what he was yesterday, for the other has
half by the entreaty and grant of the whole table. He'll
go, he says, and sowl the porter of Rome gates by th'ears.
He will mow all down before him, and leave his passage
polled.

SECOND SERVINGMAN And he's as like to do't as any   210
man I can imagine.

THIRD SERVINGMAN Do't! He will do't, for look you,
sir, he has as many friends as enemies; which friends,
sir, as it were, durst not – look you, sir – show themselves, as we term it, his friends whilst he's in directitude.

FIRST SERVINGMAN Directitude? What's that?

THIRD SERVINGMAN But when they shall see, sir, his
crest up again and the man in blood, they will out of their
burrows like conies after rain, and revel all with him.

220 FIRST SERVINGMAN But when goes this forward?

THIRD SERVINGMAN Tomorrow, today, presently. You
shall have the drum struck up this afternoon. 'Tis as it
were a parcel of their feast, and to be executed ere they
wipe their lips.

SECOND SERVINGMAN Why, then we shall have a stirring world again. This peace is nothing but to rust iron,
increase tailors, and breed ballad-makers.

FIRST SERVINGMAN Let me have war, say I. It exceeds
peace as far as day does night. It's sprightly walking,
230 audible, and full of vent. Peace is a very apoplexy,
lethargy; mulled, deaf, sleepy, insensible; a getter of
more bastard children than war's a destroyer of men.

SECOND SERVINGMAN 'Tis so. And as wars in some sort
may be said to be a ravisher, so it cannot be denied but
peace is a great maker of cuckolds.

FIRST SERVINGMAN Ay, and it makes men hate one
another.

THIRD SERVINGMAN Reason: because they then less
need one another. The wars for my money. I hope to see
240 Romans as cheap as Volscians. They are rising, they are
rising.

BOTH In, in, in, in.   *Exeunt*

IV.6   *Enter the two Tribunes, Sicinius and Brutus*

SICINIUS
We hear not of him, neither need we fear him.
His remedies are tame – the present peace
And quietness of the people, which before
Were in wild hurry. Here do we make his friends

Blush that the world goes well, who rather had,
Though they themselves did suffer by't, behold
Dissentious numbers pestering streets than see
Our tradesmen singing in their shops and going
About their functions friendly.

BRUTUS

We stood to't in good time.

Enter Menenius

Is this Menenius?   10

SICINIUS

'Tis he, 'tis he. O, he is grown most kind
Of late. Hail, sir!

MENENIUS   Hail to you both!

SICINIUS

Your Coriolanus is not much missed
But with his friends. The commonwealth doth stand,
And so would do, were he more angry at it.

MENENIUS

All's well, and might have been much better if
He could have temporized.

SICINIUS   Where is he, hear you?

MENENIUS

Nay, I hear nothing. His mother and his wife
Hear nothing from him.

Enter three or four Citizens

CITIZENS

The gods preserve you both!

SICINIUS   Good-e'en, our neighbours.   20

BRUTUS

Good-e'en to you all, good-e'en to you all.

FIRST CITIZEN

Ourselves, our wives and children, on our knees
Are bound to pray for you both.

SICINIUS   Live and thrive!

BRUTUS

    Farewell, kind neighbours. We wished Coriolanus
    Had loved you as we did.

CITIZENS   Now the gods keep you!

BOTH TRIBUNES

    Farewell, farewell.   *Exeunt Citizens*

SICINIUS

    This is a happier and more comely time
    Than when these fellows ran about the streets
    Crying confusion.

BRUTUS   Caius Martius was

30   A worthy officer i'th'war, but insolent,
    O'ercome with pride, ambitious past all thinking,
    Self-loving –

SICINIUS   And affecting one sole throne
    Without assistance.

MENENIUS   I think not so.

SICINIUS

    We should by this, to all our lamentation,
    If he had gone forth Consul, found it so.

BRUTUS

    The gods have well prevented it, and Rome
    Sits safe and still without him.

    Enter an Aedile

AEDILE   Worthy Tribunes,
    There is a slave, whom we have put in prison,
    Reports the Volsces with two several powers
40   Are entered in the Roman territories,
    And with the deepest malice of the war
    Destroy what lies before 'em.

MENENIUS   'Tis Aufidius,
    Who, hearing of our Martius' banishment,
    Thrusts forth his horns again into the world,
    Which were inshelled when Martius stood for Rome,

And durst not once peep out.

SICINIUS
Come, what talk you of Martius?

BRUTUS
Go see this rumourer whipped. It cannot be
The Volsces dare break with us.

MENENIUS   Cannot be!
We have record that very well it can,   50
And three examples of the like hath been
Within my age. But reason with the fellow
Before you punish him, where he heard this,
Lest you shall chance to whip your information
And beat the messenger who bids beware
Of what is to be dreaded.

SICINIUS   Tell not me.
I know this cannot be.

BRUTUS   Not possible.

    Enter a Messenger

MESSENGER
The nobles in great earnestness are going
All to the Senate House. Some news is coming
That turns their countenances.

SICINIUS   'Tis this slave –   60
Go whip him 'fore the people's eyes – his raising,
Nothing but his report.

MESSENGER   Yes, worthy sir,
The slave's report is seconded, and more,
More fearful is delivered.

SICINIUS   What more fearful?

MESSENGER
It is spoke freely out of many mouths –
How probable I do not know – that Martius,
Joined with Aufidius, leads a power 'gainst Rome,
And vows revenge as spacious as between

The young'st and oldest thing.

SICINIUS   This is most likely!

BRUTUS

70   Raised only that the weaker sort may wish
      Good Martius home again.

SICINIUS   The very trick on't.

MENENIUS

      This is unlikely.
      He and Aufidius can no more atone
      Than violent'st contrariety.
            Enter a second Messenger

SECOND MESSENGER

      You are sent for to the Senate.
      A fearful army, led by Caius Martius
      Associated with Aufidius, rages
      Upon our territories, and have already
      O'erborne their way, consumed with fire and took

80   What lay before them.
            Enter Cominius

COMINIUS

      O, you have made good work!

MENENIUS   What news? What news?

COMINIUS

      You have holp to ravish your own daughters and
      To melt the city leads upon your pates,
      To see your wives dishonoured to your noses –

MENENIUS

      What's the news? What's the news?

COMINIUS

      – Your temples burnèd in their cement, and
      Your franchises, whereon you stood, confined
      Into an auger's bore.

MENENIUS   Pray now, your news? –
      You have made fair work, I fear me. – Pray, your news? –

If Martius should be joined wi'th'Volscians –

COMINIUS   If?   90
He is their god. He leads them like a thing
Made by some other deity than Nature,
That shapes man better; and they follow him
Against us brats with no less confidence
Than boys pursuing summer butterflies,
Or butchers killing flies.

MENENIUS   You have made good work,
You and your apron-men, you that stood so much
Upon the voice of occupation and
The breath of garlic-eaters!

COMINIUS
He'll shake your Rome about your ears.   100

MENENIUS
As Hercules did shake down mellow fruit.
You have made fair work!

BRUTUS
But is this true, sir?

COMINIUS   Ay, and you'll look pale
Before you find it other. All the regions
Do smilingly revolt, and who resists
Are mocked for valiant ignorance,
And perish constant fools. Who is't can blame him?
Your enemies and his find something in him.

MENENIUS
We are all undone unless
The noble man have mercy.

COMINIUS   Who shall ask it?   110
The Tribunes cannot do't for shame; the people
Deserve such pity of him as the wolf
Does of the shepherds. For his best friends, if they
Should say 'Be good to Rome', they charged him even
As those should do that had deserved his hate,

And therein showed like enemies.

MENENIUS   'Tis true.
If he were putting to my house the brand
That should consume it, I have not the face
To say 'Beseech you, cease.' You have made fair hands,
You and your crafts! You have crafted fair!

COMINIUS   You have brought
A trembling upon Rome, such as was never
S'incapable of help.

TRIBUNES   Say not we brought it.

MENENIUS
How? Was't we? We loved him, but, like beasts
And cowardly nobles, gave way unto your clusters,
Who did hoot him out o'th'city.

COMINIUS   But I fear
They'll roar him in again. Tullus Aufidius,
The second name of men, obeys his points
As if he were his officer. Desperation
Is all the policy, strength, and defence
That Rome can make against them.

          Enter a troop of Citizens

MENENIUS   Here come the clusters.
And is Aufidius with him? You are they
That made the air unwholesome when you cast
Your stinking greasy caps in hooting
At Coriolanus' exile. Now he's coming,
And not a hair upon a soldier's head
Which will not prove a whip. As many coxcombs
As you threw caps up will he tumble down,
And pay you for your voices. 'Tis no matter.
If he could burn us all into one coal,
We have deserved it.

CITIZENS
Faith, we hear fearful news.

FIRST CITIZEN   For mine own part,
  When I said banish him, I said 'twas pity.
SECOND CITIZEN And so did I.
THIRD CITIZEN And so did I, and, to say the truth, so
  did very many of us. That we did, we did for the best,
  and though we willingly consented to his banishment,
  yet it was against our will.
COMINIUS
  Y'are goodly things, you voices!
MENENIUS
  You have made good work,
  You and your cry! Shall's to the Capitol?   150
COMINIUS
  O, ay, what else?   *Exeunt both*
SICINIUS
  Go, masters, get you home. Be not dismayed;
  These are a side that would be glad to have
  This true which they so seem to fear. Go home,
  And show no sign of fear.
FIRST CITIZEN The gods be good to us! Come, masters,
  let's home. I ever said we were i'th'wrong when we
  banished him.
SECOND CITIZEN So did we all. But come, let's home.
                                           Exeunt Citizens
BRUTUS
  I do not like this news.   160
SICINIUS
  Nor I.
BRUTUS
  Let's to the Capitol. Would half my wealth
  Would buy this for a lie!
SICINIUS   Pray let's go.
                                           Exeunt Tribunes

IV.7   *Enter Aufidius, with his Lieutenant*

AUFIDIUS
    Do they still fly to th'Roman?

LIEUTENANT
    I do not know what witchcraft's in him, but
    Your soldiers use him as the grace 'fore meat,
    Their talk at table and their thanks at end,
    And you are darkened in this action, sir,
    Even by your own.

AUFIDIUS   I cannot help it now,
    Unless by using means I lame the foot
    Of our design. He bears himself more proudlier,
    Even to my person, than I thought he would
10 When first I did embrace him. Yet his nature
    In that's no changeling, and I must excuse
    What cannot be amended.

LIEUTENANT   Yet I wish, sir –
    I mean for your particular – you had not
    Joined in commission with him, but either
    Have borne the action of yourself, or else
    To him had left it solely.

AUFIDIUS
    I understand thee well, and be thou sure,
    When he shall come to his account, he knows not
    What I can urge against him. Although it seems,
20 And so he thinks, and is no less apparent
    To th'vulgar eye, that he bears all things fairly
    And shows good husbandry for the Volscian state,
    Fights dragon-like, and does achieve as soon
    As draw his sword; yet he hath left undone
    That which shall break his neck or hazard mine
    Whene'er we come to our account.

LIEUTENANT
    Sir, I beseech you, think you he'll carry Rome?

AUFIDIUS

All places yield to him ere he sits down,
And the nobility of Rome are his.
The senators and patricians love him too.   30
The tribunes are no soldiers, and their people
Will be as rash in the repeal as hasty
To expel him thence. I think he'll be to Rome
As is the osprey to the fish, who takes it
By sovereignty of nature. First he was
A noble servant to them, but he could not
Carry his honours even. Whether 'twas pride,
Which out of daily fortune ever taints
The happy man; whether defect of judgement,
To fail in the disposing of those chances   40
Which he was lord of; or whether nature,
Not to be other than one thing, not moving
From th'casque to th'cushion, but commanding peace
Even with the same austerity and garb
As he controlled the war; but one of these –
As he hath spices of them all – not all,
For I dare so far free him – made him feared,
So hated, and so banished. But he has a merit
To choke it in the utterance. So our virtues
Lie in th'interpretation of the time;   50
And power, unto itself most commendable,
Hath not a tomb so evident as a chair
T'extol what it hath done.
One fire drives out one fire; one nail one nail;
Rights by rights fuller, strengths by strengths do fail.
Come, let's away. When, Caius, Rome is thine,
Thou art poor'st of all; then shortly art thou mine.

Exeunt

*

V.I   *Enter Menenius, Cominius, Sicinius and Brutus the*
           two Tribunes, with others

MENENIUS

No, I'll not go. You hear what he hath said
Which was sometime his general, who loved him
In a most dear particular. He called me father;
But what o'that? Go, you that banished him,
A mile before his tent fall down, and knee
The way into his mercy. Nay, if he coyed
To hear Cominius speak, I'll keep at home.

COMINIUS

He would not seem to know me.

MENENIUS   Do you hear?

COMINIUS

Yet one time he did call me by my name.
10   I urged our old acquaintance and the drops
That we have bled together. 'Coriolanus'
He would not answer to; forbade all names;
He was a kind of nothing, titleless,
Till he had forged himself a name i'th'fire
Of burning Rome.

MENENIUS   Why, so! You have made good work.
A pair of Tribunes that have wracked for Rome
To make coals cheap – a noble memory!

COMINIUS

I minded him how royal 'twas to pardon
When it was less expected. He replied,
20   It was a bare petition of a state
To one whom they had punished.

MENENIUS

Very well. Could he say less?

COMINIUS

I offered to awaken his regard
For's private friends. His answer to me was,

He could not stay to pick them in a pile
Of noisome musty chaff. He said 'twas folly,
For one poor grain or two, to leave unburnt
And still to nose th'offence.

MENENIUS
For one poor grain or two!
I am one of those; his mother, wife, his child,   30
And this brave fellow too – we are the grains.
You are the musty chaff, and you are smelt
Above the moon. We must be burnt for you.

SICINIUS
Nay, pray be patient. If you refuse your aid
In this so-never-needed help, yet do not
Upbraid's with our distress. But sure, if you
Would be your country's pleader, your good tongue,
More than the instant army we can make,
Might stop our countryman.

MENENIUS   No, I'll not meddle.

SICINIUS
Pray you go to him.

MENENIUS   What should I do?   40

BRUTUS
Only make trial what your love can do
For Rome towards Martius.

MENENIUS   Well, and say that Martius
Return me, as Cominius is returned,
Unheard – what then?
But as a discontented friend, grief-shot
With his unkindness? Say't be so?

SICINIUS   Yet your good will
Must have that thanks from Rome after the measure
As you intended well.

MENENIUS   I'll undertake't;
I think he'll hear me. Yet to bite his lip

50   And hum at good Cominius much unhearts me.
      He was not taken well; he had not dined.
      The veins unfilled, our blood is cold, and then
      We pout upon the morning, are unapt
      To give or to forgive, but when we have stuffed
      These pipes and these conveyances of our blood
      With wine and feeding, we have suppler souls
      Than in our priest-like fasts. Therefore I'll watch him
      Till he be dieted to my request,
      And then I'll set upon him.

BRUTUS

60   You know the very road into his kindness
      And cannot lose your way.

MENENIUS   Good faith, I'll prove him,
      Speed how it will. I shall ere long have knowledge
      Of my success.   *Exit*

COMINIUS   He'll never hear him.

SICINIUS   Not?

COMINIUS

      I tell you he does sit in gold, his eye
      Red as 'twould burn Rome, and his injury
      The gaoler to his pity. I kneeled before him;
      'Twas very faintly he said 'Rise', dismissed me
      Thus with his speechless hand. What he would do
      He sent in writing after me, what he would not,

70   Bound with an oath to yield to his conditions.
      So that all hope is vain
      Unless his noble mother and his wife,
      Who, as I hear, mean to solicit him
      For mercy to his country. Therefore let's hence,
      And with our fair entreaties haste them on.   *Exeunt*

Enter Menenius to the Watch on guard   **V.2**

FIRST WATCH
  Stay. Whence are you?
SECOND WATCH   Stand, and go back.
MENENIUS
  You guard like men, 'tis well. But, by your leave,
  I am an officer of state and come
  To speak with Coriolanus.
FIRST WATCH   From whence?
MENENIUS   From Rome.
FIRST WATCH
  You may not pass, you must return. Our general
  Will no more hear from thence.
SECOND WATCH
  You'll see your Rome embraced with fire before
  You'll speak with Coriolanus.
MENENIUS   Good my friends,
  If you have heard your general talk of Rome
  And of his friends there, it is lots to blanks   10
  My name hath touched your ears: it is Menenius.
FIRST WATCH
  Be it so; go back. The virtue of your name
  Is not here passable.
MENENIUS   I tell thee, fellow,
  Thy general is my lover. I have been
  The book of his good acts whence men have read
  His fame unparalleled haply amplified.
  For I have ever varnishèd my friends –
  Of whom he's chief – with all the size that verity
  Would without lapsing suffer. Nay, sometimes,
  Like to a bowl upon a subtle ground,   20
  I have tumbled past the throw, and in his praise
  Have almost stamped the leasing. Therefore, fellow,
  I must have leave to pass.

FIRST WATCH Faith, sir, if you had told as many lies in
his behalf as you have uttered words in your own, you
should not pass here; no, though it were as virtuous to
lie as to live chastely. Therefore go back.

MENENIUS Prithee, fellow, remember my name is Menenius, always factionary on the party of your general.

30 SECOND WATCH Howsoever you have been his liar, as
you say you have, I am one that, telling true under him,
must say you cannot pass. Therefore go back.

MENENIUS Has he dined, canst thou tell? For I would not
speak with him till after dinner.

FIRST WATCH You are a Roman, are you?

MENENIUS I am as thy general is.

FIRST WATCH Then you should hate Rome, as he does.
Can you, when you have pushed out your gates the very
defender of them, and in a violent popular ignorance
40 given your enemy your shield, think to front his revenges
with the easy groans of old women, the virginal palms of
your daughters, or with the palsied intercession of such
a decayed dotant as you seem to be? Can you think to
blow out the intended fire your city is ready to flame in
with such weak breath as this? No, you are deceived,
therefore back to Rome and prepare for your execution.
You are condemned, our general has sworn you out of
reprieve and pardon.

MENENIUS Sirrah, if thy captain knew I were here, he
50 would use me with estimation.

FIRST WATCH Come, my captain knows you not.

MENENIUS I mean thy general.

FIRST WATCH My general cares not for you. Back, I say,
go, lest I let forth your half-pint of blood. Back – that's
the utmost of your having. Back.

MENENIUS Nay, but fellow, fellow –

Enter Coriolanus with Aufidius

CORIOLANUS What's the matter?

MENENIUS Now, you companion, I'll say an errand for
you. You shall know now that I am in estimation. You
shall perceive that a Jack guardant cannot office me from   60
my son Coriolanus. Guess but my entertainment with
him. If thou stand'st not i'th'state of hanging, or of
some death more long in spectatorship and crueller in
suffering, behold now presently and swoon for what's to
come upon thee. (*To Coriolanus*) The glorious gods sit in
hourly synod about thy particular prosperity and love
thee no worse than thy old father Menenius does! O my
son, my son, thou art preparing fire for us. Look thee,
here's water to quench it. I was hardly moved to come
to thee; but being assured none but myself could move   70
thee, I have been blown out of your gates with sighs,
and conjure thee to pardon Rome and thy petitionary
countrymen. The good gods assuage thy wrath and turn
the dregs of it upon this varlet here – this, who, like a
block, hath denied my access to thee.

CORIOLANUS Away!

MENENIUS How? Away?

CORIOLANUS

Wife, mother, child, I know not. My affairs
Are servanted to others. Though I owe
My revenge properly, my remission lies   80
In Volscian breasts. That we have been familiar,
Ingrate forgetfulness shall poison rather
Than pity note how much. Therefore be gone.
Mine ears against your suits are stronger than
Your gates against my force. Yet, for I loved thee,
Take this along. I writ it for thy sake (*gives a letter*)
And would have sent it. Another word, Menenius,
I will not hear thee speak. This man, Aufidius,
Was my beloved in Rome; yet thou behold'st.

AUFIDIUS

90   You keep a constant temper.   *Exeunt*

        The Guard and Menenius stay behind

FIRST WATCH Now, sir, is your name Menenius?

SECOND WATCH 'Tis a spell, you see, of much power.
        You know the way home again.

FIRST WATCH Do you hear how we are shent for keeping
        your greatness back?

SECOND WATCH What cause do you think I have to
        swoon?

MENENIUS I neither care for th'world nor your general.
        For such things as you, I can scarce think there's any,

100   y'are so slight. He that hath a will to die by himself fears
        it not from another. Let your general do his worst. For
        you, be that you are, long; and your misery increase
        with your age! I say to you, as I was said to, Away!

                                                            Exit

FIRST WATCH A noble fellow, I warrant him.

SECOND WATCH The worthy fellow is our general. He's
        the rock, the oak not to be wind-shaken.   *Exit Watch*

V.3   *Enter Coriolanus and Aufidius with others. They sit*

CORIOLANUS

        We will before the walls of Rome tomorrow
        Set down our host. My partner in this action,
        You must report to th'Volscian lords how plainly
        I have borne this business.

AUFIDIUS   Only their ends
        You have respected; stopped your ears against
        The general suit of Rome; never admitted
        A private whisper – no, not with such friends
        That thought them sure of you.

CORIOLANUS   This last old man,

Whom with a cracked heart I have sent to Rome,
Loved me above the measure of a father,   10
Nay, godded me indeed. Their latest refuge
Was to send him; for whose old love I have –
Though I showed sourly to him – once more offered
The first conditions, which they did refuse
And cannot now accept, to grace him only
That thought he could do more. A very little
I have yielded to. Fresh embassies and suits,
Nor from the state nor private friends, hereafter
Will I lend ear to. (*Shouts within*) Ha! What shout is
   this?
(*Aside*) Shall I be tempted to infringe my vow   20
In the same time 'tis made? I will not.
   Enter Virgilia, Volumnia, Valeria, young Martius,
   with Attendants
My wife comes foremost, then the honoured mould
Wherein this trunk was framed, and in her hand
The grandchild to her blood. But out, affection!
All bond and privilege of nature, break!
Let it be virtuous to be obstinate.
What is that curtsy worth? Or those dove's eyes
Which can make gods forsworn? I melt, and am not
Of stronger earth than others. My mother bows,
As if Olympus to a molehill should   30
In supplication nod, and my young boy
Hath an aspect of intercession which
Great Nature cries 'Deny not.' Let the Volsces
Plough Rome and harrow Italy! I'll never
Be such a gosling to obey instinct, but stand
As if a man were author of himself
And knew no other kin.

VIRGILIA   My lord and husband!

CORIOLANUS
  These eyes are not the same I wore in Rome.

VIRGILIA
  The sorrow that delivers us thus changed
40 Makes you think so.

CORIOLANUS (*aside*)   Like a dull actor now
  I have forgot my part and I am out,
  Even to a full disgrace. (*Rising and going to her*) Best of
      my flesh,
  Forgive my tyranny; but do not say
  For that, 'Forgive our Romans.' O, a kiss
  Long as my exile, sweet as my revenge!
  Now, by the jealous queen of heaven, that kiss
  I carried from thee, dear, and my true lip
  Hath virgined it e'er since. You gods! I pray,
  And the most noble mother of the world
50 Leave unsaluted. Sink my knee i'th'earth;
        He kneels
  Of thy deep duty more impression show
  Than that of common sons.

VOLUMNIA   O, stand up blest!
        He rises
  Whilst with no softer cushion than the flint
  I kneel before thee, and unproperly
  Show duty as mistaken all this while
  Between the child and parent.
        She kneels

CORIOLANUS   What's this?
  Your knees to me? To your corrected son?
        He raises her
  Then let the pebbles on the hungry beach
  Fillip the stars. Then let the mutinous winds
60 Strike the proud cedars 'gainst the fiery sun,
  Murdering impossibility, to make

What cannot be slight work.

VOLUMNIA   Thou art my warrior;
I holp to frame thee. Do you know this lady?

CORIOLANUS
The noble sister of Publicola,
The moon of Rome, chaste as the icicle
That's curdied by the frost from purest snow
And hangs on Dian's temple – dear Valeria!

VOLUMNIA (*indicating young Martius*)
This is a poor epitome of yours,
Which by th'interpretation of full time
May show like all yourself.

CORIOLANUS   The god of soldiers,   70
With the consent of supreme Jove, inform
Thy thoughts with nobleness, that thou mayst prove
To shame unvulnerable, and stick i'th'wars
Like a great sea-mark, standing every flaw
And saving those that eye thee!

VOLUMNIA   Your knee, sirrah.

CORIOLANUS
That's my brave boy!

VOLUMNIA
Even he, your wife, this lady, and myself
Are suitors to you.

CORIOLANUS   I beseech you, peace!
Or, if you'd ask, remember this before:
The thing I have forsworn to grant may never   80
Be held by you denials. Do not bid me
Dismiss my soldiers, or capitulate
Again with Rome's mechanics. Tell me not
Wherein I seem unnatural. Desire not
T'allay my rages and revenges with
Your colder reasons.

VOLUMNIA   O, no more, no more!

You have said you will not grant us any thing –
For we have nothing else to ask but that
Which you deny already. Yet we will ask,
90   That, if you fail in our request, the blame
May hang upon your hardness. Therefore hear us.

CORIOLANUS

Aufidius, and you Volsces, mark; for we'll
Hear naught from Rome in private. (*He sits*) Your
    request?

VOLUMNIA

Should we be silent and not speak, our raiment
And state of bodies would bewray what life
We have led since thy exile. Think with thyself
How more unfortunate than all living women
Are we come hither; since that thy sight, which should
Make our eyes flow with joy, hearts dance with comforts,
100   Constrains them weep and shake with fear and sorrow,
Making the mother, wife, and child to see
The son, the husband, and the father tearing
His country's bowels out. And to poor we
Thine enmity's most capital. Thou barr'st us
Our prayers to the gods, which is a comfort
That all but we enjoy. For how can we,
Alas, how can we for our country pray,
Whereto we are bound, together with thy victory,
Whereto we are bound? Alack, or we must lose
110   The country, our dear nurse, or else thy person,
Our comfort in the country. We must find
An evident calamity, though we had
Our wish, which side should win. For either thou
Must as a foreign recreant be led
With manacles through our streets, or else
Triumphantly tread on thy country's ruin,
And bear the palm for having bravely shed

Thy wife and children's blood. For myself, son,
I purpose not to wait on fortune till
These wars determine. If I cannot persuade thee   120
Rather to show a noble grace to both parts
Than seek the end of one, thou shalt no sooner
March to assault thy country than to tread –
Trust to't, thou shalt not – on thy mother's womb
That brought thee to this world.

VIRGILIA   Ay, and mine,
That brought you forth this boy to keep your name
Living to time.

BOY   'A shall not tread on me!
I'll run away till I am bigger, but then I'll fight.

CORIOLANUS
Not of a woman's tenderness to be
Requires nor child nor woman's face to see.   130
I have sat too long.
       He rises

VOLUMNIA   Nay, go not from us thus.
If it were so that our request did tend
To save the Romans, thereby to destroy
The Volsces whom you serve, you might condemn us
As poisonous of your honour. No, our suit
Is that you reconcile them, while the Volsces
May say 'This mercy we have showed', the Romans
'This we received', and each in either side
Give the all-hail to thee and cry 'Be blest
For making up this peace!' Thou know'st, great son,   140
The end of war's uncertain; but this certain,
That, if thou conquer Rome, the benefit
Which thou shalt thereby reap is such a name
Whose repetition will be dogged with curses,
Whose chronicle thus writ: 'The man was noble,
But with his last attempt he wiped it out,

Destroyed his country, and his name remains
To th'ensuing age abhorred.' Speak to me, son.
Thou hast affected the fine strains of honour,
To imitate the graces of the gods,
To tear with thunder the wide cheeks o'th'air,
And yet to charge thy sulphur with a bolt
That should but rive an oak. Why dost not speak?
Think'st thou it honourable for a nobleman
Still to remember wrongs? Daughter, speak you:
He cares not for your weeping. Speak thou, boy.
Perhaps thy childishness will move him more
Than can our reasons. There's no man in the world
More bound to's mother, yet here he lets me prate
Like one i'th'stocks. Thou hast never in thy life
Showed thy dear mother any courtesy,
When she, poor hen, fond of no second brood,
Has clucked thee to the wars, and safely home
Loaden with honour. Say my request's unjust,
And spurn me back. But if it be not so,
Thou art not honest, and the gods will plague thee
That thou restrain'st from me the duty which
To a mother's part belongs. He turns away.
Down ladies! Let us shame him with our knees.
To his surname Coriolanus 'longs more pride
Than pity to our prayers. Down! An end;
      The four kneel
This is the last. So, we will home to Rome,
And die among our neighbours. Nay, behold's!
This boy, that cannot tell what he would have
But kneels and holds up hands for fellowship,
Does reason our petition with more strength
Than thou hast to deny't. Come, let us go.
      They rise
This fellow had a Volscian to his mother;

His wife is in Corioles, and his child
Like him by chance. Yet give us our dispatch.   180
I am hushed until our city be afire,
And then I'll speak a little.

CORIOLANUS
    Holds her by the hand, silent
O, mother, mother!
What have you done? Behold, the heavens do ope,
The gods look down, and this unnatural scene
They laugh at. O my mother, mother! O!
You have won a happy victory to Rome.
But for your son – believe it, O believe it –
Most dangerously you have with him prevailed,
If not most mortal to him. But let it come.   190
Aufidius, though I cannot make true wars,
I'll frame convenient peace. Now, good Aufidius,
Were you in my stead, would you have heard
A mother less? Or granted less, Aufidius?

AUFIDIUS
I was moved withal.

CORIOLANUS   I dare be sworn you were!
And, sir, it is no little thing to make
Mine eyes to sweat compassion. But, good sir,
What peace you'll make, advise me. For my part,
I'll not to Rome, I'll back with you, and pray you
Stand to me in this cause. O mother! Wife!   200

AUFIDIUS (*aside*)
I am glad thou hast set thy mercy and thy honour
At difference in thee. Out of that I'll work
Myself a former fortune.

CORIOLANUS (*to the ladies*) Ay, by and by.
But we will drink together; and you shall bear
A better witness back than words, which we,
On like conditions, will have counter-sealed.

Come, enter with us. Ladies, you deserve
To have a temple built you. All the swords
In Italy, and her confederate arms,
210   Could not have made this peace.   *Exeunt*

V.4   *Enter Menenius and Sicinius*

MENENIUS See you yond coign o'th' Capitol, yond corner-
stone?

SICINIUS Why, what of that?

MENENIUS If it be possible for you to displace it with
your little finger, there is some hope the ladies of Rome,
especially his mother, may prevail with him. But I say
there is no hope in't, our throats are sentenced and stay
upon execution.

SICINIUS Is't possible that so short a time can alter the
10   condition of a man?

MENENIUS There is difference between a grub and a
butterfly, yet your butterfly was a grub. This Martius is
grown from man to dragon. He has wings, he's more
than a creeping thing.

SICINIUS He loved his mother dearly.

MENENIUS So did he me; and he no more remembers his
mother now than an eight-year-old horse. The tartness
of his face sours ripe grapes. When he walks, he moves
like an engine, and the ground shrinks before his tread-
20   ing. He is able to pierce a corslet with his eye, talks like
a knell, and his hum is a battery. He sits in his state as a
thing made for Alexander. What he bids be done is
finished with his bidding. He wants nothing of a god but
eternity and a heaven to throne in.

SICINIUS Yes, mercy, if you report him truly.

MENENIUS I paint him in the character. Mark what mercy
his mother shall bring from him. There is no more

mercy in him than there is milk in a male tiger. That
shall our poor city find. And all this is 'long of you.

SICINIUS The gods be good unto us!   30

MENENIUS No, in such a case the gods will not be good
    unto us. When we banished him we respected not them;
    and, he returning to break our necks, they respect not us.

    Enter a Messenger

MESSENGER

    Sir, if you'd save your life, fly to your house.
    The plebeians have got your fellow Tribune
    And hale him up and down, all swearing if
    The Roman ladies bring not comfort home
    They'll give him death by inches.

    Enter another Messenger

SICINIUS   What's the news?

SECOND MESSENGER

    Good news, good news! The ladies have prevailed,
    The Volscians are dislodged and Martius gone.   40
    A merrier day did never yet greet Rome,
    No, not th'expulsion of the Tarquins.

SICINIUS   Friend,
    Art thou certain this is true? Is't most certain?

SECOND MESSENGER

    As certain as I know the sun is fire.
    Where have you lurked that you make doubt of it?
    Ne'er through an arch so hurried the blown tide
    As the recomforted through th'gates. Why, hark you!

    Trumpets, hautboys, drums beat, all together
    The trumpets, sackbuts, psalteries, and fifes,
    Tabors and cymbals and the shouting Romans
    Make the sun dance. Hark you!

    A shout within

MENENIUS   This is good news.   50
    I will go meet the ladies. This Volumnia

Is worth of consuls, senators, patricians,
A city full; of tribunes such as you,
A sea and land full. You have prayed well today.
This morning for ten thousand of your throats
I'd not have given a doit. Hark, how they joy!
    Sound still with the shouts

SICINIUS
First, the gods bless you for your tidings; next,
Accept my thankfulness.

SECOND MESSENGER
Sir, we have all great cause to give great thanks.

SICINIUS
60   They are near the city?

SECOND MESSENGER
Almost at point to enter.

SICINIUS
We'll meet them, and help the joy.   *Exeunt*

V.5   *Enter two Senators, with Volumnia, Virgilia, and*
            Valeria, passing over the stage, with other Lords

FIRST SENATOR
Behold our patroness, the life of Rome!
Call all your tribes together, praise the gods,
And make triumphant fires; strew flowers before them.
Unshout the noise that banished Martius,
Repeal him with the welcome of his mother.
Cry 'Welcome, ladies, welcome!'

ALL
Welcome, ladies, welcome!
          A flourish with drums and trumpets. Exeunt

Enter Tullus Aufidius, with Attendants   V.6

AUFIDIUS

    Go tell the lords o'th'city I am here.
    Deliver them this paper. Having read it,
    Bid them repair to th'market-place, where I,
    Even in theirs and in the commons' ears,
    Will vouch the truth of it. Him I accuse
    The city ports by this hath entered and
    Intends t'appear before the people, hoping
    To purge himself with words. Dispatch.

                                    Exeunt Attendants

        Enter three or four Conspirators of Aufidius' faction
    Most welcome!

FIRST CONSPIRATOR

    How is it with our general?

AUFIDIUS   Even so   10
    As with a man by his own alms empoisoned
    And with his charity slain.

SECOND CONSPIRATOR   Most noble sir,
    If you do hold the same intent wherein
    You wished us parties, we'll deliver you
    Of your great danger.

AUFIDIUS   Sir, I cannot tell.
    We must proceed as we do find the people.

THIRD CONSPIRATOR

    The people will remain uncertain whilst
    'Twixt you there's difference. But the fall of either
    Makes the survivor heir of all.

AUFIDIUS   I know it,
    And my pretext to strike at him admits   20
    A good construction. I raised him, and I pawned
    Mine honour for his truth; who being so heightened,
    He watered his new plants with dews of flattery,
    Seducing so my friends. And to this end

He bowed his nature, never known before
But to be rough, unswayable and free.

THIRD CONSPIRATOR
Sir, his stoutness
When he did stand for consul, which he lost
By lack of stooping –

AUFIDIUS   That I would have spoke of.
30   Being banished for't, he came unto my hearth,
Presented to my knife his throat. I took him,
Made him joint-servant with me, gave him way
In all his own desires; nay, let him choose
Out of my files, his projects to accomplish,
My best and freshest men; served his designments
In mine own person; holp to reap the fame
Which he did end all his, and took some pride
To do myself this wrong. Till at the last
I seemed his follower, not partner; and
40   He waged me with his countenance as if
I had been mercenary.

FIRST CONSPIRATOR   So he did, my lord;
The army marvelled at it. And, in the last,
When we had carried Rome and that we looked
For no less spoil than glory –

AUFIDIUS   There was it,
For which my sinews shall be stretched upon him.
At a few drops of women's rheum, which are
As cheap as lies, he sold the blood and labour
Of our great action. Therefore shall he die,
And I'll renew me in his fall. But hark!

*Drums and trumpets sound, with great shouts of the
people*

FIRST CONSPIRATOR
50   Your native town you entered like a post,
And had no welcomes home; but he returns

Splitting the air with noise.

SECOND CONSPIRATOR   And patient fools,
Whose children he hath slain, their base throats tear
With giving him glory.

THIRD CONSPIRATOR   Therefore, at your vantage,
Ere he express himself or move the people
With what he would say, let him feel your sword,
Which we will second. When he lies along,
After your way his tale pronounced shall bury
His reasons with his body.

AUFIDIUS   Say no more.
Here come the Lords.   60

    Enter the Lords of the city

ALL LORDS
You are most welcome home.

AUFIDIUS   I have not deserved it.
But, worthy Lords, have you with heed perused
What I have written to you?

ALL   We have.

FIRST LORD   And grieve to hear't.
What faults he made before the last, I think
Might have found easy fines. But there to end
Where he was to begin, and give away
The benefit of our levies, answering us
With our own charge, making a treaty where
There was a yielding – this admits no excuse.

AUFIDIUS
He approaches. You shall hear him.   70

    Enter Coriolanus, marching with drum and colours;
    the Commoners being with him

CORIOLANUS
Hail, Lords! I am returned your soldier,
No more infected with my country's love
Than when I parted hence, but still subsisting

Under your great command. You are to know
That prosperously I have attempted and
With bloody passage led your wars even to
The gates of Rome. Our spoils we have brought home
Doth more than counterpoise a full third part
The charges of the action. We have made peace
80   With no less honour to the Antiates
Than shame to th'Romans. And we here deliver,
Subscribed by th'consuls and patricians,
Together with the seal o'th'Senate, what
We have compounded on.

AUFIDIUS   Read it not, noble Lords;
But tell the traitor in the highest degree
He hath abused your powers.

CORIOLANUS
Traitor? How now?

AUFIDIUS   Ay, traitor, Martius!

CORIOLANUS   Martius?

AUFIDIUS
Ay, Martius, Caius Martius! Dost thou think
I'll grace thee with that robbery, thy stolen name
90   Coriolanus in Corioles?
You lords and heads o'th'state, perfidiously
He has betrayed your business and given up,
For certain drops of salt, your city Rome –
I say your city – to his wife and mother,
Breaking his oath and resolution like
A twist of rotten silk, never admitting
Counsel o'th'war. But at his nurse's tears
He whined and roared away your victory,
That pages blushed at him and men of heart
100   Looked wondering each at others.

CORIOLANUS   Hear'st thou, Mars?

AUFIDIUS
  Name not the god, thou boy of tears!
CORIOLANUS   Ha?
AUFIDIUS
  No more.
CORIOLANUS
  Measureless liar, thou hast made my heart
  Too great for what contains it. 'Boy'! O slave!
  Pardon me, Lords, 'tis the first time that ever
  I was forced to scold. Your judgements, my grave Lords,
  Must give this cur the lie; and his own notion –
  Who wears my stripes impressed upon him, that
  Must bear my beating to his grave – shall join
  To thrust the lie unto him.   110
FIRST LORD
  Peace, both, and hear me speak.
CORIOLANUS
  Cut me to pieces, Volsces. Men and lads,
  Stain all your edges on me. 'Boy'! False hound!
  If you have writ your annals true, 'tis there
  That, like an eagle in a dove-cote, I
  Fluttered your Volscians in Corioles.
  Alone I did it. 'Boy'!
AUFIDIUS   Why, noble Lords,
  Will you be put in mind of his blind fortune,
  Which was your shame, by this unholy braggart,
  'Fore your own eyes and ears?
ALL CONSPIRATORS   Let him die for't.   120
ALL THE PEOPLE Tear him to pieces! – Do it presently!
  – He killed my son! – My daughter! – He killed my
  cousin Marcus! – He killed my father!
SECOND LORD
  Peace, ho! No outrage. Peace!
  The man is noble and his fame folds in

This orb o'th'earth. His last offences to us
Shall have judicious hearing. Stand, Aufidius,
And trouble not the peace.

CORIOLANUS   O that I had him,
With six Aufidiuses or more – his tribe,
130   To use my lawful sword!

AUFIDIUS   Insolent villain!

ALL CONSPIRATORS
Kill, kill, kill, kill, kill him!

The Conspirators draw their swords, and kill Martius,
who falls
Aufidius stands on him

LORDS
Hold, hold, hold, hold!

AUFIDIUS
My noble masters, hear me speak.

FIRST LORD   O Tullus!

SECOND LORD
Thou hast done a deed whereat valour will weep.

THIRD LORD
Tread not upon him. Masters all, be quiet.
Put up your swords.

AUFIDIUS
My Lords, when you shall know – as in this rage
Provoked by him you cannot – the great danger
Which this man's life did owe you, you'll rejoice
140   That he is thus cut off. Please it your honours
To call me to your Senate, I'll deliver
Myself your loyal servant, or endure
Your heaviest censure.

FIRST LORD   Bear from hence his body,
And mourn you for him. Let him be regarded
As the most noble corse that ever herald
Did follow to his urn.

SECOND LORD   His own impatience
  Takes from Aufidius a great part of blame.
  Let's make the best of it.
AUFIDIUS   My rage is gone,
  And I am struck with sorrow. Take him up.
  Help three o'th'chiefest soldiers; I'll be one.   150
  Beat thou the drum, that it speak mournfully.
  Trail your steel pikes. Though in this city he
  Hath widowed and unchilded many a one,
  Which to this hour bewail the injury,
  Yet he shall have a noble memory.
  Assist.

                   Exeunt, bearing the body of Martius.
                          A dead march sounded

An Account of the Text

Still unpublished when Shakespeare died in 1616, *Coriolanus* is one of the seventeen plays that were printed for the first time in the first Folio of 1623 (F; F1), where it was originally intended to stand at the head of the Tragedies, a position which it later lost through the last-minute inclusion of *Troilus and Cressida* in the volume. Since its publication was quite regular, this version, with the authority of Shakespeare's old friends and fellow-actors, John Heminges and Henry Condell, to back it, is the sole source for the text of the play.

There are strong indications that the material Heminges and Condell placed at the printer's disposal was either a carefully prepared manuscript in Shakespeare's autograph – probably a fair copy – or a close transcript of it. In the first place *Coriolanus* is unusually long for an Elizabethan play, and it seems unlikely that it would normally have been produced in its entirety. The prompt copy would, therefore, have been a cut version, which the Folio text plainly is not. Secondly, the stage directions, while exceptionally detailed and elaborate, are in many cases of a kind that would not have been convenient in an actual performance, and appear to have been written for the benefit of a producer rather than as commands to the actors. The opening of the third scene provides a good example: *Enter Volumnia and Virgilia, mother and wife to Martius: they set them down on two low stools and sew.* This is the kind of business that is generally left to actors in rehearsal, and its inclusion suggests that when Shakespeare wrote the play he was no longer in such close touch with the company as he had been hitherto – perhaps he was already spending most of his time

at Stratford. Furthermore, many of the directions are too indefinite
to serve for a performance. *Enter seven or eight Citizens*, at the
beginning of II.3, and *Enter three or four Conspirators of Aufidius'
faction*, at V.6.8, leave things vague which the actors need to
know. Some of the directions, such as that which introduces I.7,
even have a distinct literary quality about them and look like the
author's sketch for the action and dialogue that are to follow.
Finally, there are a number of spellings which seem to be peculiar
to Shakespeare. The form *Scicinius* for *Sicinius*, which occurs in
the stage direction at II.3.137 and consistently as a speech-prefix
for the rest of the scene, as well as spasmodically in III.1, looks
like a close relation of the unusual spelling 'scilens' for 'silence',
which is to be found at line 50 of Shakespeare's part of the play
Sir Thomas More (the only piece of dramatic writing in his own
hand that still survives) and which appears no fewer than eighteen
times in the Quarto version of *Henry IV, Part II*, published in
1600, where it stands for the name of the character Silence.

But, while there is good evidence that the Folio text of
Coriolanus was set from Shakespeare's autograph, there must have
been some editorial interference with the manuscript before it
reached the printer. The mark of it is to be seen in some of the
punctuation. For instance, the Folio text at III.3.68–74 runs as
follows (here the 'long s' [ʃ] is replaced by 's' in all quotations):

> The fires i'th'lowest hell. Fould in the people:
> Call me their Traitor, thou iniurious Tribune.
> Within thine eyes sate twenty thousand deaths
> In thy hands clutcht: as many Millions in
> Thy lying tongue, both numbers. I would say
> Thou lyest vnto thee, with a voice as free,
> As I do pray the Gods.

This pointing is clearly the work of someone who simply did not
understand the sense of the passage he was dealing with, and
cannot therefore be Shakespeare's. The punctuation is, in fact,
one of the most difficult of the problems that face the editor of
this play.

There are two others. First, there is a good deal of mislineation, or what appears to be mislineation, of the verse. Quite

often one speech ends with a half-line and the next begins with a full line, and it is not easy to be sure whether the resulting irregularity is deliberate or not. For example, I.9.19–23 in the present edition appears in the following form in the Folio:

Hath ouerta'ne mine Act.
    Com. You shall not be the Graue of your deseruing,
Rome must know the value of her owne:
'Twere a Concealement worse then a Theft,
No less then a Traducement,
To hide your doings, and to silence that . . .

By using the words *You shall not be* to complete the previous half-line, the metre can be smoothed out, but this procedure does involve the loss of the emphasis which Cominius' three lines *Rome . . . Traducement* acquire from the heavy stresses and pauses which are needed to eke them out. Shakespeare's blank verse in his last period is such a flexible medium that only the insensitive can be dogmatic about it.

The other main difficulty that the Folio text raises is occasioned by the large number of misprints in it. Most of them can, however, be explained as a natural result of peculiarities in Shakespeare's handwriting, and add weight to the view that the text was set up from his autograph. To take one instance out of many: the appearance of the curious word *Contenning* at I.3.44, where it looks like the name of the Gentlewoman attending on Valeria, is probably due to his fondness for using a capital 'C' initially and to his carelessness in differentiating between 'm' and 'n'. The word he wrote was almost certainly 'contemning'.

Below are listed departures in the present text of *Coriolanus* from that of the first Folio. Obvious minor misprints are not noted, nor are changes in lineation and punctuation unless they are of special significance. A few of these alterations were made in one of the three seventeenth-century reprints of the Folio (F2, F3 and F4); these are indicated. Most of them were first made by editors during the eighteenth century. Emendations suggested by modern editors are gratefully acknowledged. In the following instances the emendation is due to the present editor: I.6.42, II.1.236, III.1.187, III.2.21 and IV.7.55.

COLLATIONS

l

I.1

26 FIRST CITIZEN] *All.*
33 SECOND CITIZEN] *All.*
55 (*and for the rest of the scene*) FIRST CITIZEN] *2 Cit.*
90 stale't] scale't
108 tauntingly] (F4; F2, *spelt* tantingly); taintingly
170 geese. You are no] Geese you are: No
212 Shouting] Shooting
214–15 Brutus, one | Sicinius Velutus, and – I] *Brutus,* | *Sicinius Velutus,* and I
230 together.] together?

I.3

44 sword, contemning. Tell] sword. *Contenning,* tell

I.4

42 trenches. Follow's!] Trenches followes.
56 lost] left
59 Cato's] *Calues*

I.5

3 *Trumpeter*] *Trumpet.*

I.6

42 truth – but for our gentlemen.] truth: but for our Gentlemen,
53 Antiates] Antients
76 O'me alone, make you a sword of me.] Oh me alone, make you a sword of me:
84 I] foure

I.9

49 shout] (F4); shoot
64, 66 Caius Martius] *Marcus Caius*

II.1

53–4 I cannot say] I can say
60 bisson] beesome
117–18 Brings 'a victory in his pocket, the] brings a Victorie in his Pocket? the

119 brows, Menenius. He] Browes: *Menenius*, hee

157–8 Caius Martius; these | In honour follows 'Coriolanus']
     Martius Caius: | These in honor followes *Martius Caius*
     Coriolanus

173 CORIOLANUS] *Com.*

196 *Brutus and Sicinius come forward*] *Enter Brutus and*
     Scicinius

226 napless] Naples

236 authority's for an end.] Authorities, for an end.

243 the war] their Warre

II.2

34 *by themselves*] *by themselues: Coriolanus stands.*

44 Caius Martius] *Martius Caius*

89 chin] (F3); Shinne

II.3

36 it. I say, if] it, I say. If

65 Ay, but not mine] I, but mine

113 hire] (F2); higher

114 wolvish toge] Wooluish tongue

242–3 And Censorinus, nobly namèd so, | Twice being by
     the people chosen censor] And Nobly nam'd, so twice
     being Censor

III.1

91 O good but] O God! but

92 reckless] wreaklesse

143 Where one] Whereon

185–6 Tribunes! ... Citizens!] *assigned to 2. Sen.*

187 MENENIUS] *All.*

229 your house] our house

230 CORIOLANUS] *Com.*

236 COMINIUS] (F2); *Corio.*

237–41 CORIOLANUS I would ... Capitol. MENENIUS Be
     gone ... another.] *Mene.* I would ... another.

286 our] one

304 SICINIUS] *Menen.*

322–3 bring him | Where] bring him in peace, | Where

III.2

21 crossings] things

40–41 noble. | But when extremities speak, I have heard you

say,] Noble, | But when extremities speake. I haue heard
you say,
78   With] Which
80   handling, say] handling: or say
115   lulls] lull

III.3
36   Throng] Through
55   accents] Actions
110   for] from

IV.1
37   VIRGILIA] *Corio.*

IV.2
17   this, fool:] this Foole,

IV.3
9   approved] appear'd

IV.4
23   hate] haue

IV.5
134   o'erbear't] o're-beate
192–3   him, directly to say the truth on't. Before Corioles he]
        him directly, to say the Troth on't before *Corioles,* he

IV.7
49   virtues] Vertue
55   fuller] fouler

V.1
14   i'th'] a'th'

V.2
17   varnishèd] (*J. Dover Wilson*); verified
61–3   Coriolanus. Guess but my . . . him. If . . . spectatorship
        and] Coriolanus, guesse but my . . . him: if . . .
        spectatorship, and

V.3
0   *Aufidius with others. They sit*] *Auffidius.*
15–17   accept, to grace him only | That thought he could do
        more. A very little | I have yielded to] accept, to grace
        him onely, | That thought he could do more: A very
        little | I haue yeelded too
42   (*Rising and going to her*)] *not in* F
50   *He kneels*] *Kneeles*
52   *He rises*] *not in* F

56 *She kneels*] not in F
57 *He raises her*] not in F
63 holp] hope
93 *(He sits)*] not in F
131 *He rises*] not in F
152 charge] change
171 *The four kneel*] not in F
177 *They rise*] not in F

v.6

57–8 second. When he lies along, | After your way his]
second, when he lies along | After your way. His
116 Fluttered] (F3); Flatter'd
131 *The Conspirators draw their swords, and kill*] Draw both
the Conspirators, and kils

2

Below are listed instances where the present edition substantially
preserves readings of the first Folio that have often, with
some measure of plausibility, been emended, or introduces an
emendation that is different from the one normally accepted.
Emendations frequently found in modern editions of the play are
given after the square bracket.

I.1

256 him; he] (F1: him, he); him! He

I.4

42 trenches. Follow's] (F1: Trenches followes); trenches
followed

I.5

4 hours] honours

I.6

42 truth – but for our gentlemen.] (F1: truth: but for our
Gentlemen,); truth. But for our gentlemen,
76 O'me alone, make you a sword of me.] (F1: Oh me
alone, make you a sword of me:); O me, alone! Make
you a sword of me?

I.9

40 beheld] upheld
46 An overture] A coverture

II.1

    178 begin at] begnaw the

    236 authority's for an end.] (F1: Authorities, for an end.);
        authorities. For an end,

    247 teach] touch

II.2

    106 Where it did mark, it took from face to foot.] (F1:
        Where it did marke, it tooke from face to foot:); Where
        it did mark, it took; from face to foot

III.1

    48 COMINIUS] CORIOLANUS

III.2

    21 crossings] (F1: things); thwartings; taxings (*C. J. Sisson*)

    32 heart] herd

IV.5

    196 boiled] broiled

    229 sprightly walking,] sprightly, waking,

IV.6

    2–4 tame – the ... hurry. Here do we make] tame. The ...
        hurry, here do make

    59 coming] come

IV.7

    55 fuller] (F1: fouler); falter

V.1

    14 i'th'] (F1: a'th'); o'th' (F4)

    16 wracked for] racked for; wrecked fair

V.2

    61–4 Coriolanus. Guess but my ... him. If ... suffering,
        behold] (F1: Coriolanus, guesse but my ... him: if ...
        suffering, behold); Coriolanus. Guess but by my ...
        him if ... suffering; behold

V.3

    15–17 accept, to grace him only | That thought he could do
        more. A very little | I have yielded to] (F1: accept, to
        grace him onely, | That thought he could do more: A
        very little | I haue yeelded too); accept; to grace him
        only | That thought he could do more, a very little |
        I have yielded to

    48 pray] prate

    179 his child] this child

The Language of the Play

The richness and vitality of Shakespeare's plays is due in no small measure to the fact that they were written at a time when the English language was developing at a rate never equalled before or since. In *Coriolanus* this trend is most obvious in the speech of Menenius, who coins words almost as he needs them, but it is also evident in such linguistic blunders as that of the Third Servingman at IV.5.215, when he speaks of *directitude* without having any idea of what he really means by this, to him, imposing term. One consequence of this rapid growth is that many of the words used by Shakespeare have now become obsolete or have disappeared entirely from modern English. (These, however, cause no difficulty to readers of the present day, since they will naturally look them up in the Commentary.) The real stumbling-block is the appearance in his writings of many other words which are still a familiar part of the English we speak, but which no longer mean to us what they meant to Shakespeare, or which had in his day an additional meaning to that which they have now. These can be extremely misleading, and it therefore seems desirable to give a list of some of the most common of them occurring in *Coriolanus*.

abuse deceive, mislead
affect desire, aim at
affection inclination, desire
attend await
but except
come off retire (military)
comfortable cheerful
determine terminate, end

discover reveal, show
discovery revelation
hardly with difficulty
owe own, possess
passing surpassingly, extremely
present immediate
presently immediately, at once
press a power raise an army

pretence intention, design   *still* always, constantly
sensible sensitive, feeling   *success* outcome, result

An additional difficulty in this particular play is an extensive use in it, as in *Antony and Cleopatra*, of shortened and colloquial forms. At first sight somewhat disconcerting to the modern reader, because of their unfamiliarity, these forms are soon accepted and, indeed, appreciated for their effect in helping to give the play that rapid and impetuous quality which is one of its most striking characteristics. The most important of them are the following:

'a he	*on't* of it
an't if it	*o'th'* of the
'has he has	*to's* to its
in's in his, in its	*to't* to it
i'th' in the	*to th'* to the
on's of his, of its	*y'are* ye are

Commentary

The Act and scene divisions are those of Peter Alexander's edition of the *Complete Works* (1951). F refers to the first Folio of Shakespeare's plays (1623). Quotations from North's Plutarch are from *Shakespeare's Plutarch*, edited by T. J. B. Spencer (1964). For colloquial forms, see The Language of the Play.

I.I

> In this scene, which not only provides the play with a bustling and arresting opening (a great advantage in a theatre where there were no lights to go down) but also establishes the central conflict out of which the rest of the action grows, Shakespeare skilfully combines two separate incidents in Plutarch's narrative into one. The first (*Shakespeare's Plutarch*, pp. 300–305) was a rebellion of the people against 'the sore oppression of usurers'. This was pacified by the diplomacy of Menenius and by the concession to the people of the right to choose five tribunes annually to defend them from 'violence and oppression'. The second uprising, which occurred shortly before the time when Coriolanus stood for the consulship, was the result of a famine in Rome (pp. 314–24). On both occasions the people expressed their dissatisfaction by refusing to do military service.

0 *mutinous*: Rebellious, riotous.

7 *Caius Martius*: The correct form of the hero's name in Latin is 'Caius Marcius'. 'Martius' is preferred in this edition, contrary to the practice of most editors, for

three reasons: it is consistently so given in F; it was the form Shakespeare found in North and in Holland's translation of Livy (see note to III.3.26–7); it indicates, and may even have influenced, Shakespeare's view of Coriolanus' character. He is a 'son of Mars'.

11 *verdict*: Unanimous decision.

15 *good*: Rich, substantial.

authority: The patricians, the ruling class.

17 *wholesome*: Good, fit to eat.

guess: Think, deduce.

18 *humanely*: Out of fellow-feeling.

18–21 *But they think ... them*: The general sense of this passage, which states the exact opposite of all that is conveyed by the word *humanely*, is: 'They prefer to keep us as we are, because the sight of our wretchedness makes them realize with pleasure precisely how well off they are.'

18 *dear*: Precious, valuable.

19 *object*: Spectacle.

inventory: Detailed list, set of meagre figures (like the citizens) representing large possessions.

20 *particularize*: Give details of.

sufferance: Distress, suffering.

22 *rakes*: 'As lean as a rake' is proverbial. Later in the scene Martius jeers at the citizens' addiction to proverbs.

26 *a very dog*: A merciless enemy.

35 *famously*: Gloriously, in a way that made him renowned.

to that end: With that purpose (the winning of personal fame) in mind.

soft-conscienced: Easy-going, with no real convictions.

37 *to be partly proud*: Partly to be proud.

38 *even to the altitude of his virtue*: The First Citizen means that Martius' pride is as excessive as his valour.

44 *Shouts within*: Shakespeare, characteristically, is thinking in terms of his stage. *within* means in the tiring-house, offstage.

46 *Capitol*: Citadel of Rome.

48 *Soft*: Stay, wait a moment.

49 *Worthy Menenius Agrippa*: It was Plutarch who supplied

Shakespeare with the groundwork for this character and suggested his affable manner with the citizens. He writes (*Shakespeare's Plutarch*, p. 303): 'The Senate . . . did send unto them certain of the pleasantest old men and the most acceptable to the people among them. Of those Menenius Agrippa was he who was sent for chief man . . .' As befits his rank, Menenius speaks blank verse, but his language is colloquial and friendly.

54 *bats*: Cudgels (the weapons of the London apprentices).

55 *FIRST CITIZEN*: F assigns this speech and the rest of the dialogue with Menenius to the Second Citizen. This must be wrong, since the Second Citizen is kindly disposed towards Menenius and Martius. It is the First Citizen who is the leader of the crowd and its mouth-piece.

61 *undo*: Ruin.

64 *For*: As for.

67 *on*: Continue on.

68 *curbs*: A curb is a chain attached to the part of a bridle known as the bit, and is used to check an unruly horse. Here it is employed figuratively to mean restraints or hindrances.

70 *your impediment*: The obstruction you create.

73 *transported*: Carried away.

74 *attends*: Awaits.

75 *helms*: Helmsmen, pilots.

81 *piercing*: Oppressive, severe.

90 *stale't*: Make it stale.

92 *fob off*: Dispose of, or get rid of, by a trick.
   disgrace: Misfortune, calamity.

96 *gulf*: Bottomless pit, whirlpool.

98 *Still*: Always, continually.

99 *where*: Whereas.
   instruments: Organs.

100 *devise*: Ponder, deliberate.

101 *participate*: Participating.

102 *affection*: Inclination, wish.

105–6 *a kind of smile,* | *Which ne'er came from the lungs*: A

supercilious smile, as distinct from a belly-laugh –
Menenius makes the belly very much a patrician.

108 *tauntingly*: F reads *taintingly*, which has been explained
as 'so as to put to shame', but *tauntingly* fits the manner
in which the belly eventually gives its answer.

110 *envied his receipt*: Envied it for what it received.
fitly: Justly (used ironically).

112–22 *Your belly's answer ... belly answer*: The reversal of
roles here, with the First Citizen taking up the allegory
and Menenius asking the questions, is a fine example
of Shakespeare's skill in breaking up a piece of narrative to give it dramatic life.

113–17 *The kingly crownèd head ... our fabric*: The analogy
between the state and the human body was one of the
great commonplaces of Shakespeare's time. The head,
as the seat of reason, was king of the little state of man;
and the heart, as the seat of understanding, was the
place of counsel and deliberation.

116 *muniments*: Supports.

118 *'Fore me*: Upon my word.

119 *cormorant*: Greedy, insatiable (frequently applied to
usurers in Shakespeare's day).

120 *sink*: Cesspool.

124 *you'st*: You'll (provincial).

128 *incorporate*: United in one body.

131 *shop*: Workshop.

134 *to the court, the heart, to th'seat o'th'brain*: To the court
or place of counsel (that is, the heart) and thence to
the throne itself (that is, the brain).

135 *cranks*: Winding passages.
offices: Inferior rooms.

136 *nerves*: Sinews, muscles.

143 *flour*: In F this word is *Flowre*. It is clearly intended to
carry the sense of 'fine essence' in addition to its literal
meaning.

148 *digest*: Understand, interpret (with a play on the normal
sense).

149 *weal o'th'common*: Welfare of the state.

157–8 *Thou rascal ... to win some vantage*: A *rascal* was a deer in poor condition (*worst in blood*), but the word could also be used of a dog, which fits this context better. Dr Johnson paraphrases thus: 'Thou that art a hound, or running dog of the lowest breed, lead'st the pack, when anything is to be gotten.'

161 *have bale*: Get the worst of it, be destroyed.

162 *Thanks*: This entry is a telling one. Dismissing compliments with a single word, Martius rounds on the citizens.

164 *scabs*: This word has two meanings, both of which are relevant: (1) scabs raised by scratching oneself; (2) scurvy rogues. Martius regards the people's grievances as superficial and self-inflicted.

167 *nor peace*: Neither peace.

168 *proud*: High-spirited (and, therefore, ungovernable).

171 *the coal of fire upon the ice*: This image is probably an allusion to the Great Frost of 1607–8, when the Thames was frozen over and 'pans of coals' were placed on the ice to enable people to warm their hands.

172–4 *Your virtue is . . . justice did it*: Your peculiar quality is to make a hero of the man whose offence subjects him to the law, and to curse the justice that punishes him.

182 *garland*: Pride, chief ornament.

186 *seeking*: Suit, petition.

191 *side*: Take sides with.

193 *feebling*: Depreciating, making weak.

195 *ruth*: Pity.

196 *quarry*: Heap of slaughtered deer.

197 *quartered*: Cut into four pieces (the punishment inflicted on traitors in Shakespeare's day).

198 *pick*: Pitch, hurl.

199 *almost*: Some editors emend to 'all most'.

201 *passing*: Extremely, exceedingly.

209 *To break the heart of generosity*: To give the final blow to the nobility – Latin *generosus*, of good birth.

212 *Shouting their emulation*: Rivalling each other in shouting.

215 *'Sdeath*: God's death (an oath).

218 *Win upon power*: Take advantage of the power already

won to win more.

218–19   *themes | For insurrection's arguing*: Subjects for rebels to discuss.

   223   *vent*: Get rid of.

   227   *to't*: That is, to the test.

   230   *together*: Against each other. F reads *together?*, but it is inconceivable that Cominius should not know of the long-standing rivalry between Martius and Aufidius.

   232   *party*: Side.

   237   *I am constant*: I keep my word.

   239   *Stand'st out*: Do you refuse to take part?

   245   *Right worthy you priority*: You fully deserve pride of place.

   249   *puts well forth*: Blossoms, makes a fine show.
         stay behind: F reads *Manent*.

   254   *moved*: Moved to anger, exasperated.
         spare to gird: Refrain from mocking at.

256–7   *The present wars ... so valiant*: The present wars eat him up with increased pride in his own valour. Many editors read 'The present wars devour him!' – that is, 'May the coming wars eat him up!'

   258   *Tickled*: Flattered, gratified.
         success: Fortune, result.

260–61   *to be commanded | Under*: To be under the command of.

261–2   *Fame, at the which he aims ... graced*: Fame is thought of at first as an object to be aimed at, hence the use of *which*; then as a goddess whose favours Martius has received, hence the use of *whom*.

   269   *Opinion*: (1) Honour, reputation; (2) public opinion.
         sticks: Is set.

   270   *demerits*: Deserts, merits.

   275   *dispatch*: Final arrangements.

   276   *More than his singularity*: With an even greater display of pride and self-importance than usual.

I.2

Plutarch does not mention Aufidius until after the banishment of Coriolanus (*Shakespeare's Plutarch*, p. 334) though he does say then that they 'had encountered many times together'. Shakespeare, with the dramatist's feeling

for conflict, introduces the rivalry between them into his
first scene and brings on Aufidius himself in the second.

2 *entered in*: Acquainted with, in the secret of.

4 *What*: What things, what plans.

6 *circumvention*: Knowledge to circumvent it.

9 *pressed a power*: Levied an army.

20 *pretences*: Plans, designs.

22 *appeared*: Became apparent.

 discovery: Disclosure.

24 *take in*: Capture.

 almost: Even.

27 *Let us alone*: Trust us.

28 *set down before's*: Besiege us.

 for the remove: To raise the siege.

32 *parcels*: Parts, portions.

1.3

This quiet domestic scene, which is of Shakespeare's
own invention, is in marked contrast to the public scenes
preceding it. Through it he conveys much about
Coriolanus' upbringing and his relationship with his
mother, which is vital for the further development of
the action. The *two low stools* would indicate to his
audience that the scene is set indoors.

2 *comfortable sort*: Cheerful manner.

10 *such a person*: Such a fine figure of a man.

 it: This fine figure.

11 *hang by th'wall*: Be a mere ornament.

 made it not stir: Did not give it movement.

13 *a cruel war*: The war against the Tarquins, in which
Coriolanus saved the life of a fellow-soldier and was
'crowned . . . with a garland of oaken boughs' for doing
so (*Shakespeare's Plutarch*, p. 298).

18 *But had he died*: Virgilia's first words indicate her nature;
she is concerned for life.

25 *surfeit*: Spend his time in self-indulgence.

34 *Come on, you cowards*: These words look forward to
the next scene and prepare the way for it. They also
show whence the hero derives his attitude towards his
fellow-soldiers.

34 *got*: Begotten.

37 *tasked*: Employed, set a task.

37–8 *to mow | Or all or lose his hire*: Either to mow the whole (of the field) or to lose his wages.

41 *trophy*: Monument.

Hecuba: Wife of Priam, king of Troy, and mother of Hector, the Trojan champion.

44 *At Grecian sword, contemning. Tell Valeria*: F reads: 'At Grecian sword. *Contemning*, tell *Valeria*' – the compositor having apparently taken *Contemning* to be the name of the gentlewoman.

46 *bless*: Guard, protect.

47–8 *He'll beat Aufidius' head below his knee . . . neck*: This proud boast is a piece of unconscious irony.

48 *Usher*: A male attendant on a lady.

52 *How do you both*: How are you both?

You are manifest housekeepers: You have clearly settled down to a day indoors.

53 *spot*: Embroidered pattern of small flowers, fruits and the like.

60 *confirmed*: Resolute, determined.

66 *mammocked*: Tore to shreds.

69 *crack*: Young rascal.

72 *will not out*: Will not go out.

83 *Penelope*: Wife of Ulysses, king of Ithaca. During the long absence of her husband after the siege of Troy she was pressed to marry one of her many suitors. She put them off by pretending that she could not marry until she had finished a shroud she was weaving. At night she undid the work she had done in the day, so that the shroud was never completed.

85 *moths*: Used with a double meaning: (1) the insects; (2) parasites, referring to the suitors of Penelope who lived in the house of Ulysses and consumed his goods.

86 *sensible*: Sensitive, capable of feeling.

100–101 *They nothing doubt prevailing and to make it brief wars*: The sense is: 'They are confident of victory and that the campaign will be a short one.'

106 *disease our better mirth*: Spoil our pleasure, which will
   be better without her.

110 *at a word*: Once for all.

I.4

   This scene opens the war with the Volsces which takes
   up the rest of the act. The scene divisions, introduced
   by the eighteenth-century editors, are misleading,
   because the action is continuous. The material is
   drawn largely from Plutarch (*Shakespeare's Plutarch*,
   pp. 306–14).

 4 *spoke*: Encountered.

 7 *Summon*: Call to a parley.

 9 *'larum*: Alarum, call to arms. Shakespeare uses these
   noises offstage to keep his audience aware of the other
   battle between Cominius and the Volsces, which is
   taking place at the same time as the assault on Corioles.

10 *Mars*: Roman god of war.

12 *fielded*: In the battlefield.

14–15 *No, nor a man that fears you less ... a little*: The sense
   is: 'No, and there is not a man here but fears you less
   than he does, if that is possible, since his fear of you
   is infinitesimal.' Shakespeare often intensifies the force
   of a negative by writing 'less' where modern usage
   would require 'more'. Cf. *Troilus and Cressida*, I.1.25–6:
   'Patience herself, what goddess e'er she be, | Doth
   lesser blench at sufferance than I do.'

17 *pound us up*: Shut us up as in a pound (an enclosure for
   stray cattle, a pinfold).

20 *List*: Hark, listen to.

21 *cloven*: Which is being cut to pieces.

22 *our instruction*: A lesson to us.
   the army of the Volsces: The Volscian troops within the
   city who make an unexpected sally.

25 *proof*: Sound, impenetrable.

29 *Alarum ... cursing*: This stage direction, while calling
   for a battle of some length, fails to indicate what Martius
   does before he re-enters *cursing*, since he is given no
   exit. He must drive some of the Volsces offstage on
   the one side, while the rest of them press back the

Romans on the other. It also leaves the activities and whereabouts of Titus Lartius obscure until he re-enters at 49.

30 *contagion of the south*: The warm south and south-west winds brought mists which were thought to breed the plague – cf. Caliban's curse on Prospero (*The Tempest*, I.2.323–4): 'A south-west blow on ye | And blister you all o'er!'

31 *You herd of – Boils*: F reads *you Heard of Byles*. The broken sentence, together with the heavy use of alliteration running through this speech, gives a powerful impression of Martius' boiling rage.

32–3 *abhorred | Farther than seen*: Loathed (on account of your stink) before you are even in sight.

36 *Pluto*: God of Hades, the classical hell.

38 *agued*: Shivering.
Mend: Do better.
home: Into the midst of the enemy.

42 *Follow's*: Follow us! F reads *As they vs to our Trenches followes*. This makes no sense, and many editors emend to 'followed'. It has also been suggested that *followes* is a stage direction that has crept into the text. *Follow's* is, however, a good colloquialism and carries on the sense and idiom of *Look to't. Come on!* at 40.
Another alarum . . . shut in: F reads *Another Alarum, and Martius followes them to gates, and is shut in*. This is a general account anticipating what is about to happen in the next seven lines, rather than a precise direction, but it would have its value for an actor about to be involved in an extended bout of hand-to-hand fighting. A more explicit stage direction follows at 45.

43 *seconds*: Supporters.

49 *To th'pot*: To the stew-pot, referring to the way in which meat is cut up before being placed in it. The soldiers' slang is a sardonic comment on Martius' stirring call to action.

54 *answer*: Cope with, face.

55 *sensibly*: With his sensitive body.
senseless: Insensitive.

56 *stand'st*: Thou standest.

  lost: F reads *left*, but the comparison that follows between Martius and a carbuncle (a red precious stone) demands *lost*.

59 *Cato's*: F reads *Calues*, an obvious mistake since Shakespeare is following North, who writes: 'For he was even such another as Cato would have a soldier and a captain to be' (*Shakespeare's Plutarch*, pp. 306–7). The Cato referred to is Cato the Censor, 234–149 BC, who was born 250 years after Coriolanus' death.

64 *fetch him off*: Rescue him.

  make remain alike: Stay with him, share his fate.

I.5

3 *murrain*: Plague (literally, a disease of cattle).

4 *movers*: Active men (ironical).

5 *drachma*: Greek coin of small value, worthless when cracked.

6 *Irons of a doit*: Weapons worth a farthing.

  hangmen: The Elizabethan hangman was allowed to keep the clothes of his victims as a perquisite.

12 *make good*: Hold, secure.

18 *physical*: Good for my health (blood-letting being the treatment in Shakespeare's day for all the ills that flesh is heir to).

21 *charms*: Magic spells.

23 *Prosperity*: Success.

23–4 *Thy friend no less | Than those*: May she be no less a friend to thee than to those.

I.6

1 *Breathe you*: Take a rest, catch your breath.

  are come off: Have got clear.

3 *retire*: Retreat.

4 *struck*: Been striking blows.

5 *By interims and conveying gusts*: At intervals and by means of gusts of wind carrying the noise.

6 *The Roman gods*: The sense is vocative.

7 *successes*: Fortunes.

10 *issued*: Sallied forth.

16 *briefly*: A short time ago.

17 *confound*: Waste.

25 *tabor*: Small drum.

29 *clip*: Embrace.

32 *to bedward*: Toward bed, showing us the way to bed.

36 *Ransoming him or pitying*: Releasing a man for ransom or remitting it out of pity.

42 *He did inform the truth – but for our gentlemen*: He told the truth – except in so far as our gentlemen were concerned. In F the line runs: *He did informe the truth: but for our Gentlemen,* a punctuation that has led many editors to take *our gentlemen* as a sarcastic allusion to *The common file.* It seems doubtful that Martius would, even in scorn, describe soldiers who had run away as *gentlemen.* What happens is that with his customary respect for truth he comes to the support of the Messenger, and then recollects that he was seconded in his counter-attack by 'a few men' (*Shakespeare's Plutarch*, p. 306). Furthermore, it is most unlikely that he would not make an exception for Titus Lartius at least.

44–5 *budge | From*: Flinch from, give way before.

53 *vaward*: Vanguard.

   Antiates: Men of Antium (the chief city of the Volsces and the home of Aufidius). The word is three-syllabled, as though written *Antiats*, which is the form it actually takes in F at I.6.59.

55 *heart of hope*: The man on whom all their hopes depend.

60 *delay the present*: Make any delay now.

61 *advanced*: Raised aloft.

62 *prove*: Try the fortunes of.

69–70 *fear | Lesser*: Fear less for.

76 *O'me alone, make you a sword of me*: This is one of the most difficult passages in the play. F reads: *Oh me alone, make you a sword of me:* – words which can be interpreted as expressive of surprise, protest or delight, and punctuated accordingly. The present editor's view is that Martius is enraptured to receive such a response – the rest of this speech is unusually courteous – and offers himself to the army as a sword to be made use

of against the enemy.

77 *outward*: Insincere, superficial.

78 *But is*: That is not.

83 *As cause will be obeyed*: As circumstances require.

84 *I shall*: F reads *foure shall*, but it is difficult to imagine
    Martius leaving the task of selection to four nameless
    men, especially when he has just said (81) that he intends
    to do it himself. Dover Wilson suggests that the capital
    'I' in Shakespeare's handwriting might have been
    mistaken for the numeral '4'.

    draw out: Pick.

    command: Troop, body of men.

86 *ostentation*: Demonstration of enthusiasm.

1.7

The stage direction with which the scene opens is in
effect a summary of what follows. It may well represent part of the author's plot or scenario.

1 *ports*: Gates.

3 *centuries*: Companies of the Roman army, each con-
   sisting originally of one hundred men.

7 *guider*: Guide.

1.8

The duel between Martius and Aufidius, to which
this scene is devoted, is a Shakespearian addition to
Plutarch's narrative.

0 *at several doors*: At different doors, from opposite sides
   of the stage.

4 *fame and envy*: Hated fame.

7 *Holloa*: Pursue with shouts.

12 *of your bragged progeny*: Belonging to the ancestors you
    boast of. Aeneas, the legendary founder of the Roman
    state, was, like Hector the scourge of the Greeks, a
    Trojan.

14 *Officious*: Meddling, giving unwanted assistance.

15 *In your condemnèd seconds*: By seconding me in such a
    damned cowardly fashion.

1.9

0 *retreat*: The trumpet call to bring back troops from the
   pursuit of the enemy.

2   *Thou't*: Thou wouldst.

4   *attend*: Listen.

    shrug: Shrug their shoulders in disbelief.

5   *admire*: Marvel.

6   *gladly quaked*: Pleasurably agitated.

    dull: Spiritless, stupid.

7   *fusty*: Mouldy-smelling.

10 *of*: In the form of. Cominius means that the battle Martius has just taken part in was a mere snack in comparison with the large dinner (of fighting) that he had already eaten in Corioles.

12 *caparison*: Trappings (of a horse).

14 *charter*: Privilege, right.

18 *effected his good will*: Carried out his intentions.

19 *overta'en*: Surpassed (implying that Martius himself has not accomplished all that he set out to do).

22 *traducement*: Slander, calumny.

24 *to the spire and top of praises vouched*: Proclaimed in the highest possible terms of praise.

25 *but modest*: Only moderate praise.

26 *sign*: Token.

29 *not*: Not hear themselves remembered.

30 *'gainst*: When exposed to.

31 *tent themselves with death*: Cure themselves by causing your death. A *tent* was a roll of bandage used for probing wounds and for keeping them open in order to prevent their festering.

32 *good and good store*: Good in quality and plenty of them.

35–6 *at | Your only choice*: According to your own personal wishes, exactly as you choose.

44 *Made all of false-faced soothing*: Given over entirely to hypocritical flattery.

44–6 *When steel grows ... overture for th'wars*: This is a difficult and much disputed passage. Assuming that *overture*, which frequently means an 'opening' in Elizabethan English, is here used for the man who makes the opening, the present editor interprets it thus: 'When arms and armour grow as soft as the court-parasite's silken clothes, let the parasite be made the spear-head of the attack.' Shakespeare probably had in mind two passages from North which he had just been using. In the first, Martius, in Corioles, finding himself surrounded by the enemy, 'made a lane through the midst of them'. In the second, leading his men against the Antiates, 'he made such a lane through them and opened a passage into the battle of the enemies' (*Shakespeare's Plutarch*, pp. 308 and 310). Many editors emend *overture* to 'coverture', giving the sense 'let a covering of silk [instead of armour] be made for the parasite when he goes to war'.

47 *For that*: Because.

48 *foiled*: Defeated.

debile: Feeble.

without note: Unnoticed.

49 *shout me forth*: Cry me up.

51 *little*: Slight achievement.

51–2 *dieted | In*: Fattened on.

52 *sauced*: Spiced, seasoned.

54 *give*: Report.

56 *means his proper harm*: Intends to commit suicide.

61 *trim belonging*: Either 'fine trappings' or 'the equipment that goes with him', since each of these words can be taken as a noun or an adjective.

65 *addition*: Title, mark of distinction.

68 *fair*: Clean.

71 *undercrest*: Support as if it were my crest, live up to.

72 *To th'fairness of my power*: As creditably as I can.

76 *best*: Leading citizens.

articulate: Negotiate, come to terms.

81 *lay*: Lodged.

82 *used*: Treated. In North the man concerned is 'an honest wealthy man, and now a prisoner, who, living before in great wealth in his own country, liveth now a poor prisoner in the hands of his enemies' (*Shakespeare's Plutarch*, p. 312). By making the man poor, Shakespeare increases an audience's sense of Martius' magnanimity and fundamental decency.

I.10

This little scene has a double function within the structure of the play as a whole. First, it has the effect of increasing the tension when, in IV.4, Coriolanus decides to enter Aufidius' house. Secondly, in showing Aufidius abandoning the ideals of honour and chivalrous emulation for the ways of treachery, it prepares for the denouement.

2 *on good condition*: On favourable terms.

5 *be that I am*: Be one who refuses to accept defeat.

6 *good condition*: Sound state, well-being. The wordplay is an expression of Aufidius's bitterness.

7 *part that is at mercy*: Defeated side.

14 *in an equal force*: On fair terms.

15 *potch*: Thrust, make a stab (a vulgar word for an action Aufidius recognizes as mean).

18 *stain*: Disgrace.

19 *Shall fly out of itself*: (It) shall change its nature.

20 *naked*: Defenceless, without his sword.

22 *Embarquements*: Embargoes, restraints.

23 *rotten*: Corrupt with age, worn out.

25 *upon my brother's guard*: With my brother posted to protect him.

26 *the hospitable canon*: The law of hospitality.

32–3 *that to the pace of it | I may spur on my journey*: So that I may not be left behind by the speed of events.

II.1

Serving as a link between the war with the Volsces, which is now over, and the struggle for power within Rome itself, which is about to begin, this scene is almost entirely of Shakespeare's own invention. In it he draws extensively on his knowledge and observation of London life. The houses and buildings described are wholly English, the crowd is a London crowd, and the Tribunes are depicted as self-important City magistrates. The baiting of them by Menenius is a piece of satirical comedy, contrasting strongly with the scenes of action which precede and follow it. It also reminds an audience of the class conflict with which the play began, and prepares them for its renewal.

1 *augurer*: Soothsayer, member of the Roman priesthood who studied omens.

15 *enormity*: Irregularity of conduct, vice.

19 *topping*: Surpassing.

21 *censured*: Judged, thought of.

22 *right-hand file*: Patricians (the right-hand file being the place of honour in the army in Shakespeare's day).

27–8 *a very little thief of occasion will rob you of a great deal of patience*: The slightest pretext will make you extremely impatient.

34–5 *wondrous single*: Extraordinarily feeble.

36–8 *turn your eyes . . . selves*: See yourselves as others see you.

43 *known well enough*: Pretty notorious.

45 *hot wine*: Wine made into a hot drink with the addition of sugar, spices, and so on, generally known as mulled wine (a popular drink in Elizabethan England).

46 *Tiber*: The river on which Rome stands, here used for water generally.

46–7 *something imperfect in favouring the first complaint*: Somewhat at fault for deciding cases too quickly in favour of the plaintiff, without waiting to hear the other side. Menenius is making a favourable contrast between his own expeditious handling of cases and the dilatory methods of the Tribunes which he describes later.

47 *tinder-like*: Inflammable, quick-tempered.

48 *motion*: Cause, provocation.

48–9 *converses more . . . forehead of the morning*: Is more used to staying up late at night than to rising early in the morning.

50 *spend*: Get rid of.

51 *wealsmen*: Men devoted to the public good, statesmen.

52 *Lycurguses*: Wise legislators, Lycurgus being the legendary lawgiver of Sparta.

52–3 *if the drink you give me . . . crooked face at it*: If I do not like what you say, I show my displeasure in my looks.

55–6 *the ass in compound with the major part of your syllables*:
      A large element of the fool in most of what you say.

58 *tell*: Say, relate.

58–9 *the map of my microcosm*: My face, since the face indi-
      cates by its expression what is going on within the little
      world of man, just as a globe shows the main features
      of the big world.

60 *bisson conspectuities*: Blear-eyed insights; *conspectuities*
   is a nonce-word. Menenius is, to use a modern phrase,
   blinding the Tribunes with science. F reads *beesome
   Conspectuities*.

61 *character*: Character-sketch. 'Characters' – in the sense
   of brief witty delineations of human types – were about
   to become something of a literary craze at the time
   when *Coriolanus* was written. The first book of
   Characters in English, Joseph Hall's *Characters of Vices
   and Virtues*, appeared in 1608.

64 *caps*: Doffing of caps as a mark of respect.
   legs: Genuflections, bows.

65 *wholesome*: Which might be spent more profitably.

66 *cause*: Case in a court of law.
   orange-wife: Woman who sells oranges.
   faucet-seller: One who sells taps for barrels.

67 *rejourn*: Put off, postpone.

68 *audience*: Hearing.

69 *party and party*: One litigant and another.

70 *mummers*: Actors in a dumb show who conveyed their
   meaning by their facial expressions.

70–71 *set up the bloody flag against*: Declare war on.

72 *bleeding*: Unhealed, undecided.

76–8 *a perfecter giber ... bencher in the Capitol*: More
      successful as a wit at a dinner party than as a statesman
      dealing with national affairs.

80 *subjects*: In two senses: (1) creatures; (2) topics.

83 *botcher*: Mender of old clothes.

86 *Deucalion*: The counterpart in classical mythology of
   Noah: survivor, along with his wife Pyrrha, of the
   Flood.

88 *Good-e'en*: A form of 'good even', this salutation means

'good evening', but it was used at any time after noon. Cf. *Romeo and Juliet*, II.4.107–10.

89 *conversation*: Society.

being: You being, since you are. The use of a participle with a pronoun implied in a pronominal adjective (here 'your' in *your conversation*) is fairly common in Shakespeare.

92 *the moon*: Diana, the goddess of chastity. Menenius's speech becomes courtly and complimentary when he addresses members of his own class, and especially ladies.

98–9 *prosperous approbation*: Confirmed success.

109 *gives me an estate of*: Endows me with.

110 *make a lip at*: Mock.

111 *Galen*: Famous Greek physician (AD 129–99), still regarded as an authority in Shakespeare's day.

112 *empiricutic*: Quackish. This word, which appears in F as *Emperickqutique*, is not to be found elsewhere and seems to be a coinage of Menenius'. There would seem to be some proverbial basis for it, however, because George Herbert writes in his *Jacula Prudentum* (No. 1044): 'The words ending in *Ique* do mock the Physician (as Hectique, Paralitique, Apoplectique, Lethargique).'

112 *to this preservative*: Compared with this means of preserving life and health.

117 *Brings 'a*: Provided he brings.

119 *On's brows*: Volumnia means that the sign of victory, the oaken garland, is on Coriolanus' head, not in his pocket.

121 *disciplined*: Thrashed.

125 *An*: If.

126 *fidiused*: Treated as Aufidius was.

127 *possessed*: Informed.

130 *name*: Honour, credit.

134 *purchasing*: Achieving.

142–3 *stand for his place*: Be a candidate for the consulship. Volumnia has her son's career already planned for him, and sees his scars, which she reckons up so eagerly, as so many qualifications for office.

143 *Tarquin*: Tarquinius Superbus, the last king of Rome,

who was expelled from the city and, when he attempted
to win back his throne, was finally defeated at the battle
of Lake Regillus about 496 BC.

153 *nervy*: Muscular, sinewy.

154 *advanced*: Raised, uplifted.

declines: Falls.

sennet: Notes on a trumpet or cornet to herald a stage
procession.

Titus Lartius: Though he says nothing, Titus Lartius
must be present in this scene, since Menenius refers at
179 to *three* (Cominius, Titus and Coriolanus). Yet he
has no right to be so, because he was left in Corioles
at I.9.74–5 and he is still there at II.2.36 when the
Senate decides to *send for* him. It looks, therefore, as
though II.1, or at least this part of it, was composed at
a different time from Act I and II.2.

157 *With fame*: Along with fame.

to: In addition to.

157–8 *these | In honour follows 'Coriolanus'*: The name
Coriolanus follows these names as a mark of honour.
North, who explains Roman nomenclature in detail,
writes: 'The third [name] was some addition given,
either for some act or notable service ... or else for
some special virtue they had' (*Shakespeare's Plutarch*,
p. 313).

164 *prosperity*: Success.

He kneels: This stage direction, which appears as *Kneeles*
in F and is probably Shakespeare's own, emphasizes
the right and proper relationship between mother and
son. It was normal in Elizabethan England for a son to
kneel when receiving his mother's blessing. The whole
ceremony suffers a violent and shocking reversal in V.3
where Volumnia kneels to her son.

166 *deed-achieving honour*: Honour won by deeds.

168 *gracious*: Lovely.

177 *light and heavy*: Joyful and sad.

182 *grafted to your relish*: Implanted with a liking for you.

190 *change of honours*: New honours or titles.

191 *inherited*: Realized, taken possession of. Volumnia sees

her son as the heir who has come into the estate and
titles that she had long hoped would be his.

196 *sway with*: Rule over. Coriolanus' answer to Volumnia
marks the beginning of the rift between the mother,
who has her son's future all mapped out for him, and
the son himself, who wishes to go his own way.

197 *sights*: Eyes.

199 *rapture*: Fit.

200 *chats*: Gossips about.

kitchen malkin: Slatternly kitchenmaid.

201 *lockram*: Piece of hempen fabric.

reechy: Dirty, grimy.

202 *bulks*: Wooden projections in front of Elizabethan
shops, used for displaying wares.

203 *leads*: Lead-covered roofs.

ridges horsed: Ridges (on the roofs of houses) covered
with spectators sitting astride them as though on horse-
back.

204 *variable complexions*: All sorts of people.

205 *Seld-shown flamens*: Priests rarely seen in public.

207 *vulgar station*: Place in the crowd.

209 *nicely gawded*: Skilfully made-up.

spoil: Ravages.

210 *Phoebus*: The sun. In Shakespeare's day sunburn was
not fashionable.

pother: Fuss, turmoil.

213 *posture*: Bearing.

216 *temperately transport*: Carry in a balanced, self-
controlled manner.

217 *From where he should begin and end*: From the right
beginning to the proper conclusion.

218–20 *Doubt not . . . forget*: Be sure that the commoners, whom
we represent, will, because of their long-standing
hostility to him, forget.

223 *As*: As that.

226 *napless*: Threadbare.

229 *miss*: Go without.

230 *carry*: Win, obtain.

but: Except.

234 *as our good wills*: As our interest demands.

236 *To him, or our authority's for an end*: In F this line runs:
To him, or our Authorities, for an end. Most editors emend
as follows: 'To him or our authorities. For an end,'
taking 'For an end' to mean 'To this end'. As compared
with this change of punctuation and sense, the reading
adopted involves a minimum of interference with the
text and makes good sense, *for* meaning 'on the way
to, destined for' as in 'we are for the dark' (*Antony and
Cleopatra*, V.2.194).

237 *suggest*: Insinuate to.

238 *still*: Always.

240 *Dispropertied*: Deprived of their essential nature, made
a farce of.

243 *provand*: Provender.

247 *teach*: Lecture (as Coriolanus did in I.1). Many editors
emend to 'touch': that is, touch to the quick, inflame.

247–8 *which time shall not want, | If he be put upon't*: Which
time will surely come, if he is provoked into doing
it.

249–50 *his fire | To kindle their dry stubble*: The spark setting
him alight that will then kindle those who are like dry
stubble. The language is very compact, but the main
idea is clear enough: both Coriolanus and the people
are extremely inflammable.

258 *Jove*: Jupiter (chief god of the Romans).

261–2 *carry with us ears ... hearts for the event*: See and hear
what passes, but keep our hearts fixed on our purpose.

II.2

This scene is built on a striking contrast between the
quiet opening, with its shrewd appraisals of Coriolanus'
character and of his attitude towards the people, and
the pomp and circumstance of the public ceremony that
follows.

5 *vengeance*: Frightfully.

7 *hath*: Often emended, unnecessarily, to 'have'. The use
of 'there is', 'there hath', etc., before a plural subject
is very common in Shakespeare.

13 *in*: Of.

14 *carelessness*: Indifference to public opinion.

16 *waved indifferently*: Would be wavering impartially.

19 *discover him their opposite*: Reveal him as their opponent.

20 *to seem to affect*: To give the impression of cultivating.

24 *degrees*: Steps.

26–7 *bonneted, without ... report*: Went cap-in-hand and, without doing anything else whatever to earn it, won immediate popularity.

34 *Lictors*: Attendants on the Roman magistrates. In F this stage direction ends with the words *Coriolanus stands*, but this must be wrong, since at 64 comes the explicit direction, supported by the dialogue, *Coriolanus rises, and offers to go away*.

35 *determined of*: Settled about.

38 *gratify*: Show our gratitude for.

39 *stood for*: Defended.

42 *well-found*: Fortunate.

45 *remember*: Acknowledge our debt to.

47–9 *make us think ... stretch it out*: Cause us to feel that our state has not the means to repay him fully rather than that we are unwilling to strain those means to the utmost.

51 *Your loving motion toward*: Your kind influence with.

52 *yield*: Assent to.
convented: Convened, met.

53 *treaty*: Proposal for an agreement.

56 *blessed*: Happy, glad.

58 *off*: Off the point, irrelevant.

63 *tie*: Oblige, constrain.

64 *offers*: Makes ready, prepares, tries.

69 *disbenched*: Unseated, caused to rise.

71 *soothed*: Flattered.

72 *as they weigh*: According to their worth.

75 *monstered*: Turned into marvels.

80–120 *I shall lack voice. The deeds of Coriolanus ... To ease his breast with panting*: Cominius' formal oration, or *laus*, of Coriolanus is one of the finest pieces of epic poetry in English. Its basic assumption, which is also that of epic, is contained in the sentence *It is held . . . haver* (81–3). This derives almost literally from Plutarch, who writes: 'Now in those days valiantness was honoured in Rome above all other virtues; which they call *virtus*, by the name of virtue itself, as including in that general name all other special virtues besides' (*Shakespeare's Plutarch*, p. 297).

85 *singly counterpoised*: Equalled by any other individual.

86 *made a head for*: Raised an army against.

87 *Beyond the mark*: Beyond the reach, beyond the powers.

89 *Amazonian chin*: Beardless chin, the Amazons being female warriors in classical mythology.

93 *on his knee*: On to his knee.

94 *act the woman in the scene*: Take the female part in the action, like the boy-actors of the Elizabethan stage.

95 *meed*: Reward.

96–7 *His pupil age | Man-entered thus*: Having started his apprenticeship in the style of one who had already completed it.

99 *lurched all swords of the garland*: Robbed all other soldiers of their glory, stole the show.

101 *speak him home*: Find words to do him justice.

105 *stem*: Prow.

stamp: Tool or die for stamping a mark or design on some softer material.

106–7 *took . . . foot. | He . . . blood*: F reads *tooke from face to foot: | He was a thing of Blood*, which most editors emend to 'took; from face to foot | He was a thing of blood,'. To the present editor the alteration seems unnecessary, since the passage has much in common with, and appears to have grown out of, the speech of the Bloody Captain in I.2 of *Macbeth*. The action described in the words *it took from face to foot* is the same as that of Macbeth when he fought Macdonwald 'Till he unseamed him from the nave to the chops' (22), except that the movement of the sword is downwards, not upwards.

took: Double meaning: (1) made an impression; (2) destroyed.

108 *timed with*: Regularly accompanied by.

109 *mortal*: Fatal (because it seemed death to enter it).

    which: The city rather than the gates.

110 *shunless destiny*: Probably the memento mori, the bony representation of death, which was such a common motif in the art of the Middle Ages and the Renaissance, especially from about the beginning of the fifteenth century to the middle of the seventeenth. In *Measure for Measure* Shakespeare writes (III.1.11–13): 'Merely thou art death's fool, | For him thou labour'st by thy flight to shun, | And yet runn'st toward him still.'

111 *reinforcement*: Fresh assault.

111–12 *struck | Corioles like a planet*: Blasted it. Planets were believed to be capable of exerting a malignant influence, and the planet involved here is indubitably Mars.

112–13 *Now all's his, | When*: No sooner is all his than.

114 *ready sense*: Hearing alert for the sound of battle.

    doubled: Twice as strong as before.

115 *Requickened*: Revived, reanimated.

    fatigate: Weary.

117 *reeking*: Steaming (like a stream of blood).

118 *spoil*: Massacre.

119 *stood*: Stood still, stopped.

120 *Worthy*: Heroic, deserving the highest praise.

121 *He cannot but with measure fit*: He cannot help but measure up to.

125 *misery*: Utter poverty.

127 *To spend the time to end it*: To spend his life in doing great actions, which to him is an end in itself.

135 *naked*: Exposed to view.

137 *pass*: Omit.

138 *voices*: Votes.

139 *Put them not to't*: Don't press them too hard.

142 *your form*: The form which custom prescribes to you.

142–3 *It is a part | That I shall blush in acting*: From this point onwards, to the end of Act III, the feeling that he is playing a shameful role, instead of being his own true self, is constantly with Coriolanus.

148 *stand upon't*: Make an issue of it, insist on it.

150 *purpose*: Proposal.

154 *require*: Make his request of them.

155 *what*: That what.

II.3

With this scene the great central section of the play, dealing with the clash between Coriolanus and the people, begins. The material on which it is based comes from North but Shakespeare alters it radically. In the source Coriolanus shows no reluctance about appearing in the market-place and exhibiting his wounds to the citizens. The reluctance is on their side; but after he had shown them his scars:

... there was not a man among the people but was ashamed of himself to refuse so valiant a man. And one of them said to another:
  'We must needs choose him Consul; there is no remedy.'

Nevertheless, he fails to secure the consulship, because on the day of the election:

... the love and good-will of the common people turned straight to an hate and envy toward him, fearing to put this oYce of sovereign authority into his hands, being a man some-what partial toward the nobility and of great credit and authority amongst the patricians, and as one they might doubt would take away altogether the liberty from the people. (*Shakespeare's Plutarch*, pp. 317–20)

There is no suggestion in Plutarch that the people have been manipulated by their Tribunes.

1 *Once*: Once for all, in a word.

13–14 *a little help will serve*: It will not need much effort on our part.

15 *stuck not*: Did not hesitate.

18 *abram*: Dark brown.

21–2 *their consent of one direct way*: Their agreement to go in one direction.

31 *rotten*: Unhealthy, corrupting (cf. I.4.30, and note).

33–4 *You may*: Go on, have your little joke.

36 *that's no matter, the greater part carries it*: That doesn't matter; the vote need not be unanimous, a majority is enough.

42 *by particulars*: To individuals, one by one.

47 *you are not right*: You are mistaken.

55 *think upon*: Think kindly of. This phrase – badly chosen by the normally diplomatic Menenius – was part of the Elizabethan beggar's patter and, as such, it rankles with Coriolanus.

56–7 *like the virtues | Which our divines lose by 'em*: As they forget the virtuous precepts which our priests throw away on them.

59 *Enter three of the Citizens*: There is some confusion here. The stage direction demands three Citizens and there are three parts, though the First Citizen has only one brief speech. On the other hand, Coriolanus describes them as *a brace* when they first appear, and as they go he remarks, *There's in all two worthy voices begged* (79–80), from which it would seem that only two Citizens were intended to be on the stage.

65 *Ay, but not mine*: F reads *I, but mine*. The Third Citizen's question in the next line makes it clear that the word 'not' has been omitted.

73 *The price is to ask it kindly*: This answer throws a great deal of light on Shakespeare's attitude to the citizens – one of them at least can give Coriolanus a lesson in manners.

79 *A match*: A bargain, agreed!

84 *stand*: Agree.

90–92 *You have been a scourge . . . common people*: The Fourth Citizen is the only one who makes any attempt to employ the tactics which, as Brutus reveals later in the scene, the Tribunes had instructed the people to use.

94 *common*: Cheap, promiscuous.

96 *condition*: Form of behaviour.

gentle: Aristocratic, gentleman-like.

99 *be off to them*: Raise my hat to them.

100 *bewitchment*: Enchanting manners.

popular man: Demagogue, one who curries popular favour.

107 *seal*: Confirm.

112–23 *Better it is to die ... will I do*: Coriolanus' sarcasms, which the citizens fail to understand, and his refusal to show his wounds, reveal how unbearable the whole business is becoming to him. Left alone for a few moments, he expresses his outraged feelings in a soliloquy which acquires added bite from the use of heroic couplets, the vehicle of satire.

114 *wolvish toge*: Toga which makes me look like a wolf (in sheep's clothing). F reads *Wooluish tongue*. It seems probable that the compositor, finding the unfamiliar word 'toge' in the manuscript, read it as 'tõge': that is, the abbreviated form of *tongue*.

115 *Hob and Dick*: This was the equivalent of 'Tom, Dick and Harry'. *Hob* was the rustic version of 'Robert'.

that does appear: Who make their appearance.

116 *needless vouches*: Formal confirmations that are unnecessary, since he has already been appointed by the Senate.

118 *antique time*: Old-fashioned institutions.

120 *to o'erpeer*: To be able to see over the top of it.

126 *Watched*: Done guard duty.

138 *limitation*: Appointed time.

139 *Endue*: Endow.

144 *upon your approbation*: To ratify your election.

172 *no further with you*: No further use for you.

173 *ignorant to see't*: Too simple-minded to see it.

176 *lessoned*: Instructed. It is by touches like this that Shakespeare extends the whole scope of the play. An audience is made aware that an intensive course of political indoctrination (of which they have seen nothing) has been given to the people by the Tribunes.

180 *body of the weal*: Commonwealth.

arriving: Reaching, attaining to.

183 *plebeii*: Plebeians.

186 *stood for*: Was a candidate for.

188 *Translate*: Change, transform.

190 *touched*: Tested the quality of.

193 *As cause had called you up*: When some crisis had aroused you.

195 *article*: Any condition or stipulation.

199 *free*: Frank, undisguised.

203 *heart*: Courage. The idea of the heart as the seat of counsel is also relevant.

  cry: Protest.

204 *rectorship*: Rule, governance.

204–7 *Have you ... tongues*: Have you before this occasion denied your votes to a man who asked for them in the right way, and do you now bestow them on one who mocked instead of asking?

211 *piece*: Add to, eke out.

217 *safer*: Sounder.

218 *Enforce*: Stress, make a point of.

219 *forget not*: Do not fail to mention.

220 *weed*: Garment, apparel.

223 *apprehension*: Perception, ability to understand the meaning of.

  portance: Behaviour.

227 *No impediment between*: Provided that no hitch occurred in the interim.

234 *read lectures*: Gave lessons.

237–44 *The noble house ... ancestor*: This passage is a paraphrase of the opening words of Plutarch's *Life* (*Shakespeare's Plutarch*, p. 296). There is a fine irony in the fact that the information about Coriolanus' noble origins is given by his enemies as part of their plot to ruin him.

242–4 *And Censorinus ... great ancestor*: F reads, *And Nobly nam'd, so twice being Censor, | Was his great Ancestor*. It is plain that something has been omitted, and editors have supplied the missing words from North. An alternative reconstruction is: 'And Censorinus that was so surnamed | And nobly naméd so ...'

243 *censor*: Important Roman magistrate, who maintained the official list of citizens and controlled public morals.

248 *Scaling*: Weighing.

250 *sudden*: Hasty.

251 *putting on*: Instigation.

252 *presently*: Immediately.

drawn your number: Collected a crowd.

255 *put in hazard*: Ventured.

256 *Than stay, past doubt, for greater*: Than wait for the chance of a bigger and surer one.

258–9 *observe and answer | The vantage of his anger*: Look out for and take full advantage of the opportunity his anger will provide.

III.1

This important scene, in which the political divisions in Rome come to a head, is based on North (*Shakespeare's Plutarch*, pp. 320–27). Shakespeare, however, enriches the original enormously by adding a fine ironical opening of his own. Knowing nothing of the activities of the Tribunes, Coriolanus and those about him take it for granted that he is now Consul and behave as though his term of office had already begun. At the moment when he is about to be confronted with civil disorder and to be tested as a statesman, the hero is wholly taken up with Aufidius and the Volsces.

1 *made new head*: Raised a fresh army.

3 *swifter composition*: Coming to terms the more quickly.

5 *road*: Inroads, incursions.

6 *worn*: Worn down, exhausted.

7 *ages*: Lifetimes.

9 *On safeguard*: Under safe-conduct.

16 *To hopeless restitution*: Beyond all hope of recovery.

so: Provided that, so that.

19–20 *I wish I had a cause ... To oppose his hatred fully*: A pregnant piece of unconscious irony.

23 *prank them*: Dress themselves up, flaunt themselves.

24 *Against all noble sufferance*: Beyond the endurance of the nobility.

29 *passed*: Been approved by.

36 *rule*: Control.

43 *repined*: Complained, expressed regret.

47 *sithence*: Since.

48 *You are like to do such business*: The present edition follows F in assigning this line to Cominius. Many editors give it to Coriolanus on the grounds that the abbreviated names used in F (*Cor.* and *Com.*) are easily confused and that Brutus' answer is directed to Coriolanus. It could, however, be equally intended for Coriolanus' party.

48–9 *Not unlike* | *Each way to better yours*: Likely to make a better job of providing for the welfare of the state than you are.

52 *that*: That arrogance.

55 *are out of*: Have strayed from.

58 *abused*: Misled, deceived.

   paltering: Trickery, equivocation.

60–61 *dishonoured rub*: Dishonourable obstacle.

   laid falsely: Treacherously placed.

   plain way: Level track. All three images in these lines are taken from the game of bowls.

65 *For*: As for.

66 *meiny*: Multitude, crowd.

67–8 *Regard me ... themselves*: Take note that I am no flatterer, so that in what I say they will really see themselves as they are.

70 *cockle*: Tares, darnel. Shakespeare found this word in North (*Shakespeare's Plutarch*, p. 322) and it suggested to him the parable of the wheat and the tares in the Bible (Matthew 13:24–30) which he uses at 71–2.

78 *till their decay*: Till death.

   measles: Punning on (1) the disease; (2) scabs, scurvy wretches.

79 *tetter*: Cover the skin with scabs. Cf. *Hamlet*, I.5.71–3: 'And a most instant tetter barked about, | Most lazar-like, with vile and loathsome crust | All my smooth body.'

85 *patient*: Calm.

89 *Triton*: Minor sea god who served as trumpeter to Neptune.

90 *from the canon*: Out of order, unconstitutional.

Cominius' point is that the Tribunes can only express
the will of the people; they have no right to lay down
the law. Coriolanus expands the same idea in his speech
that follows.

91 *O good*: F reads *O God!*, which gives a possible sense
but not the parallel that seems to be required by *grave
but reckless* at 92.

93 *Hydra*: Many-headed monster of Greek mythology.
When one of its heads was cut off, two more replaced
it.

95 *horn*: Wind instrument of that name.
o'th'monster's: Of the monster. Shakespeare sometimes
uses the double genitive.

96 *turn your current in a ditch*: Divert your stream (of
power) into a ditch.

97–8 *If he have power, | Then vail your ignorance*: If this man
really has power, let your negligence that gave it him
vail (or bow down) before him.

99 *learned*: Wise.

101 *have cushions by you*: Sit beside you in the Senate.

103–4 *When, both your voices blended . . . palates theirs*: When
the voices of the plebeians are blended with those of
the senators, the dominant flavour of the compound
will taste more of populace than of Senate.

106 *popular*: Plebeian.
bench: Senate, governing body.

109 *up*: In action, exerting power.

110 *confusion*: Chaos.

111–12 *take | The one by th'other*: Use one to destroy the other.

114 *as 'twas used*: As was customary.

120 *more worthier*: Cf. IV.7.8 and note.

121 *our recompense*: Our reward to them for services done.

122 *Being pressed*: When they were conscripted.

123 *navel*: Nerve centre.
touched: Threatened.

124 *thread*: Pass through one by one.

129 *All cause unborn*: Utterly without justification.
native: Origin.

130 *frank*: Generous.

131 *bosom multiplied*: Multiple stomach, the stomach of the many-headed monster.

134 *greater poll*: Larger number of heads, majority.

137 *cares*: Concern for the state.

142 *Seal*: Confirm.
    double worship: Divided sovereignty.

144 *Insult*: Behave insolently.
    without: Beyond.
    gentry: High birth.

145 *conclude*: Come to a decision.

146 *omit*: Neglect, disregard.

148 *slightness*: trifling, vacillation.

148–9 *Purpose so barred . . . purpose*: When sound policy is so obstructed, it follows that nothing effective is accomplished.

152 *doubt*: Fear.

154 *To jump a body with a dangerous physic*: To risk giving a dangerous treatment to a body.

156 *The multitudinous tongue*: Those who speak for the multitude, the Tribunes.

157 *The sweet*: The sweets of office.

159 *integrity*: Unity, wholeness.

162 *answer*: Answer for it.

163 *despite*: Scorn, contempt.

164 *bald*: Witless (as well as hairless).

166 *th'greater bench*: The Senate.

167 *When what's not meet, but what must be, was law*: When that which was not right, but which was nevertheless unavoidable, was made law.

169 *Let what is meet be said it must be meet*: Let it be said that the right thing to do shall be done.

172 *Aediles*: Subordinate officials who assisted the Tribunes.

174 *Attach*: Arrest.
    innovator: Revolutionary.

176 *answer*: Interrogation, trial.

177 *surety*: Go bail for.

180 *respect*: Thought, consideration.

185–8 *Tribunes! Patricians! Citizens! What ho! . . . out of breath*: F assigns 185–6 to 2 *Sen.*, 187 to *All.* and 188 to *Mene.*

It is clear, however, that 185–6 must belong to the mixed crowd of patricians and citizens. The allocation of 187 is doubtful. In this edition it is given to Menenius because he is the only person interested in peace and because his uttering it adds further point to his statement *I am out of breath.*

189 *speak*: Make a speech.

193 *at point to lose*: On the point of losing.

205 *distinctly ranges*: Is clearly arranged in a definite order. Shakespeare is probably thinking of the courses of brick or stone which go to make up a building. Cf. 'the wide arch | Of the ranged empire' (*Antony and Cleopatra*, I.1.33–4). But implicit in the image is the Elizabethan idea of the hierarchical state, which is in grave danger at this point.

211 *present*: Immediate.

212 *th'rock Tarpeian*: The Tarpeian rock was a cliff on the Capitoline hill in Rome from which traitors were thrown headlong down.

228 *beat in*: Driven off the stage.

230 *naught*: Lost, ruined.

230–31 *Stand fast! | We have as many friends as enemies*: F gives this speech to *Com*. The difficulty about this assignment is that at 244–9 Cominius is in favour of retreat, not of fighting. Coriolanus alone wants to make a stand.

234 *cause*: Disease, illness.

235 *tent*: Treat, cure.

236 *Come, sir, along with us*: F gives this line to *Corio.*, but he must be the character addressed, not the speaker.

237–41 *I would they were barbarians . . . another*: F assigns these lines to *Mene.*, which is clearly a mistake. The first three are in the idiom of Coriolanus, and, unless he speaks them, there is no point in Menenius's plea, *Put not your worthy rage into your tongue.*

241 *One time will owe another*: Another time will pay for this.

243 *Take up*: Take on, cope with.

244 *'tis odds beyond arithmetic*: Their numbers are infinitely greater than ours.

245–6 stands | *Against a falling fabric*: Resists (that is, tries to prop up) a falling building.

247 *tag*: Rabble.

248 *o'erbear*: Overwhelm.

255 *Neptune*: God of the sea in classical mythology. He was armed with a trident (or three-pronged spear).

256 *His heart's his mouth*: He speaks what he feels.

271 *sure on't*: For certain.

273–4 *Do not cry havoc ... warrant*: Do not call for indiscriminate slaughter in a case where your licence to hunt is strictly limited. The situation is now the reverse of that which existed in I.1, where Coriolanus thought of himself as the hunter and of the people as the quarry.

275 *holp*: Helped.

make this rescue: To 'make rescue' was a technical term in English law, meaning to use force in order to release a man from custody – a very serious offence.

284 *peremptory*: Determined, resolved.

286 *our danger*: F reads *one danger*, but the sense demands the contrast between 'our danger' and 'our death'.

290 *deservèd*: Deserving, meritorious.

302 *clean kam*: Quite wrong, utterly misleading.

304–6 *The service of the foot ... was*: F assigns these words to Menenius, but he has already made the point (294–5) that the diseased limb (Coriolanus) can be cured. Gangrene, however, is incurable and requires amputation of the affected limb, which is precisely what Menenius wishes to avoid. The lines are, in fact, the logical continuation of Sicinius' remark at 293, *He's a disease that must be cut away.*

311 *unscanned swiftness*: Unthinking haste.

312 *process*: Proper form of law.

320 *bolted*: Refined, carefully considered. To 'bolt' meal was to pass it through a sieve or cloth in order to separate the flour from the bran.

323–4 *answer by a lawful form,* | *In peace, to his utmost peril*: Stand his trial peacefully even though his life be at stake.

III.2

For Coriolanus this scene is critical, for he finds himself
faced with a conflict of loyalties. It owes practically
nothing to Plutarch, who merely says that at this junc-
ture the patricians were divided, their younger members
being intransigent while 'the most ancient Senators'
favoured some sort of compromise with the people
(*Shakespeare's Plutarch*, pp. 330–31).

  4 *precipitation*: Headlong drop, precipice.
  5 *Below the beam of sight*: Farther than the eye can reach.
  7 *I muse*: I wonder, am puzzled.
  9 *woollen vassals*: Slaves clad in coarse woollens.
9–10 *things created* | *To buy and sell with groats*: Born to be
      mere petty traders.
 12 *ordinance*: Rank.
 18 *Let go*: Enough! desist!
 21 *crossings*: F reads *things*, which is unmetrical and makes
      no sense. The emendation accepted by most editors,
      'thwartings', is not a word that is to be found elsewhere
      in Shakespeare's work as a noun. C. J. Sisson suggests
      'taxings' as graphically probable; *crossings* is good
      Shakespearian English – Glendower tells Hotspur,
      'Cousin, of many men | I do not bear these crossings'
      (*Henry IV, Part I*, III.1.35–6) – and it links up with the
      verb *to cross* at 23, just as *dispositions* links up with
      disposed at 22.
 23 *Ere they lacked power*: While they still had power, before
      they lost power.
 29 *apt*: Yielding, compliant.
 32 *stoop to th'heart*: Most editors emend *heart*, the reading
      of F, to 'herd'. But *stoop to th'heart*, meaning 'humble
      his very inmost self', makes good sense and anticipates
      Coriolanus' own words at 99–101: *Must I* | *With my
      base tongue give to my noble heart* | *A lie that it must
      bear?* F's reading points straight to the central issue of
      this scene: whether Coriolanus will preserve his essen-
      tial nobility of spirit intact or not.
 33 *fit*: Madness.
      physic: Medicine, medical treatment.

39–41 *You are too absolute ... say*: F reads: *You are too*
       absolute, | Though therein you can neuer be too Noble, |
       But when extremities speake. I haue heard you say. Many
       editors accept the F text as it stands, taking *But when*
       to mean 'except when'. This, however, is not
       Volumnia's point. What she is saying is that when it
       comes to the push, as she has heard Coriolanus himself
       admit, honour and policy can be reconciled.

39   *absolute*: Intransigent.

41   *extremities speak*: Absolute necessity demands.

42   *policy*: Stratagems.
       unsevered: Inseparable.

51   *stands in like request*: Is equally requisite.
       force: Urge.

52   *lies you on*: Is incumbent on you.

53   *instruction*: Prompting, manner expressive of your
       feelings.

55   *roted*: Learned by rote and spoken with no sincerity.

57   *Of no allowance*: Bearing no valid relationship.

59   *take in*: Capture.

64   *I am*: I represent, I speak for.

68   *inheritance*: Obtaining, winning.

69   *that want*: That failure to fawn.

71   *Not*: Not only.

72–86 *I prithee now, my son ... person*: This speech, which
       calls for a great deal of appropriate gesture, since
       Volumnia is showing her son how to behave as well as
       telling him what to say, must have been a great oppor-
       tunity for the boy-actor who first played the part. For
       the modern editor, however, it offers some puzzles,
       since it is one long involved sentence, liberally
       sprinkled with parentheses.

73   *this bonnet*: The cap on his head, which she either points
       to or possibly removes and handles.

74   *be with them*: Comply with their wish, get round them.

75   *bussing*: Kissing. At this point Volumnia demonstrates
       how to curtsey.

76   *Action*: Gesture.

77–80 *waving thy head ... to them*: F reads:

>   . . . wauing thy head,
> Which often thus correcting thy stout heart,
> Now humble as the ripest Mulberry,
> That will not hold the handling: or say to them,

The only way to make any sense of this as it stands is to regard *Which* as referring to *thy head* and to take *humble* as a verb in the imperative. Even so *or* is redundant, since Volumnia is not recommending alternative courses of action but one single procedure in which gesture is succeeded by speech. In this edition, therefore, *or* is omitted and *Which* emended to *With*.

77 *waving thy head*: Moving your head up and down in sign of repentance.

78 *thus*: Here Volumnia beats her breast or makes some such gesture of self-chastisement.

85 *theirs*: According to their wishes.

91 *in a fiery gulf*: Into a fiery pit or chasm.

94 *make strong party*: Gather a strong faction about you.

99 *unbarbed sconce*: Uncovered head (a sign of great respect).

102 *plot*: Piece of earth (that is, his body).

103 *mould*: Used in two senses: (1) form; (2) earth.

106 *discharge to th'life*: Play convincingly.

113 *choired with*: Sang in tune with.

114 *Small*: High-pitched.

115 *babies lulls*: Lulls dolls.

116 *Tent*: Lodge, encamp.
    take up: Fill up.

117 *glasses of my sight*: Eyeballs.

123 *inherent*: Fixed, irremovable.

127 *Thy dangerous stoutness*: The danger created by your obstinacy.

130 *owe*: Own, possess. Volumnia means that Coriolanus' pride is of his own making (she has had no part in it!) and he must take the responsibility for it.

132 *mountebank*: Win by trickery and the use of patter.

133 *Cog*: Swindle, wheedle. Coriolanus's use of words like

this is expressive of the self-disgust he feels at agreeing to act like a cheap-jack.

143 *by invention*: With trumped-up charges.

III.3

Based largely on North (*Shakespeare's Plutarch*, pp. 325–33), this scene is the climax of the struggle for political power in Rome. Shakespeare heightens the effect of it all in two ways: first, by giving greater prominence to the care and deliberation with which the Tribunes make their arrangements for the organization of the crowd; secondly, by making Coriolanus far more defiant and vociferous than he is in Plutarch, where he is taken by surprise and merely seeks to excuse himself.

3 *Enforce him*: Ply him hard.

envy: Malice, hatred.

9 *voices*: Cries in chorus, claque.

10 *by th'poll*: According to the list of voters. For a full discussion of the voting procedure at this point in the play, see Geoffrey Bullough's *Narrative and Dramatic Sources of Shakespeare*, vol. V, pp. 466–70. The voting was, in fact, by tribes (as is indicated at 11), a method that was bound to give the plebeians a majority; but Shakespeare was misled by North, who, following the French of Amyot, adds some detail which does not appear at all in Plutarch's Greek. After relating how the Tribunes insisted that the voting should be by tribes, North continues: 'for by this means the multitude of the poor needy people ... came to be of greater force, because their voices were numbered by the poll' (*Shakespeare's Plutarch*, pp. 331–2). The final clause in this sentence, for which there is no equivalent in Plutarch, seems to have given Shakespeare the impression that the method of voting was the same as that adopted at an English parliamentary election, where heads were counted, and where the volume of noise created in support of a candidate appears to have carried at least as much weight as the number of votes cast for him. See J. E. Neale, *The Elizabethan House of Commons* (1963), pp. 81–2.

12 *presently*: Immediately

18 *i'th'truth o'th'cause*: In the justice of the case. For an audience in 1608 or thereabouts these words would probably have had a distinctly Puritan ring.

26–7 *have his worth | Of contradiction*: Have his pennyworth of answering back (that is, give as good as he gets). The phrase may well be a memory of Philemon Holland's translation of *The Romane Historie of T. Livy* (1600). There Livy writes that the Commons complained that they had no hope of food and sustenance, 'unlesse the Tribunes be delivered and yeelded prisoners hand and foot bound to *C. Martius*, unlesse he might have his penniworths of the backe and shoulders of the commons of Rome' (*Sources of Shakespeare*, ed. Bullough, vol. V, p. 501).

29 *looks*: Promises, looks likely.

32 *piece*: Piece of money, coin.

33 *bear the knave by th'volume*: Put up with being called knave to any extent.

36 *shows*: Ceremonies.

40 *Audience*: Attention!

42 *this present*: The matter in hand. North writes (*Shakespeare's Plutarch*, p. 331): 'Martius ... said that thereupon he did willingly offer himself to the people, to be tried upon that accusation ... "conditionally", quoth he, "that you charge me with nothing else besides". They promised they would not.'

43 *determine*: End, be settled.

45 *Allow*: Acknowledge the authority of.

57 *envy you*: Show ill will towards you.

64 *seasoned*: Established, mature.
   wind: Insinuate (a charge that comes well from the Tribunes!).

68 *fold in*: Envelop, enfold.

69 *their traitor*: Traitor to them.
   injurious: Insultingly libellous.

81 *capital*: Punishable by death.

85 *You*: Coriolanus' contempt springs from the fact that 'service' to him means only military service.

97 *not*: Not only.

102 *precipitation*: Being thrown.

114 *estimate*: Reputation, honour.

120 *cry*: Pack.

121 *reek*: Foggy vapours.

124–33 *And here remain with your uncertainty ... without blows*:
Here, perhaps, are to be seen the first glimmerings, as
yet incompletely formulated, of the hero's decision to
turn against Rome.

129 *finds not till it feels*: Foresees nothing until it experi-
ences it.

130–31 *Making but reservation ... foes*: Leaving none in the city
except yourselves who are always your own worst
enemies.

132 *abated*: Humbled, abject.

135 *Exeunt Coriolanus ... Patricians*: F reads *Exeunt
Coriolanus, Cominius, with Cumalijs*, the compositor
having apparently mistaken '*cum aliis*', the Latin for
'with the others', for a personal name.

140 *vexation*: Torment of mind, mortification. In this
moment of triumph Sicinius' customary political
sagacity deserts him. The advice he gives to the people
is taken, and the manner in which Coriolanus is hooted
out of the city rankles deeply with him and helps to
inspire his determination to be revenged.

IV.I

Nowhere else in the play does Coriolanus appear to
better advantage than in this scene of leave-taking
which is developed out of a few lines in North, relating
how he took 'his leave of his mother and wife, finding
them weeping and shrieking out for sorrow, and ...
comforted and persuaded them to be content with his
chance' (*Shakespeare's Plutarch*, p. 333).

3–9 *You were used ... cunning*: The same sentiments,
expressed in much greater detail, are to be found in
Troilus and Cressida, I.3.17–54.

4 *extremities was*: Great crises were.

7–9 *fortune's blows ... A noble cunning*: The syntax is loose
– as it often is in colloquial speech – but the sense

comes through: 'when fortune strikes her hardest blows, one needs the training of a gentleman to take them as a gentleman should'.

11 *conned*: Studied, learned by heart.

13 *the red pestilence*: Probably typhus, which caused a red eruption of the skin.

15 *lacked*: Missed.

17 *Hercules*: The most popular hero of classical mythology, who carried out twelve stupendous 'labours' or tasks.

26 *fond*: Foolish.

27 *wot*: Know.

29 *Believe't not lightly*: Believe firmly, be assured of this.

32 *or exceed the common*: Either do something exceptional.

33 *cautelous*: Crafty, deceitful.
    practice: Stratagems.

36 *wild exposure*: Rash exposure of yourself.

37 *O the gods*: F assigns this exclamation to *Corio*. but the words are in the idiom of Virgilia (cf. 12).

41 *repeal*: Recall.

49 *of noble touch*: Of proved nobility (like gold that has passed the test of the touchstone).

55–7 *If I could shake off but one seven years ... foot*: A nice touch that is very much in character – Coriolanus's exile has made Menenius feel seven years older, just as his triumph made him feel seven years younger at II.1.109–11.

IV.2

In keeping with the symmetrical structure of the play, this scene, which brings the central part of the action to a close, is like a mirror image of II.1, the scene with which this part of the action began. At the end of II.1 the Tribunes, fearing Coriolanus, were laying plans for his overthrow; at the opening of this scene those plans have been successful. At the beginning of II.1 Menenius was baiting the Tribunes; at the end of this scene Volumnia is cursing them. Like II.1, it owes nothing to Plutarch.

16 *mankind*: Sicinius uses the word in the sense of 'mad' (cf. *The Winter's Tale*, II.3.67, where Leontes calls

Paulina 'A mankind witch') but Volumnia takes it in its normal sense of 'belonging to the human race'.

18 *foxship*: Low cunning.

24 *in Arabia*: That is, in the desert, where the Tribunes would not have a crowd of plebeians behind them.

31 *unknit*: Untied.

32 *The noble knot*: The close bond, of service on his part and gratitude on the part of Rome, which held them together.

34 *Cats*: Used as a term of contempt – Volumnia's feminine equivalent for the word *curs* that her son is so fond of using.

48 *told them home*: Rebuked them thoroughly, given them a piece of your mind.

52 *faint puling*: Feeble whimpering.

53 *Juno-like*: Resembling Juno (chief goddess of the Romans and wife of Jupiter).

IV.3

This little scene, involving two minor characters who do not appear elsewhere in the play, acts as a kind of prologue to the final movement of the action which is now about to begin. Set, as it is, somewhere between Rome and Antium, it indicates the direction in which events are moving and brings the wars between Rome and the Volsces back into the story. More important still, it introduces the idea of treachery which is to have a dominant function in this last phase of the play.

4–5 *my services are, as you are, against 'em*: I am in your pay. The treachery of this Roman anticipates the treachery of Coriolanus.

9 *favour*: Face, countenance.

approved: F reads *appear'd*. The objections to this reading, which some commentators explain as 'made manifest', are that it is not used elsewhere by Shakespeare as a transitive verb and that it does not give the required sense. Adrian is not too sure of Nicanor's face, but his half-recollection of it is *approved* (that is, confirmed or reinforced) by his memory of Nicanor's voice.

28 *them*: The Volsces.

33 *He cannot choose*: He is bound to.

39 *centurions*: Officers each of whom commanded a century
(see note to I.7.3).

39–40 *their charges*: The troops under their command.

40 *distinctly billeted*: Separately enrolled, on a list giving
each man's name.

in th'entertainment: Receiving pay.

43 *present*: Immediate.

IV.4

This scene and IV.5 are really one continuous scene
set at Aufidius' house in Antium. The material on which
they are based is derived, with some elaboration, from
North, whose account of the hero's entry into Antium
and of his meeting with Aufidius is already highly
dramatic (*Shakespeare's Plutarch*, pp. 334–8).

0 *Enter Coriolanus in mean apparel, disguised and muffled*:
This graphic stage direction gives an impression of
utter poverty and dereliction, whereas North is very
explicit that Coriolanus has only put on this *mean
apparel* as a disguise.

3 *'fore my wars*: In the face of my attacks.

12–26 *O world, thy slippery turns . . . service*: This soliloquy,
the most important of the very few that occur in
the play, is not a piece of reflection, still less of self-
examination. It is rather an attempt by Coriolanus to
find some sort of justification for embarking on a course
of action that he has decided to undertake without
properly understanding his own motives. He adopts a
pose of complete cynicism which is foreign both to his
nature and to his training.

12 *slippery turns*: Fickle changes.

17 *On a dissension of a doit*: Over some dispute about the
merest trifle.

19–20 *Whose passions and whose plots . . . take the one the other*:
Whose passions have kept them awake at night plot-
ting how to destroy each other.

22 *interjoin their issues*: Unite their designs.

23–4 *My birthplace hate I . . . enemy town*: The paradoxical quality of this statement emphasizes the 'unnaturalness' of the feeling it expresses.

25 *give me way*: Grant my request, fall in with my plans.

IV.5

2 *fellows*: Fellow-servants.

8–9 *go to the door*: Get out.

14 *companions*: Rogues, rascals.

17 *th'art*: Thou art (colloquial).

18 *brave*: Insolent.

25 *avoid*: Leave, quit.

32 *station*: Place to stand in.

34 *batten*: Grow fat.

40 *the canopy*: The sky; cf. *Hamlet*, II.2.299–300, 'This most excellent canopy, the air'.

44 *kites and crows*: These birds are scavengers, living on carrion.

46 *daws*: Proverbially foolish birds.

48–50 *meddle*: There is a quibble here. In the first case *meddle* has the normal meaning of 'interfere', but in the second it carries the sense of 'have illicit sexual relations'.

52 *trencher*: Plate or platter.

64 *tackle*: Rigging of a ship (referring to Coriolanus' dress).

65 *vessel*: Used in two senses: (1) ship; (2) the body as the vessel that contains the soul.

68–104 *My name . . . service*: This speech is very close to North's prose (see *Shakespeare's Plutarch*, p. 337), which it follows at times almost word for word.

71 *painful*: Arduous.

74 *memory*: Reminder, memorial.

85 *in mere spite*: Out of pure spite.

86 *To be full quit of*: To settle my account completely with, to get my own back on.

88 *of wreak*: Ready for revenge.

that wilt: So that you are eager to.

89–90 *stop those maims | Of shame*: Close up those shameful wounds.

90 *through*: Throughout.

94 *cankered*: Corrupted.

95 *under fiends*: Devils of hell.
96 *prove*: Try.
111 *grainèd ash*: Tough lance (*grainèd* means straight-grained, a straight-grained shaft being stronger than a cross-grained one).
112 *clip*: Embrace.
113 *The anvil of my sword*: These words refer to Coriolanus, whose armour the sword of Aufidius has so often struck like the blows of a hammer on an anvil. Cf. the First Player's lines in *Hamlet* (II.2.487–90):

> And never did the Cyclops' hammers fall
> On Mars's armour, forged for proof eterne,
> With less remorse than Pyrrhus' bleeding sword
> Now falls on Priam.

119 *dances*: Sets dancing.
    rapt: Enraptured.
123 *target*: Shield.
    brawn: Muscular arm.
124 *out*: Outright, thoroughly.
125 *several*: Separate, different.
134 *o'erbear't*: F reads *o're-beate*, but an object to the verb is clearly required, and *o'erbear* is a favourite word of Shakespeare's to describe the action of a flood (cf. III.1.248).
139 *absolute*: Incomparable.
141 *commission*: Command.
    set down: Decide, appoint.
153–4 *gave me*: Suggested to me.
156–7 *set up a top*: Start a top spinning.
166–7 *a greater soldier than he you wot one*: You know of one greater soldier than he.
169 *it's no matter for that*: Never mind about that.
192 *directly*: Without ambiguity.
193 *scotched*: Slashed.
194 *carbonado*: Rasher for grilling.
196 *boiled*: Many editors emend to 'broiled', because carbonadoes were broiled. But boiling seems just as

likely a method for cannibals to adopt in preparing
their victims for the table.

198 *he is so made on*: He is made so much of.

199 *at upper end*: In the place of honour.

201 *bald*: Bare-headed. Elizabethan men normally kept their
hats on when indoors.

202 *sanctifies himself with's hand*: Touches his hand as
though it were a sacred relic. The language is that of
Elizabethan love poetry and may be compared with
Romeo's words to Juliet, 'If I profane with my unwor-
thiest hand | This holy shrine' (*Romeo and Juliet*,
I.5.93–4).

204 *bottom*: Essential part, gist.

207 *sowl*: Pull, lug.

209 *polled*: Shorn, stripped bare.

215 *directitude*: As the First Servingman's question indicates, this word is a verbal blunder, a piece of nonsense
resulting from the speaker's desire to be impressive. He
does not know what it means himself, but obviously
intends to imply something like 'discredit'.

218 *in blood*: In good condition, full of hope and vigour.

219 *conies*: Rabbits.

221 *presently*: Immediately.

223 *parcel*: Part, portion.

229–30 *It's sprightly walking, audible, and full of vent*: War is
imagined here as a hunting-dog, walking along in a
sprightly manner, giving tongue, and eager to pick up
the scent of its quarry. Cf. 'the dogs of war', *Julius
Caesar*, III.1.273.

231 *mulled*: Stupefied, dull.

IV.6

The first part of this scene, up to the entrance of the
Aedile at 37, is of Shakespeare's own invention and
forms an ironical contrast with what is to follow. The
latter part of it is based loosely on Plutarch.

2 *His remedies are tame*: The remedies against Coriolanus
are tame. Sicinius is still thinking of Coriolanus as a
disease, just as he did in III.1, and is contrasting the
wild state of the people then, when they served as an

antidote to him, with their present peaceful condition.
F reads *His remedies are tame, the present peace*, which
many editors emend to 'His remedies are tame. The
present peace', taking *His remedies* as 'his means of
redress'.

10 *stood to't*: Made a stand, put up a fight.

33 *assistance*: Associates, partners.

34–5 *We should by this . . . found it so*: In this sentence *should*
carries the sense of 'should have', owing to the introduction of the conditional clause with *had*.

45 *inshelled*: Drawn in.

47 *what*: Why.

49 *break*: Break terms.

52 *reason with*: Talk with, question.

54 *information*: Source of information.

59 *coming*: Coming in. Many editors emend to 'come' in
order to avoid the jingling effect after *going* at the end
of 58.

61 *raising*: Incitement, starting of a rumour.

63 *seconded*: Supported.

68 *as spacious as between*: Big enough to include.

73 *atone*: Become reconciled.

74 *violent'st contrariety*: Opposite extremes.

79 *O'erborne their way*: Crushed everything in their way.

82 *holp*: Helped.

83 *city leads*: Lead-covered roofs of the city.

86 *in their cement*: Down to their foundations.

88 *auger's bore*: The small hole made with an auger.

96 *flies*: This reading is taken from F. It results in an
awkward repetition, and may well have been produced
by the compositor's eye catching the end of the previous
line – 'Butter-flies' – in the manuscript he was working
from. The present editor thinks, for two reasons,
that Shakespeare may well have written 'calves'.
First, because calves were closely associated with
butchers in his mind – see *Love's Labour's Lost*,
V.2.253–5, *Henry VI, Part II*, IV.2.25–7 and, above all,
III.1.210–12:

> And as the butcher takes away the calf,
> And binds the wretch, and beats it when it strays,
> Bearing it to the bloody slaughter-house . . .

Secondly, because the alliterative pattern of 94–6, with its heavy use of the letter 'b', seems to demand a word that alliterates with *confidence* and *killing* to complete it.

97 *apron-men*: 'Mechanicals', manual workers who wore leather aprons.

98 *the voice of occupation*: The votes of handicraftsmen.

101 *As Hercules did shake down mellow fruit*: The last of the twelve labours of Hercules was to obtain the golden apples from a tree in the Hesperides (the end of the world) which was guarded by a dragon.

105 *who resists*: Whoever resist.

114 *charged*: Would be entreating.

116 *showed*: Would appear.

119 *made fair hands*: Made a fine job of it (ironical).

120 *crafted*: Used in two senses: (1) carried out a piece of work; (2) intrigued, acted craftily.

124 *clusters*: Crowds, mob.

127 *obeys his points*: Obeys him in every point.

136 *coxcombs*: Fools' heads.

139 *coal*: Piece of charcoal.

150 *cry*: Pack of hounds.

162–3 *Would half my wealth | Would buy this for a lie*: How gladly would I give half my fortune to prove this a lie!

IV.7

A striking feature of Shakespeare's dramatic art is its economy, of which this scene is an excellent example. Based partly on North (*Shakespeare's Plutarch*, pp. 347–8), it serves two different purposes. Its first function is to explain the reasons for Aufidius's turning against Coriolanus, and so to prepare the way for the catastrophe. But Shakespeare also takes this opportunity to sum up his hero's character, as it has appeared so far, and to give a number of possible interpretations

of his earlier behaviour, and especially of his failure
in the central movement of the action.

5 *darkened*: Eclipsed, put in the shade.

   action: Campaign.

6 *by your own*: By your own action (in making Coriolanus
his fellow-general).

7 *means*: Remedies (against Coriolanus).

8 *more proudlier*: Shakespeare often uses double comparatives and superlatives in order to give added emphasis.
Cf. *more worthier*, III.1.120.

11 *changeling*: Fickle thing.

13 *for your particular*: Where your own interests are
concerned.

15 *Have*: Would have. Most editors emend to 'had' in order
to bring the construction into line with *had* in 13 and
again in 16; but this kind of shift in construction is a
fairly common feature of Shakespeare's later style.

   borne the action of yourself: Conducted the campaign
alone, by yourself.

22 *husbandry for*: Management of, concern for the welfare
of.

23 *achieve*: Accomplish his intention.

34–5 *As is the osprey to the fish . . . sovereignty of nature*: This
is an allusion to the belief that fish, recognizing the
kingly status of the osprey, turned up the whites of
their bellies to him so that he might seize them more
easily.

35–53 *First he was . . . done*: In these lines Aufidius's role is
almost that of a Chorus, providing explanations for
Coriolanus's actions and at the same time insisting on
his *merit* (48). The inconclusive nature of the analysis
suggests that Shakespeare wishes his audience to realize
that there is an element of mystery at the heart of the
tragedy.

37 *even*: Without losing his balance. The idea expressed
is almost a repetition of Sicinius' words at II.1.216–17:
'He cannot temperately transport his honours | From
where he should begin and end'.

38–9 *out of daily fortune ever taints | The happy man*: As a result of uninterrupted success always infects the fortunate man.

40 *disposing of*: Making the best use of.

43 *casque*: Helmet (representing the military life).
    cushion: Seat of office (representing the civil life).

44 *austerity and garb*: Austere manner, rigid discipline.

45–7 *but one of these ... feared*: Having suggested three possible reasons for Coriolanus' failure, Aufidius goes on to say that one of his explanations, not all of them, must be the right one, but he cannot say which it is, because to the observer the hero shows traces of them all.

46 *spices*: Touches, traces.

47 *free*: Absolve.

48 *a merit*: That is, his valour.

49 *To choke it in the utterance*: To choke any mention of the one fatal fault before it can be spoken.

49–55 *So our virtues ... fail*: The best commentary on this difficult passage, which is concerned with the transient and insecure nature of human achievement, is provided by Ulysses' great speech, 'Time hath, my lord, a wallet at his back ...', in *Troilus and Cressida* (III.3.145–89).

50 *Lie in th'interpretation of the time*: Are at the mercy of any construction the world chooses to set on them.

51–3 *And power, unto itself most commendable ... done*: And power, which carries its own commendation with it so long as it is active, has no more certain grave than the public acknowledgement of its achievements. The basic idea is that men's awareness of great deeds can only be kept alive by more great deeds; as soon as deeds are transformed into words, they lose their lustre and become tarnished. Moreover, success leads to defeat.
    evident: Inevitable, certain.
    chair: Public rostrum from which speeches are made.

54–5 *One fire drives out one fire; one nail one nail; | Rights by rights fuller, strengths by strengths do fail*: These two lines are made up of proverbial statements. The first two are to be found in M. P. Tilley's *Dictionary of the Proverbs in England in the Sixteenth and Seventeenth*

Centuries, where they appear as F277 and N17. The
fourth is in Erasmus's *Adagia* (949 C), where it is given
in the following form: '*Fortis in alium fortiorem incidit.
Dici solitum, ubi quis nimium fretus suis viribus, aliquando
nanciscitur, a quo vincatur*' ('The strong man meets a
stronger. Usually said when a man who relies too much
on his own unaided power eventually lights on one
who proves too much for him'). The present editor has
been unable to trace the third, but it must be parallel
with the others. The central idea in each case is that
any force can only be overcome by a stronger force of
the same kind. For this reason the reading *fuller* is
adopted in 55 in place of F's *fouler*, giving the sense
'rights are frustrated by stronger rights, strengths by
greater strengths'. For *fuller* meaning 'stronger' cf.
Othello, II.1.6, 'A fuller blast ne'er shook our battle-
ments.' Most editors emend 'fouler' to 'falter'.

V.I

Plutarch relates how the near approach of Coriolanus'
forces to Rome 'appeased the sedition and dissension
betwixt the nobility and the people' to such an extent
that the Senate agreed to the people's demand that his
banishment should be repealed. They therefore sent
ambassadors to him, choosing for the purpose 'Martius'
familiar friends and acquaintance'. Shakespeare
heightens the dramatic effect by replacing the name-
less friends of his source with Cominius and Menenius,
and by sending them separately, instead of as members
of the same delegation (see *Shakespeare's Plutarch*,
pp. 345–7).

3 *In a most dear particular*: With the warmest personal
affection.

5 *knee*: Make your way on your knees. Shakespeare has
in mind the behaviour of Christian penitents when
approaching shrines.

6–7 *coyed | To hear*: Showed disdain when hearing.

14 *i'th'fire*: F reads *a'th'fire*, but forging is done in a fire,
not out of it.

16 *wracked for*: Menenius, who is given to coining words,

has here combined 'wrack', meaning 'ruin', with 'rack', meaning 'make a great effort', and produced a portmanteau word, signifying 'toiled to disastrous effect'. Many editors read 'wrecked fair', and others 'racked for'.

17 *memory*: Memorial.

20 *bare*: Bare-faced, impudent.

23 *offered*: Tried, ventured.

28 *nose th'offence*: Smell the offensive matter.

35 *In this so-never-needed help*: In this crisis when help was never so badly needed as it is now.

38 *instant army*: Army mobilized on the spur of the moment.

45 *grief-shot*: Stricken with grief.

47–8 *after the measure | As you intended well*: In proportion to your good intentions.

50 *hum at*: Say 'hum' to (a sign of displeasure).

51 *taken well*: Approached at the right time. It is characteristic of Menenius, the bon viveur, that he should attach so much importance to a good dinner as a means of putting a man in an amiable frame of mind.

55 *conveyances*: Channels.

58 *dieted to*: In the mood – following a good meal – to listen to.

62 *Speed how it will*: Let it turn out as it will, no matter what the upshot may be.

64 *sit in gold*: Sit on a golden chair. North writes: 'he was set in his chair of state, with a marvellous and an unspeakable majesty' (*Shakespeare's Plutarch*, p. 347).

65 *his injury*: His sense of the wrong done to him.

70 *Bound with an oath*: This phrase applies equally to both sets of conditions (the concessions he is willing to make and the concessions he is unwilling to make), which, Coriolanus has sworn, must be accepted completely by the Romans.

72 *Unless*: Except for, if it were not for. Cf. *All's Well that Ends Well*, IV.1.4–6: 'we must not seem to understand him, unless some one among us, whom we must produce for an interpreter.'

V.2

This scene, set in the Volscian camp before Rome, has a double function. With its mixture of humour and pathos, it acts as a contrast to the sustained tension of the great scene that is to follow it. At the same time it depicts a further sapping of the hero's resolution. Cominius, his old general, has not left Coriolanus entirely unmoved – "Twas very faintly he said "Rise"' (V.1.67). Now Menenius, who has been the nearest thing to a father that Coriolanus has ever known, touches his feelings even more closely and, in doing so, prepares the ground for the arrival of his family.

  0 *Watch*: Sentries, military guard.

 10 *lots to blanks*: A thousand to one (referring to lottery tickets).

 13 *passable*: Current, valid (with a pun on 'giving the right to pass').

 14 *lover*: Dearest friend.

 17 *varnishèd*: F's reading *verified* is unsatisfactory because it does not connect in any way – as it should – with *size*; *varnishèd*, probably spelled 'vernished' in the manuscript, does, and gives a typically Shakespearian pun, since *size* means not only magnitude but also the sticky wash used by artists.

 19 *lapsing*: Slipping, collapsing.

 20 *upon a subtle ground*: On a tricky green.

 21 *tumbled past the throw*: Overshot the mark.

 22 *stamped the leasing*: Given falsehood the stamp of truth.

 29 *factionary on the party of*: Active in the support of.

 40 *front*: Confront, oppose.

 43 *dotant*: Dotard.

 50 *use me with estimation*: Treat me with respect.

58–9 *say an errand for you*: Deliver the message for you. Menenius intends to have his say first.

 60 *Jack guardant*: Jack-in-office on guard.
    office: Officiously withhold.

61–2 *Guess but my entertainment with him. If*: Many editors emend to 'Guess but by my . . . him if'.

 69 *hardly*: With difficulty.

71 *your gates*: The gates of your native city.

75 *block*: Punning on (1) obstruction; (2) blockhead.

79 *servanted*: Put in subjection.

79–80 *I owe | My revenge properly*: My revenge is my own affair.

80 *remission*: Power to pardon.

81–3 *That we have been familiar ... much*: The ungrateful forgetfulness of my services, which you and the Roman nobility have shown, shall poison the memory of our friendship rather than that I will allow any sense of pity to remind me of how great that friendship was.

94 *shent*: Rebuked.

100 *slight*: Insignificant, worthless.

by himself: By his own hand.

102 *long*: For a long time.

105–6 *The worthy fellow is our general ... oak not to be wind-shaken*: A most powerful piece of unconscious irony.

V.3

Deeply indebted to North, whom Shakespeare follows almost word for word when writing Volumnia's appeal to her son, this scene is the climax of the play. The setting for it is described in some detail by the source, which runs as follows:

Now was Martius set then in his chair of state, with all the honours of a general; and, when he had spied the women coming afar off, he marvelled what the matter meant; but afterwards, knowing his wife, which came foremost, he determined at the first to persist in his obstinate and inflexible rancour. But overcome in the end with natural affection, and being altogether altered to see them, his heart would not serve him to tarry their coming to his chair, but, coming down in haste, he went to meet them; and first he kissed his mother and embraced her a pretty while, then his wife and little children; and nature so wrought with him that the tears fell from his eyes, and he could not keep himself from making much of them, but yielded to the affection of his blood, as if he had been violently carried with the fury of a most swift-running stream. (*Shakespeare's Plutarch*, pp. 352–3)

3 *plainly*: Openly, straightforwardly.

11 *godded*: Idolized, made a god of.

latest refuge: Last resource.

15–17 *And cannot now accept, to grace him only* | *That thought he could do more. A very little* | *I have yielded to*: Many editors read: 'And cannot now accept. To grace him only | That thought he could do more, a very little | I have yielded to.'

A very little | *I have yielded to*: I did not yield much.

20–37 *Shall I be tempted to infringe my vow . . . kin*: These lines must be an aside, since the hero is not likely to reveal intimate feelings of this kind either to the Volsces or to the suppliants.

21 *Enter Virgilia, Volumnia, Valeria, young Martius, with Attendants*: Many editors add the words 'in mourning habits' after *Enter*, though there is no clear indication either in the text or in North that the women are so dressed. From what Volumnia says at 94–6, rags would seem to be more appropriate.

25 *bond and privilege of nature*: The natural ties of love and affection that bind the family together.

26 *obstinate*: Hard-hearted.

30 *Olympus*: Mountain in Greece, home of the gods in classical mythology.

32 *aspect of intercession*: Pleading look.

38 *These eyes are not the same I wore in Rome*: I see things differently now.

39 *delivers*: Presents.

41 *out*: At fault. For this use of the word *out* in a technical theatrical sense, see *Love's Labour's Lost*, V.2.151–74.

46 *the jealous queen*: Juno, the guardian of marriage.

48 *virgined it*: Remained chaste.

pray: Many editors emend to 'prate', but Coriolanus has just sworn by Juno and may, therefore, well think of himself as praying. Moreover, 'prate' is an ugly word with which to describe the tender adoration with which he has just greeted Virgilia.

51 *more impression*: A deeper mark (both metaphorically and literally).

52–6 *O, stand up blest . . . parent*: This speech is deliberately ironical. Volumnia knows precisely how to exert pressure on her son.

52 *blest*: Lucky, fortunate.

54 *unproperly*: Unfittingly, against all propriety.

57 *corrected son*: The son whom you have chastised.

58 *hungry*: Barren. The essential idea behind the passage is that a reversal of the whole natural order of things is taking place when a pebble, one of the most insignificant things in creation, can strike, or show contempt for, the stars.

61 *Murdering impossibility*: Making nothing seem impossible.

64 *Publicola*: Traditionally one of the first consuls of Rome, in 509 BC. He is the subject of one of Plutarch's *Lives*.

66 *curdied*: Congealed.

67 *Dian*: Diana, goddess of chastity.

68 *epitome*: Abridgement of a book or discourse.

69 *by th'interpretation of full time*: Time is imaged as a preacher or scholar developing a complete discourse from his *epitome* or notes.

70 *The god of soldiers*: Mars.

73 *To shame unvulnerable*: Incapable of dishonour.
   stick: Stand firm and stand out.

74 *sea-mark*: Conspicuous object serving as a navigational guide to sailors.
   standing: Withstanding.
   flaw: Gust of wind, sudden storm.

80 *forsworn to grant*: Sworn not to grant.

81 *Be held by you denials*: Be regarded by you as a refusal to answer your requests.

82 *capitulate*: Parley, discuss terms.

83 *mechanics*: Workmen, handicraftsmen (used here in a contemptuous sense to mean 'low fellows, rabble').

90 *fail in*: Fail to grant.

95 *bewray*: Reveal.

103 *to poor we*: Shakespeare occasionally uses *we* where modern usage would require 'us'. Cf. the words of

Brutus after the killing of Caesar: 'and let no man abide this deed | But we the doers' (*Julius Caesar*, III.1.94–5).

104 *capital*: Fatal, deadly.

112 *evident*: Certain, inevitable.

114 *foreign recreant*: Traitorous deserter to a foreign state.

119 *purpose*: Propose, intend.

120 *determine*: End.

121 *grace*: Favour, mercy.

124 *Trust to't, thou shalt not*: Be sure you shall not march without treading.

129–30 *Not of a woman's tenderness to be | Requires nor child nor woman's face to see*: Coriolanus means: 'I shall grow effeminate and womanish if I do not stop looking at them.' The rhyme has the effect of giving the statement a gnomic quality.

129–31 *Not of . . . long*: Probably spoken as an aside.

136 *while*: So that at the same time.

139 *the all-hail*: A general acclamation.

146 *it*: His reputation for nobility.

149–53 *Thou hast affected the fine strains of honour . . . oak*: These lines are a statement of what Volumnia wishes her son to say: namely, that he has given the impression of pursuing revenge out of over-refined sentiments of personal honour, in order that in the end he may behave like Jove, who terrifies men with his *thunder*, but, in his mercy, only directs his lightning at an oak.

151 *the wide cheeks o'th'air*: Maps in Shakespeare's time depicted the four winds issuing from the swollen cheeks of cherubs.

152 *sulphur*: Lightning.
    bolt: Thunderbolt.

153 *rive*: Split.

157 *childishness*: The natural instinctive appeal to the affections that a child has.

162 *fond of*: Wishing for.

166 *honest*: Honest with yourself, truthful.

167 *restrain'st*: Keep back, withhold.

170 *'longs*: Belongs, is due.

176 *reason*: Argue for.

179 *his child*: Some editors emend to 'this child'.

182 *Holds her by the hand, silent*: Shakespeare found the hint
     for this direction – one of the most telling in any of
     his plays – in North, whose narrative he alters subtly
     at this point in a way that makes it far more dramatic.
     The source runs:

> And with these words herself, his wife, and children fell
> down upon their knees before him. Martius, seeing that, could
> refrain no longer, but went straight and lift her up, crying
> out:
>   'Oh mother, what have you done to me?'
> And holding her hard by the right hand,
>   'Oh mother,' said he, 'you have won a happy victory for
> your country, but mortal and unhappy for your son. For I
> see myself vanquished by you alone.' (*Shakespeare's Plutarch*,
> p. 357)

190 *mortal*: Fatally.

191 *true*: According to my promise.

192 *convenient*: Proper, appropriate.

195 *withal*: By it.

203 *former fortune*: Fortune like my former one.

205 *which*: That is, the treaty.

208 *a temple built you*: Here Shakespeare has worked in a
     later passage from North, describing how the grateful
     Senate decided to grant the ladies whatever they should
     ask for: 'And they only requested that they would build
     a Temple of Fortune of the Women' (*Shakespeare's
     Plutarch*, p. 359).

V.4

     As a prelude to the catastrophe, Shakespeare moves the
     action back to Rome once more for some final ironies.
     Menenius' picture of Coriolanus is a sketch of him as
     he was, not as he is. But the behaviour of the people
     has not altered – they are as variable as they ever were.

7–8 *stay upon*: Wait for.

11   *differency*: Dissimilarity.

19   *engine*: Instrument of war – probably a battering ram.

21 *his hum*: His way of saying 'hum' (see note to V.1.50).
   battery: Military assault.
   state: Throne, chair of state.

21–2 *as a thing made for Alexander*: Like a statue of Alexander
   the Great.

26 *in the character*: To the life.

29 *'long of you*: Because of you.

36 *hale*: Drag, pull.

40 *are dislodged*: Have left their positions (military term).

46 *blown tide*: Tide driven by the wind. Shakespeare may
   well have been thinking of the tide, with an east wind
   behind it, racing through the arches of London Bridge.

48–9 *The trumpets, sackbuts, psalteries, and fifes,* | *Tabors and
   cymbals*: This list of musical instruments was probably
   suggested by the biblical catalogue (Daniel, 3:5): 'the
   cornet, trumpet, harp, sackbut, psaltery, dulcimer, and
   all instruments of music' (Geneva Bible, 1587).
   sackbuts: Bass trumpets rather like trombones.
   psalteries: Stringed instruments.

56 *Sound still with the shouts*: A command to those responsible for noises off in Shakespeare's theatre.

V.5

There is, of course, no change of location and no proper
scene division. All that happens is that Sicinius and the
Messenger go off on one side of the stage to meet the
procession, and return with it. The scene is the ironical counterpart to Coriolanus' return in II.1. Then
Rome rejoiced over his victory; now it rejoices over
his defeat – by his mother.

5 *Repeal him*: Recall him from exile.

V.6

In Plutarch Coriolanus returns to Antium after yielding
to his mother, and it is there that he meets his death
(*Shakespeare's Plutarch*, pp. 360–62). It seems as though
Shakespeare began this final scene with the same location in mind, for at 50 the First Conspirator describes
the place as Aufidius' *native town*, and there are further
references to Antium – none of them very obvious –
at 73 and 80. Then, when Shakespeare came to write

Aufidius' speech beginning at 88, he suddenly realized in the course of composition how much more dramatically appropriate Corioles would be, and made the switch, knowing that no audience would have noticed the earlier references to Antium. The play has come full circle. Once again Coriolanus is back at the scene of his victory, *alone*, as he was in I.4.53–4, *To answer all the city*.

4 *theirs*: Their. This use of *theirs* as a pronominal adjective before the noun has been explained as follows: 'It is felt that the ear cannot wait till the end of the sentence while so slight a word as *her* or *their* remains with nothing to depend on' (E. A. Abbott, *A Shakespearian Grammar* (1884), p. 161).

5 *Him*: He whom.

6 *ports*: Gates.

14 *parties*: Supporters.

15 *Of*: Out of.

17–19 *The people will remain uncertain ... all*: The Volscian mob, Shakespeare emphasizes, is as unstable as the Roman mob.

difference: Disagreement.

20–21 *admits | A good construction*: Is capable of a good interpretation.

22 *truth*: Loyalty.

heightened: Exalted.

23 *plants*: Used figuratively for position and dignities.

26 *free*: Outspoken.

27 *stoutness*: Obstinate pride.

32 *gave him way*: Gave way to him.

34 *files*: Ranks.

35 *designments*: Undertakings, enterprises.

37 *end*: Gather in as a harvest.

40–41 *He waged me with his countenance ... mercenary*: He paid me with his patronage as though I were a hired soldier. It is Coriolanus's natural and habitual assumption of authority that galls Aufidius.

43 *had carried*: Might have taken.

44 *There was it*: That was the thing.

45 *my sinews shall be stretched upon him*: My forces shall be strained to the utmost against him.

50 *post*: Messenger.

54 *at your vantage*: Seizing your opportunity.

57 *along*: Stretched out dead.

58 *After your way his tale pronounced*: The story of his actions as you will tell it.

59 *reasons*: Version of the matter.

64 *made*: Committed.

65 *easy fines*: Light punishment.

67 *levies*: Work of raising an army.

   answering: Repaying.

68 *charge*: Expenses.

73 *hence*: From Antium, which he left at the end of IV.5.

   subsisting: Continuing.

75 *prosperously I have attempted*: My efforts have proved successful.

78 *Doth more than counterpoise a full third part*: Exceed by more than a third.

84 *compounded*: Reached an agreement.

85 *traitor in the highest degree*: Traitor of the most criminal kind. Cf. *Richard III*, V.3.197: 'Perjury, perjury, in the highest degree.'

93 *drops of salt*: The tears of Volumnia and Virgilia, which Aufidius has already described as *drops of women's rheum* (46).

95 *oath and resolution*: Sworn purpose.

96 *twist*: Plaited thread.

96–7 *never admitting | Counsel o'th'war*: Never taking counsel of his fellow-officers.

99 *heart*: Courage.

100 *others*: The others.

102 *No more*: That is, no more than a boy.

107 *his own notion*: His own sense of the truth.

113 *edges*: Swords.

114 *there*: Recorded there.

118 *blind fortune*: Sheer good luck.

121 *presently*: At once.

127 *judicious*: Judicial, according to law.

Stand: Stop.

128–30 *O that I had him ... sword*: His mother's son to the last, Coriolanus almost repeats her words to Sicinius at IV.2.23–5.

131 *The Conspirators draw their swords, and kill*: F reads *Draw both the Conspirators, and kils*.

139 *did owe you*: Had for you.

141 *deliver*: Show.

146 *impatience*: Rage, anger.

150 *I'll be one*: I'll be the fourth – four being the usual number required to remove a corpse decently from the stage. Cf. *Hamlet*, V.2.389–90: 'Let four captains | Bear Hamlet like a soldier ...'

152 *Trail your steel pikes*: At military funerals in Elizabethan England the trained bands of the City carried their pikes at the trail (that is, with the butt-end near the ground and the point sloping forward) as a sign of mourning.

153 *unchilded*: Deprived of children.

155 *a noble memory*: North writes:

Howbeit it is a clear case, that this murder was not generally consented unto of the most part of the Volsces. For men came out of all parts to honour his body, and did honourably bury him, setting out his tomb with great store of armour and spoils, as the tomb of a worthy person and great captain. (*Shakespeare's Plutarch*, p. 362)

It is with just this impression of his hero's nobility and greatness that Shakespeare seeks to leave his audience.

PENGUIN SHAKESPEARE

HENRY IV, PART I
WILLIAM SHAKESPEARE

WWW.PENGUINSHAKESPEARE.COM

Prince Hal, the son of King Henry IV, spends his time in idle pleasure with dissolute friends, among them the roguish Sir John Falstaff. But when the kingdom is threatened by rebellious forces, the prince must abandon his reckless ways. Taking arms against a heroic enemy, he begins a great and compelling transformation – from irresponsible reprobate to noble ruler of men.

This book includes a general introduction to Shakespeare's life and the Elizabethan theatre, a separate introduction to *Henry IV, Part I*, a chronology of his works, suggestions for further reading, an essay discussing performance options on both stage and screen, and a commentary.

Edited by: Peter Davison

With an introduction by Charles Edelman

General Editor: Stanley Wells

Penguin Shakespeare

HENRY IV, PART II
WILLIAM SHAKESPEARE

WWW.PENGUINSHAKESPEARE.COM

Angered by the loss of his son in battle, the Earl of Northumberland supports another rebellion against King Henry IV, bringing the country to the brink of civil war. Sick and weary, the old King sends out his forces, including the unruly Sir John Falstaff, to meet the rebels. But as the conflict grows, he must also confront a more personal problem – how to make his reprobate son Prince Hal aware of the duties he must bear, as heir to the throne.

This book includes a general introduction to Shakespeare's life and the Elizabethan theatre, a separate introduction to *Henry IV, Part II*, a chronology of his works, suggestions for further reading, an essay discussing performance options on both stage and screen, and a commentary.

Edited by Peter Davison

With an introduction by Adrian Poole

General Editor: Stanley Wells

PENGUIN SHAKESPEARE

HENRY VI, PART II
WILLIAM SHAKESPEARE

WWW.PENGUINSHAKESPEARE.COM

Henry VI is tricked into marrying Margaret – lover of the Earl of
Suffolk, who hopes to rule the kingdom through her influence. There is
one great obstacle in Suffolk's path, however – the noble Lord
Protector, whom he slyly orders to be murdered. Discovering this
betrayal, Henry banishes Suffolk, but with his Lord Protector gone the
unworldly young King must face his greatest challenge: impending
civil war and the rising threat of the House of York.

This book includes a general introduction to Shakespeare's life and the
Elizabethan theatre, a separate introduction to *Henry VI, Part II*, a
chronology of his works, suggestions for further reading, an essay
discussing performance options on both stage and screen by Rebecca
Brown, and a commentary.

Edited by Norman Sanders

With an introduction by Michael Taylor

General Editor: Stanley Wells

Penguin Shakespeare

KING LEAR
WILLIAM SHAKESPEARE

WWW.PENGUINSHAKESPEARE.COM

An ageing king makes a capricious decision to divide his realm among his three daughters according to the love they express for him. When the youngest daughter refuses to take part in this charade, she is banished, leaving the king dependent on her manipulative and untrustworthy sisters. In the scheming and recriminations that follow, not only does the king's own sanity crumble, but the stability of the realm itself is also threatened.

This book includes a general introduction to Shakespeare's life and the Elizabethan theatre, a separate introduction to *King Lear*, a chronology of his works, suggestions for further reading, an essay discussing performance options on both stage and screen, and a commentary.

Edited by George Hunter

With an introduction by Kiernan Ryan

General Editor: Stanley Wells

PENGUIN SHAKESPEARE

MACBETH
WILLIAM SHAKESPEARE

WWW.PENGUINSHAKESPEARE.COM

Promised a golden future as ruler of Scotland by three sinister witches, Macbeth murders the king to ensure his ambitions come true. But he soon learns the meaning of terror – killing once, he must kill again and again, and the dead return to haunt him. A story of war, witchcraft and bloodshed, *Macbeth* also depicts the relationship between husbands and wives, and the risks they are prepared to take to achieve their desires.

This book includes a general introduction to Shakespeare's life and the Elizabethan theatre, a separate introduction to *Macbeth*, a chronology of his works, suggestions for further reading, an essay discussing performance options on both stage and screen, and a commentary.

Edited by George Hunter

With an introduction by Carol Rutter

General Editor: Stanley Wells

PENGUIN SHAKESPEARE

OTHELLO
WILLIAM SHAKESPEARE

WWW.PENGUINSHAKESPEARE.COM

A popular soldier and newly married man, Othello seems to be in an enviable position. And yet, when his supposed friend sows doubts in his mind about his wife's fidelity, he is gradually consumed by suspicion. In this powerful tragedy, innocence is corrupted and trust is eroded as every relationship is drawn into a tangled web of jealousies.

This book includes a general introduction to Shakespeare's life and the Elizabethan theatre, a separate introduction to *Othello*, a chronology of his works, suggestions for further reading, an essay discussing performance options on both stage and screen, and a commentary.

Edited by Kenneth Muir

With an introduction by Tom McAlindon

General Editor: Stanley Wells

PENGUIN SHAKESPEARE

RICHARD III
WILLIAM SHAKESPEARE

WWW.PENGUINSHAKESPEARE.COM

The bitter, deformed brother of the King is secretly plotting to seize the throne of England. Charming and duplicitous, powerfully eloquent and viciously cruel, he is prepared to go to any lengths to achieve his goal – and, in his skilful manipulation of events and people, Richard is a chilling incarnation of the lure of evil and the temptation of power.

This book includes a general introduction to Shakespeare's life and the Elizabethan theatre, a separate introduction to *Richard III*, a chronology of his works, suggestions for further reading, an essay discussing performance options on both stage and screen by Gillian Day, and a commentary.

Edited by E. A. J. Honigmann

With an introduction by Michael Taylor

General Editor: Stanley Wells

PENGUIN SHAKESPEARE

JULIUS CAESAR
WILLIAM SHAKESPEARE

WWW.PENGUINSHAKESPEARE.COM

When it seems that Julius Caesar may assume supreme power, a plot to destroy him is hatched by those determined to preserve the threatened republic. But the different motives of the conspirators soon become apparent when high principles clash with malice and political realism. As the nation plunges into bloody civil war, this taut drama explores the violent consequences of betrayal and murder.

This book includes a general introduction to Shakespeare's life and the Elizabethan theatre, a separate introduction to *Julius Caesar*, a chronology of his works, suggestions for further reading, an essay discussing performance options on both stage and screen, and a commentary.

Edited by Norman Sanders

With an introduction by Martin Wiggins

General editor: Stanley Wells

PENGUIN SHAKESPEARE

KING JOHN
WILLIAM SHAKESPEARE

WWW.PENGUINSHAKESPEARE.COM

Under the rule of King John, England is forced into war when the French challenge the legitimacy of John's claim to the throne and determine to install his nephew Arthur in his place. But political principles, hypocritically flaunted, are soon forgotten, as the French and English kings form an alliance based on cynical self-interest. And as the desire to cling to power dominates England's paranoid and weak-willed king, his country is threatened with disaster.

This book includes a general introduction to Shakespeare's life and the Elizabethan theatre, a separate introduction to *King John*, a chronology of his works, suggestions for further reading, an essay discussing performance options on both stage and screen, and a commentary.

Edited by R. L. Smallwood

With an introduction by Eugene Giddens

General Editor: Stanley Wells

PENGUIN SHAKESPEARE

TIMON OF ATHENS
WILLIAM SHAKESPEARE

WWW.PENGUINSHAKESPEARE.COM

After squandering his wealth with prodigal generosity, a rich Athenian gentleman finds himself deep in debt. Unshaken by the prospect of bankruptcy, he is certain that the friends he has helped so often will come to his aid. But when they learn his wealth is gone, he quickly finds that their promises fall away to nothing in this tragic exploration of power, greed, and loyalty betrayed.

This book includes a general introduction to Shakespeare's life and the Elizabethan theatre, a separate introduction to *Timon of Athens*, a chronology of his works, suggestions for further reading, an essay discussing performance options on both stage and screen, and a commentary.

Edited by G. R. Hibbard

With an introduction by Nicholas Walton

General Editor: Stanley Wells

Read more in Penguin

PENGUIN SHAKESPEARE